SEARCHING THE SOUL

Academic Introductions for Beginners

Volume One	**Wisdom for Thinkers: An Introduction to Christian Philosophy**
Volume Two	**Power in Service: An Introduction to Christian Political Thought**
Volume Three	**What Then *Is* Theology?: An Introduction to Christian Theology**
Volume Four	**Searching the Soul: An Introduction to Christian Psychology**
Volume Five	**Probing the Past: An Introduction to Christian History**

SEARCHING THE SOUL

An Introduction to Christian Psychology

WILLEM J. OUWENEEL

PAIDEIA PRESS

PAIDEIA PRESS,
P.O. Box 500, Jordan Station,
Ontario, Canada L0R 1S0
www.paideiapress.ca

Library & Archives Canada
ISBN 978-0-88815-258-9

2nd printing cover design and layout by Steven R. Martins,
project manager, Paideia Press

Printed in the United States of America

"I praise you, for I am fearfully and wonderfully made. Wonderful are your works; my soul knows it very well."
~ **Psalm 139:14**

"Who knows a person's thoughts except the spirit of that person, which is in him?"
~ **1 Corinthians 2:11a**

"The word of God is living and active, sharper than any two-edged sword, piercing to the division of soul and of spirit, of joints and of marrow, and discerning the thoughts and intentions of the heart."
~ **Hebrews 4:12**

Table of Contents

About the Author

Willem J. Ouweneel (1944) earned his Ph.D. in biology at the University of Utrecht (The Netherlands, 1970), his Ph.D. in philosophy at the Free University in Amsterdam (The Netherlands, 1986), and his Ph.D. in theology at the University of the Orange Free State in Bloemfontein (Republic of South Africa, 1993). Among many other things, he has been professor of the Philosophy of Science for the Natural Sciences at the University for Christian Higher Education in Potchefstroom (Republic of South Africa, 1990-1998), and professor of Philosophy and Systematic Theology at the Evangelical Theological Faculty in Leuven (Belgium, 1995-2014. He is a prolific writer (mainly in Dutch, and has preached in more than thirty countries. Several times he was a candidate for Dutch Christian political parties.

Foreword

The present volume is a total re-editing of the book that appeared in 2009 with the same publisher, under the title *Heart & Soul: A Christian View of Psychology*. This was a translation of a Dutch book of mine, titled *Hart en ziel: Een christelijke kijk op de psychologie* (1984). This book in its turn was an abridged edition of a much more extensive study, titled *Psychologie: Een christelijke kijk op het mentale leven* (1984, "Psychology: A Christian View of Mental Life"). Together with my Ph.D. dissertation on Christian philosophical anthropology (i.e., the philosophical doctrine of Man), titled *Christelijke transcendentaal-antropologie: Een sympathetisch-kritische studie van de wijsgerige antropologie van Herman Dooyeweerd* (1986, "Christian Transcendental Anthropology: A Sympathetic-Critical Study of the Philosophical Anthropology of Herman Dooyeweerd"; commercial edition: *De leer van de mens* ["The Doctrine of Man"]), the three books form as it were a kind of trilogy on philosophical anthropology and psychology.

Understanding the present book demands some basic knowledge of fundamental philosophical ideas. Therefore, for a proper understanding of the present introduction to Christian psychology, I highly recommend that you begin by reading the first volume of this series: *Wisdom for Thinkers: An Introduction to Christian Philosophy*. Many ideas in the present volume will be hard to understand without knowledge of this first volume, which forms the foundation for this whole series. Apart from that, it would also be very useful to read beforehand the third volume: *What Then Is Theology?: An Introduction to Christian Theology.*

Bible quotations in this book are usually from the English Standard Version. When other translations are used, this is indicated.

Willem J. Ouweneel
Zeist (The Netherlands)
Spring 2014

Chapter One
PSYCHOLOGY & CHRISTIANITY

Quite a number of people come into contact with a psychologist at some time or other. During childhood they may have had to take a psychological test, perhaps at school. Or perhaps they took such a test later in life during a medical examination for military service, or when applying for a certain job. There are also people who have made the acquaintance of an industrial psychologist, or have been treated by a so-called clinical psychologist when they were having mental problems. In all these examples, we are talking only about *applied* psychology. There are also many psychologists who engage in scientific research, without reflecting very much about the possible applications of what they are doing. They collect psychological knowledge as an aim in itself, simply because they are interested in one of the most fascinating phenomena in the universe: Man.

Ordinarily, the public is largely unaware of their work. These psychologists study such matters as emotions and sense perception (sight, sound, smell, taste), cognition and learning processes, creativity and imagination, memory and mental disorders, intelligence and instincts, social and economic behavior, moral and religious behavior, etc. From this small list we can see that psychologists are involved with a tremendous range of problems, and it is not so easy to spell out just what all these problems have in common. Or perhaps I could put the question another way: In all of this research that I have just described, what could we identify as the *psychical*—the subject matter of "psychology"?

What Is Psychology?

A little warning beforehand: do not confuse the word "psychical" with "psychic," which is often used for paranormal and occult matters. The psychical is simply that which is studied by psychologists. "Psychology" comes from the Greek *psyche* ("soul"), and in the past, when psychology was still part of philosophy and not yet an experimental science (see chapter 5), it was quite common to describe psychology as the study of the "soul." However, the word "soul" has so many different meanings, and especially so many unfavorable connotations, that nowadays most psychologists prefer to avoid the term. They would rather say that psychology is the study of psychical, or mental, processes, or even more simply, the study of human behavior (whereby, in the earlier days of psychology, the question whether there is something psychical "behind" our behavior was often left open). I will come back to this matter in greater detail below.

Another little terminological point: it is very common to speak of psycho*logical* problems, whereas what people mean is *psychical* problems. "Psychological" problems would literally mean problems within the science of psychology. This linguistic error is due to the tremendous influence of rationalism in our culture. We also encounter it in expressions like "geo*logical*" layers (instead of earth layers) and socio*logical* issues (instead of social issues). The point is not very important, but it *is* characteristic of our rationalistic Western civilization.

To come back to our definition of psychology, one can say that the many problems and areas studied by psychology all have something in common, which makes them the study object of psychologists. Let us start off by asserting that this "something" is exclusive to humans (and animals). It relates to phenomena that we do not encounter in connection with inanimate things or plants. The phenomena in question are very characteristic of *human beings,* and to some degree they are also found in the (higher) animals (to *what* extent we will have to find out later). Already at this point it is important to note that many psychical phenomena, such as the invention of new instruments, speech, abstract thinking (like calculus), creative, social and artistic behavior, scientific thinking, moral reasoning, religious considerations and deeds, occur *only* in human beings. Thus, psychology appears to be the special science that studies above all the being or essence of Man. Many would even call it the *science of Man par excellence.*

Now, there are several other sciences, such as historiography, linguistics, sociology, economics, aesthetics, legal sciences, and ethics, which also qualify as *humanities* (sciences of Man). Yet on closer examination we see that among all of these, psychology seems to occupy a central place (see chapter 7). Psychology touches on linguistics because linguistics is keen to find out how it is that people learn and use languages. It touches on sociology because sociology is interested in how the human individual behaves in groups. It touches on economics because economics tries to understand patterns of consumer behavior, for example. It touches on the legal sciences and ethics because it tries to understand the psychical background of certain legal and moral appraisals we make. And so on.

We see, then, that psychologists concern themselves with a wide range of questions, all of which have to do with the "human being," or, more specifically, with Man's inner (psychical and spiritual) life, as well as the external behavior governed by his inner life. This external behavior is implemented in interaction with Man's environment. In these two sentences I have managed to say a whole mouthful: they sum up just about everything that is important to mention at this point. Psychology deals with what goes on inside a person *as well as* with his outward behavior; it focuses on what originates in the person himself *and* the influence of the environment. When psychology is compared to the other humanities,which all study certain aspects of human existence, it appears to stand out among them as a science that poses the question of the nature of the human being *as such*. Apart from philosophical anthropology—which is not a special science, but part of philosophy—psychology seems to be the special science occupied with what Pierre Teilhard de Chardin (1881-1955) called *le phénomène humaine* (the human phenomenon).

Of course, it is quite presumptuous to undertake such a study. How could we come to know anything meaningful about the deepest "being" of Man? For almost a century and a half, psychology has been a so-called "experimental" science; that is to say, it tries to obtain knowledge by making observations and performing experiments. But is it really possible to learn something about the profoundest aspects of Man's being by simply *watching* human beings and *listening* to them in various circumstances? After all, that is what happens during observation and experiment.

In the past, many people thought that it was indeed possible to map out the mystery of Man through scientific observation (and presumably there are many such people still around). Moreover, they believed that science was a "neutral" and "objective" affair, in other words, a human activity in which one could engage without being caught up in prejudices of any sort (see my *Wisdom for Thinkers* for more on this erroneous way of thinking Today, we know better. We now realize that not one of the human activities we undertake is "neutral," "objective," or "unprejudiced," to say nothing of the scientific work we do. Later on we shall see that this very science—psychology—has provided us with evidence that *all* of our observations are indeed "colored" and "prejudiced." We all carry within ourselves a fund of experiences, learned "reflexes," positive and negative affections, attitudes, preconceived ideas, habits, affections, memories, orientations, and predispositions. As a rule, we are aware of them only dimly, if at all—and even then, many of them still escape our notice. Nevertheless, as we will see, they give a certain "color" to all our observations. They make us see what we want to see—even as scientists—and they make us blind to that which we wish to avoid.

Who Is Man?

Everywhere in our lives we see evidence that we are subjective and biased, even when we are engaged in scientific work. And where would we find such factors more fully at work than in the science in which we study "ourselves," the science whose field of investigation is the human being? Thus every psychologist, when he sets out to do his work, is already operating with some partly unconscious preconceived ideas as to who and what a human being really is. Let us take an obvious example: all the early psychologists—and of course there are still many of them around today—were evolutionists, that is, people who believe that Man's being could be explained from his animal origin. As a consequence, they were very strongly tempted to highlight everything Man and (higher) animals had in common, and to trivialize everything in which Man differed drastically from animals.

These and other ideas determine the psychologist's choice of experiments and influence the explanations he offers of the data yielded by his experiments. Today, Christians who choose to work in psychology confront the problem that the researchers who developed the science were not Christians at all. This might not be so serious if we were talking about a field such as mechanical engineering or dentistry. However, we are talking here about a science that, from the outset, has insisted that it is able to tell us something of great importance about who and what the "human being" is, and this in a purely scientific way.

By the way, we should take note of another terminological matter with great consequences, namely, the difference between "Who is Man?" and "What is Man?" If you are, for instance, a materialist or an evolutionist—which is often virtually the same thing—you are not interested in the first question, because the "Who" suggests that Man is essentially different from animals, which are never "whos" but only a "what" and a "which." Here you can instantly see one of the biases at work in psychology: only Christians, Jews, or Muslims will emphasize the meaning of the question "*Who* is Man?" as was done, for instance, by the Jewish thinker, Abraham J. Heschel (1907-1972). Only Man—and God, and angels, for that matter—are "whos," and as such essentially different from all lower organisms. "Personhood" is to be assigned to Man (and God, and angels), not to animals.

It is true that psychologists nowadays are on the average more modest about the pretentious claims of psychology than they used to be. Nevertheless, the idea that psychologists know everything there is to know about the human phenomenon continues to crop up. But then, the founders and early practitioners of experimental psychology all had one thing in common: not only evolutionism, as I have just mentioned, but also the conviction that any relationship Man might have with some God was something they considered beyond their sphere of operations, or something they denied altogether. This means that these psychologists had, on an *a priori* basis, excluded something that, to the Christian, is the *very essence* of Man. Therefore we may conclude that the many things that secular psychologists "discover" about Man may be quite interesting to a certain extent. However, at best these things can be nothing more than half-truths, since, according to Christians, they start with a mistaken view of Man. In other words: their psychology is grounded in the wrong philosophical anthropology.

For this reason alone, it is not enough for those Christians who choose to work in psychology to pray to God to preserve them from such influences. They would not thereby guarantee a truly critical-Christian approach to their discipline. What they really need is a *radically Christian psychology,* one that has been constructed anew from the ground up, from its foundations. Such a Christian psychology would start with the revealed Word of God. This divine revelation, which is contained in the Bible, gives us not only the highest truth about God but also the highest truth about Man as the image of God. This truth is of such a nature that it can never be acquired by experimental means; it can be obtained only through divine revelation. This deepest truth discloses the true nature of Man to us. To put it in biblical language, it reveals the *heart* of Man.

Later we will discuss the meaning of the word "heart" in the Bible (see chapter 9). But at this point I emphasize only that it has nothing to do with the hollow muscular organ in our chest cavity that pumps our blood. In the Bible, the heart is to be understood as the innermost depth of Man, the central or pivotal point in which all that is Man "comes together" and finds its unity. It is the place where Man is at his "Mannest," as someone has put it.

Not only that, but we must also recognize that it is in his heart that Man is centrally related to a higher reality. Man is a temporal, earthly being, but at the same time he is a being destined for eternity. As Ecclesiastes 3:11 tells us, God "has put eternity into man's heart". Man is a unique being in that he stands on the boundary between time and eternity. In his corporeal existence he takes part in the immanent, empirical world. In his heart he takes part in the transcendent, invisible, eternal, celestial world of God (or, of the gods, the false idols and ideologies, the powers of darkness). This is vital to any Christian anthropology: (a) Man's being is not limited to the empirical world but is centered in his relationship to the higher world, and (b) this world is either the world of God, or the world of the demons.

Is There a Christian Psychology?

Of course mine is not the first book ever to concern itself with the relationship between Christianity and psychology. Many Christians before me have written on this subject. I undertook to write this book because I am convinced that many of these other attempts need some fundamental correction. However, to begin with something positive, most of the other books on the subject are, like mine, critical of the view of Man that underlies secular psychology, and of the view that glorifies "neutral, objective" science. The truth is that there is simply no such science. The current psychology usually has a foundation which is evolutionist, materialistic, existentialist, postmodern, or something similar. This being the case, there is also room for a psychology with a Christian foundation. For Christians, this ought in fact to be the only possible option.

The scientist who nevertheless persists in believing that there is a "neutral" psychology is, first, probably a specialist in a small field, who does not have a proper overview of psychology as a whole. Usually, he does not even *think* very much about his science as a whole, much less about its foundation and starting points. The reason is that most psychologists, like most other special scientists, receive little or no training in philosophy, either in (a) the philosophy of science (German: *Wissenschaftsphilosophie*; Dutch: *wetenschapsfilosofie*), or in (b) philosophical anthropology (a foundation for all the humanities), or in (c) the special philosophy (German: *Fachphilosophy*; Dutch: *vakfilosofie*) of psychology, in which its place is defined among the other humanities, and among the special sciences in general.

Second, any psychologist believing in a "neutral" psychology is probably an adherent of *scientism*. This is the philosophical doctrine which says that the full, genuine truth about Man, or about anything, can be acquired only through science (in this case psychology), or through the humanities in general. Scientism rejects the idea that a "religious" book like the Bible could say anything meaningful about the nature of Man, because religious "myth" is "unscientific."

Even some Christians may, to a certain extent, be adherents of scientism. Where this is the case, they split their lives into two parts. On Sunday they believe in God and his Word, while from Monday to Saturday they believe in science—and the two never meet. Such Christians try to maintain two truths co-existing uneasily side by side: the truth of God for their spiritual lives, and the "truth" of science for the rest of their lives. They live in two worlds, and if they are really serious about this, in the end they must inevitably be torn apart. The reason is that ultimately Man cannot live with two truths, especially when they often collide. Eventually, one truth will devour the other. In practice unfortunately, this usually means that scientific "truth" will devour biblical truth.

Biblicism

In opposition to this scientism stands an equally mistaken view which I call *biblicism*. This is the view of certain Christian psychologists—but far more often of theologians, preachers, and laymen!—who go to the opposite extreme by declaring that only the Bible has anything meaningful to say about Man. They speak of a "biblical psychology" because, according to them, true psychology is found exclusively in the Bible. Genuine truth, including the truth about Man, cannot exist independently of God's Word-revelation. On many websites, this approach is vehemently defended, and as a result, the Bible is placed over against psychology. This is wrong for at least three reasons:

1. First, by "psychology"—I mean the psychology they are opposing, not their own "biblical psychology"—these biblicists mean *secular* psychology; apparently they cannot even *conceive* of a truly scientific psychology rooted in a Christian-philosophical view of cosmic reality and knowledge.

2. Second, most Christian websites that warn their readers about the "dangers" of psychology usually refer only to psychotherapy. They forget, or do not know, that psychology is so much more than just clinical psychology, or psychotherapy. We call the latter *applied* psychology; this should be carefully distinguished from *basic* or *pure* psychology, which is an empirical and experimental science directed at gathering theoretical knowledge about Man's mental life and the behavior associated with it.

3. Thirdly, the Bible and psychology are incomparable entities. At best, you can juxtapose the Bible and the Qur'an, or Christian psychology and secular psychology. However, for many people the Bible and Christian psychology are one and the same thing, because *all* their ideas about psychology are taken from the Bible.

There is only one element of truth in this notion of a "biblical psychology." To be sure, the Bible is by no means a handbook of psychology, not even of its basic principles. At the same time, it is perfectly true to say that *without* the Bible, psychology cannot give us any real information about the true nature, the deepest essence, of Man. In the final analysis, the truth about Man's essential being goes back to divine revelation, because, as we will see, this essence of Man lies *outside* himself, in his relationship to God. People who do not know God and his Word cannot possibly know the true nature of Man because Man, as the image of God, has been designed for a relationship with God. This relationship (*or* the lack thereof, which implies a relationship with a different, darker, higher reality) determines the essence of Man.

However—and this is the important point in contrast to all biblicism—we must remember that not everything we could possibly know about Man is recorded in the Bible. *The Bible is true, but not all truth is in the Bible.* There is much *more* to be known about Man than what has been given in the Scriptures. God tells us about Man that which we otherwise could never have known. But basically, God does *not* tell us in the Bible anything about Man that we can find out ourselves. This is in fact true for all possible subjects: God reveals to us things that we could never discover on our own. For the rest, he has equipped us with sense organs and an intellect to unravel the other mysteries of cosmic reality. God has told us about Man as the image of God, and about the *heart* of Man as the focal point of his existence, knowing that we would be able by ourselves to find out about the nervous system, hormones, perception, sensation, spiritive life, reflexes, instincts, affections, emotions, drives, deliberations, creativity, defense mechanisms, cognitive dissonance, etc. (see the following chapters).

The fact that God left so much to *us* to find out is actually something to rejoice over, because it means that the curious among us will still have many things to discover about the phenomenon of Man. This is where psychology and the other humanities come in. Any investigator who is determined to ground his work in the Word of God will find that he has all the opportunity he could possibly desire to carry out systematic, experimental studies of human emotional and intellectual life, and of human behavior.

There is plenty of room for experimental psychology. However, such a psychology should be built upon a Christian anthropology, itself rooted in the divine revelation about Man.

In summary, when some people contend that psychology cannot provide us with any true knowledge of Man, what they are really talking about is current, secular, scientistic psychology. To be sure, secular psychology does contain a lot of truth elements about Man. Truth is so intrusive that not even the atheist could miss all of it. Therefore, we can definitely learn a lot from secular psychology. However, current psychology lacks the broad perspective of the Truth. It is not capable of placing all its truth elements in the framework of the divine revelation about the essence of Man. Conversely, Christians are able to isolate those truth elements from secular psychology only on the basis of a Christian-philosophical view of cosmic reality and knowledge.

Separatism

Besides scientism and biblicism, there is a fourth secularist error that Christians can commit with respect to psychology, which I call *separatism.* It is the idea that both psychology and theology command fields of their own, which should not be confused with one another but kept separated. Now, there is indeed something to be said for this claim. Psychology and theology are both special sciences, and as such, each must have its own field of investigation. But we must be careful here not to equate theology with the Bible, or with Christianity. Psychology has only a very indirect connection to theology, but it has everything to do with a Christian worldview, which is rooted in the Bible. And in the formation of such a Christian worldview, theology can be of inestimable help.

Once again, we bump into our old friend Scholasticism (discussed extensively in two earlier volumes of this series, *Wisdom for Thinkers* and *What Then Is Theology*? This is the view (common in the medieval era, but also in early Protestantism) that *sacred* theology is about divine things, while the other (*profane*) secular sciences are about secular things. According to this view, a Christian psychology is by definition impossible because anything "Christian" belongs to the domain of theology and the sacred.

Scholasticism is the Christian version of scientism, in that it too views (profane) science as a neutral, objective, unprejudiced enterprise.

The central issue involved is this: theology allegedly studies Man's spiritual life, while psychology studies Man's mental life. Theology studies Man's religion, while psychology studies Man's religious behavior. In practice this means that when you have spiritual problems, you go to the theologian (pastor, Christian counselor) for help and when you have mental (emotional) problems you go to the (clinical) psychologist for help. The error in this type of thinking catches the eye immediately: the spiritual and the mental, religion and religious behavior, are inextricably interwoven. They can be distinguished, but they cannot be separated.

Man's inner life is an indissoluble unity, which cannot be sliced up in such a way that there is a piece for the pastor and another piece for the psychologist. However, it *is* true to say that theology is occupied with the pistical aspects of Man's functioning, and psychology with the perceptive and sensitive aspects (just as biology is occupied with the biotic aspect, sociology with the social aspect, ethics with the moral aspect, etc.). These, and many more, modalities of Man's functioning are investigated in their coherence and unity within philosophical anthropology. And all of them, theology, psychology, and philosophy (as well as biology, sociology, ethics, etc, find their unity in a Christian worldview that is itself rooted in the divine Word-revelation. How this works out practically in Christian counseling will be explained in the last three chapters of this book.

Integrationism

We now come to a fifth error that can be made when Christians think about psychology. After scientism, biblicism and (Scholastic) separatism, there is what I would like to call *integrationism*. For instance, in 1979, John D. Carter and S. Bruce Narramore published their book, *The Integration of Psychology and Theology*. In 1984, William T. Kirwan published a book with the noteworthy subtitle, *A Case for Integrating Psychology and Theology*. Nowadays,

Fuller Theological Seminary has a School of Psychology, where they advocate the same thing, which they refer to as an "integration" of theology and psychology. Although these Christians speak about this kind of "integration" with the best of intentions, and apparently with good *practical* results, as a matter of principle they are mistaken.

First, it should be recognized that psychology and theology, as distinct special sciences, must remain separated. All special sciences have their own specific field of investigation, and should be carefully kept apart. You cannot mix, fuse, or integrate them, nor should you try to.

Second, the investigators I have mentioned are too quick to take what they call "psychology" for granted, only partially realizing that it is current, secular psychology. This psychology does not become any better when "integrated" with theology. As the prophet Haggai said, holy meat that touches common food does not make that food holy as well; but anything unclean that comes in contact with holy food makes it unclean (Hag. 2:12-13). Similarly, mixing Christian theology with "pagan" psychology does not make the psychology any better, but it will definitely make your theology worse. In this respect, there is a correspondence between biblicism and integrationism: both understand by "psychology" *only current, secular* psychology, which is then rejected by biblicists and accepted by scientists and separatists, as well as integrationists.

Third, the investigators I have mentioned speak about "theology" whereas in fact they mean the Bible, or a Christian worldview. They *say* they want an integration of psychology and theology, but what they *mean*—I hope—is a true Christian psychology, which is firmly rooted in a biblical worldview. What they should be looking for is not a blending of current, secular psychology with theology, but what we might call a conversion of current psychology to a biblical worldview. There is no way theology can provide such a worldview, because it is not even equipped to do so (see my *What Then Is Theology?* for more details). Instead, abiblical worldview is supplied instead by the Bible. That is no word play, but an essential point. We do not want a psychology rooted in theology, but we want *all* the special sciences, *including theol-*

ogy, to be rooted in a Christian worldview, which is based on the divine Word-revelation alone.

What I am saying is that current, secular psychology needs to be converted—that is, turned around—in a radical way, i.e., right down to its roots (the word radical is from the Latin *radix,* meaning "root". Its edifice must be taken apart brick by brick, and each brick must be examined individually to see whether it is useful. Some bricks will have to be thrown away, whereas others will still be usable once they have gone back into the oven again. Moreover, many new bricks will be needed. This selecting and cleansing of bricks cannot be done in a merely "intuitive" way. On the contrary, it is of prime importance to realize that the whole edifice that we call psychology will have to be rebuilt *on a new foundation,* the foundation of a thoroughly biblical worldview, by means of a Christian philosophy of science and a Christian philosophical anthropology.

"Biblical Psychology"

Such a claim requires some clarification. The fact is that one cannot simply base psychology on the Bible. It has often been said that the Bible is not a manual for science. It is not a textbook for psychology either, nor for any other special science for that matter, not even for theology (see again my *What Then Is Theology?*). The point is, however, that there are some authors who have nonetheless written books on what they call "biblical psychology," i.e., some psychology supposedly extracted from the Bible. The famous Christian writer, Oswald Chambers (1874-1917), wrote a book by this title, but in fact he meant only "biblical wisdom." A certain Matthew Cohn has a "Biblical Psychology" website. In 2003, the psychologist Stephen H. Farra began to promote his ideas about "biblical psychology," and recently published the book, *The Biblical Model of Human Psychology*. Several other authors have published books on "biblical psychiatry," but, in spite of all their good intentions, I am sorry to say that all these authors are basically mistaken.

These authors suggest that there is a thing that deserves the name "psychology," which can be derived from the Bible—whereas in reality, the Bible contains a lot of wisdom but nothing that could be properly called "science,"—and this includes psychology and psychiatry. Of course, every person is free to supply us with his definitions. If you want to call biblical wisdom about Man "psychology," you are perfectly free to do so. But you should realize that you are placing yourself outside scientific discourse, for your biblical wisdom is something very different from what *scientists*—non-Christians as well as Christians—call psychology. It is quite simple: psychology is a theoretical-scientific enterprise, and the Bible does not contain a grain of what we call theory or science (as long as you do your best to understand what theory and science are, without resorting to your own private definitions

When writers use the terms "biblical psychology" or "biblical psychiatry," what they mean by them is a collection of biblical statements about Man, his inner life, and his behavior. But what a collection of such statements gives us, at most, is a set of practical insights into human life, but, while these insights are extremely important, they do not count as scientific psychology. At best, such knowledge could be said to belong to our Christian *worldview,* which also contains a certain view of Man (German: *Menschanschauung;* Dutch: *mensbeschouwing*). Such a worldview precedes, underlies and conditions all science. The biblical wisdom about Man *is* of essential significance for a Christian approach to psychology, *but as such it is not psychology.* It belongs at best to the *starting points* of a Christian psychology.

Christian-Philosophical Starting Points

There is more that precedes, underlies, and conditions a scientific psychology. The special philosophy of psychology must also provide answers to such questions as: What, strictly speaking, *is* science? What is the difference between practical wisdom—such as biblical wisdom—about Man and theoretical-scientific psychological knowledge about Man? In what sense is scientific psychology more than just a collection of practical insights? What is *the psychical* that we investigate in psychology? How do we gather experimental data about it? And how is it related to other aspects of Man (such as the logical, the social, the economic, the juridical, the moral, etc.)?

Please note that these questions are *never* dealt with, directly or indirectly, in the Bible. This fact in itself is already sufficient to show that the idea of a biblical psychology is an inner contradiction. The Bible does not deal with science, not even with the principles of science. The questions we have mentioned above are dealt with in the special philosophy of psychology, which forms the foundation for psychology. This special philosophy of psychology itself must be rooted in a general Christian-philosophical view of cosmic reality and knowledge. This philosophy itself must be rooted in a biblical worldview. Such a Christian worldview must be formed in the *spirit* and *light* of Scripture, possibly with the help of theology.

In the earlier volumes of this series, I have argued that a Christian approach to any special science can only be properly realized in the framework of a radical Christian philosophy, including a Christian anthropology. When we proceed in such a fashion, the answers we come up with are not "biblical" in the sense that we have simply extracted them from the Bible. Yet we can affirm that they are "faithful to the Bible," i.e. faithful to the way the Bible commonly speaks about Man and all his facets, and to the universal instruction given in Scripture.

In a certain sense, we might say that we all have something of the "primordial psychologist" within us: we all have a certain amount of knowledge of people, or general insight into the nature of human beings (German: *Menschenkenntnis;* Dutch: *mensenkennis*). Every day we form opinions about other people, especially about the motives behind their behavior. We judge what makes people tick. However, a *real* psychologist is someone who, in virtue of his training, is able to turn such opinions into general *theories* in an abstract, critical, and systematic fashion (see my *Wisdom for Thinkers*). He is not so much interested in how John or Jane Doe behaves, but how people behave in general, under all possible different circumstances. He is looking for *general patterns* in human behavior. He then proceeds to test such theories empirically and/or experimentally. Our general insight into the human phenomenon is of a *practical* nature, while psychological knowledge of the human phenomenon is of a *theoretical* nature.

When it comes to the *structure* of psychology, a good psychologist is one who does his work according to the highest academic principles. When it comes to the *direction* of psychology, a good psychologist is one whose work is grounded in a radical Christian philosophy, especially a Christian philosophical anthropology, which is itself based on a biblical worldview. The ideal psychologist is good in both respects—although we must always bear in mind, of course, that the perfect psychologist does not exist. "Even" Christian psychology remains faulty work undertaken by fallible human beings, since we see "in a mirror dimly," and know only "in part" (1 Cor. 13:12).

The Usefulness of a Christian Psychology

Of course at this point one might wonder whether there are really Christians sitting around waiting for a Christian psychology to be developed. Would such a psychology truly be useful? I am convinced that the answer is yes—otherwise I would not have written this book! To begin with, it is always a fine and useful thing to study the wonderful works of God in creation: "Great are the works of the Lord, studied by all who delight in them" (Ps. 111:2). This is even truer when we are talking about the human being, who is God's masterpiece: "I praise you, for I am fearfully and wonderfully made. Wonderful are your works; my soul knows it very well" (Ps. 139:14). *Good* psychology, by which I mean psychology that is faithful to Scripture on the one hand, and critical, thorough, and systematic on the other, teaches us a great deal about human beings, and at the same time instructs us about ourselves. Thus anyone who studies Christian psychology will, as a side-effect, get to know *himself* better, and that is always a welcome thing.

Such knowledge becomes even more useful when applied in practice. This is what happens in Christian counseling. The world calls it psychotherapy, but in the church it is known as pastoral care (cf. e.g., 1 Pet. 5:1-15). The two are not precisely the same thing. If your problems are more of a spiritual nature, you go to your pastor, or a pastoral assistant. If your problems are more of a mental nature, you go to a therapist. But, as I have already said, the two must not be separated. The best thing to do is go to a pastor with sufficient psychological training, or to a psychotherapist with sufficient theological training.

Most students of psychology are especially interested in "clinical psychology," and Christians also will take a keen interest in the implications of a Christian psychology for Christian clinical psychology, or for counseling, or whatever you wish to call it. On the one hand, there seems to be an ever-growing number of people in the Western world who need psychical-spiritual help. On the other hand, the number of non-Christian—or even anti-Christian—approaches to psychotherapy is on the rise. Many Christians, feeling burdened with mental problems, can no longer see the forest for the trees. In their struggle they feel they have been delivered up to the "pagans," and in many cases they are justified in feeling this way.

What they badly need are Christian counselors who have not been wounded and scarred by worldly psychotherapies. These are counselors who are not confused as to what role the Christian faith can, and should, play in the process of counseling. These are counselors who are armed with a thorough and intimate knowledge of the Bible *and* of Christian psychology, and know just how to use this knowledge in practical counseling. If all this is to be achieved, a lot of rubble will first have to be cleared away. Professional counselors are not the only ones who are in need of new reflection on these matters. Ordinary people need it too, regardless of whether they have as yet come into contact with counselors. And this book is also intended for non-psychologists.

However, there is one thing that I must add at this point. This book deals not just with counseling, but with Christian psychology in general. Indeed, our reflection needs to start with Christian psychology in general. You should like that! It is a fine thing to discover more about ourselves in a general way, not just about ourselves when we have mental or spiritual problems. Psychology is in the first place about healthy, "normal" people! Moreover, we need to start with Christian psychology in general because we can only make progress in constructing a science of Christian counseling if we have first understood something of what a Christian psychology in general might be.

Interest

You may be interested in the phenomenon of Man without being particularly interested in psychology. This is most likely because you are less interested in science, and more in the practical aspects of what humans are and do. That is quite understandable, and there is nothing wrong with you (although it does make it much less likely for you to have picked up this book in the first place). The opposite would be less understandable, i.e., if you were interested in psychology, but totally *un*interested in the human phenomenon. That would be weird! Psychology is about you and me. It deals with what goes on inside us as human beings, and how what goes on inside governs our behavior. You might also say that it deals with Man's mental life, or his "soul," or his "mind," or whatever else you might like to call it.

These are all just words, of course, which mean one thing to one person and something quite different to another. Therefore we shall have to look critically at all these words in due course. But for now I would rather stick with a somewhat vague description and say that a book about psychology basically deals not only with human behavior but with "what goes on inside a person." The Bible, as the written form of God's self-revelation, trains a strong spotlight on Man and illumines our human existence. If we did not have that spotlight, we would get nowhere and would stumble around in the dark because we would miss the most essential knowledge that we should possess about Man.

The candlelight of secular psychology does not bring to light anything that really gets to the heart of the matter (or of Man At best, secular psychology sheds some light on Man's surface, on certain peripheral phenomena, although it may *claim* to tell us something about Man's inner being. For instance, it may assert that Man is nothing but living matter; all his behavior can be reduced to the activities of atoms and molecules. Or it may claim the opposite: matter is in fact a form of "mind"; everything is "mind," and Man is the organism in which "mind" has unfolded itself most clearly. However, nothing of this touches in the least what Man really is: a creature made in the image and likeness of God (Gen. 1:26, 28). Where this is not known, or known but not believed, psychologists can only scratch at the surface of the human phenomenon. Even then, they can arrive at great insights, from which Christian psychologists can definitely benefit. But they lack an anthropological perspective in which all these insights find their proper place, in the true coherence of the phenomenon of Man.

God's Word is a spotlight that illumines the whole of our existence. As David says, "In your light we see light" (Ps. 36:9b). But if we are to apprehend the *details* properly, we must take out a magnifying glass and *investigate* the human phenomenon. We opt now for scientific refinement, though continuing to walk in the light that the Bible sheds on Man as a whole. This is the way in which a truly Christian psychology can be developed. In such a psychology, we do our work not by the light of a flickering candle but with the assistance of a powerful spotlight. In the splendid light that the Bible sheds over the whole creation, we can carry out scientific experimentation to bring to light a host of details that remain hidden from the uncritical onlooker.

Christian psychology makes grateful use of that gloriously radiant light of Scripture. We can also understand it as a magnifying glass which enables us to learn innumerable interesting details about ourselves that otherwise we would not have seen. At times those details delight us, and at other times they shock us, but we must take all of them seriously to heart. Thus we learn more about ourselves and also about our fellow human beings, and in the process we discover more about the greatness of our Creator, in whose image and likeness Man was created. Ultimately, this raises Christian psychology—knowledge of Man intertwined with knowledge of God—to a form of worship.

Chapter Two
STARTING POINTS FOR A CHRISTIAN PSYCHOLOGY

There was a time when many people thought that scientists were investigators who collected empirical facts in an unbiased way, and then constructed theories based on these facts. Today there are still people who think along such lines, even scientists. But a great many scientists now realize that this is simply not the case. For one, there is no such thing as an "unbiased" scientist, as I emphasized in chapter 1. For another, you cannot just "collect facts," for you would not know where to start. When scientists collect their data, they have a very specific purpose in mind; there is something they are looking for. They collect very selectively.

The reason is that scientists do not begin by just collecting facts. They start with a number of preconceived ideas—perhaps derived from earlier investigations—which they intend to test by means of further research. They do not move from facts to theories, but from theories (or more simply, ideas) to facts, and then back to their theories.

Moreover, we should realize that scientists always start their research with a number of very *general* ideas about the nature of the world, about what kind of thing Man is, about what knowledge is, about what science is, and so forth. Often these general ideas exist in a half-conscious form; many scientists are not aware of them, and do not even think about them. These ideas are of such a fundamental or *a prioric* nature that they cannot be experimentally tested. They belong to the realm of faith, to the scientist's basic beliefs, to his worldview. This worldview precedes, underlies, and conditions all his scientific work, whether or not the scientist is conscious of it. No psychologist will start a study concerning certain aspects of the human phenomenon without certain preconceived ideas—of which he may have little or no awareness—about who and what Man is. Let us look a little more closely into this matter.

Man: Who and What Is He?

Suppose you wanted to build a bridge, or develop a new kind of denture, or formulate a physical theory about the nature of light. Would your worldview play a major role in this enterprise? Would a Christian build a "Christian" bridge, and would it differ from a "Jewish" or "Islamic" or "atheist" bridge? I think it goes without saying that it would not. But if we undertook to expand our knowledge about human beings by developing new theories, then it would be very important what sort of view of Man we would presuppose. On the basis of his worldview, every psychologist, right at the outset, adopts a certain general point of view on the question of who and what Man is. What are we? Ennobled apes, or image-bearers of God? The difference is colossal. There may be some psychologists who deny that they start with a certain view of Man, but they are simply fooling themselves and others.

The history of psychology (see chapter 5) makes it very clear how much the famous pioneer psychologists were influenced in their research by their respective views of Man. Usually, Christian psychologists are honest enough to admit that they start their scientific work with a Christian view of Man. It is for this reason that some other scientists have accused Christian psychologists of being biased—and it is perfectly true! But the point to understand here is that *all* psychologists are biased and that they *all* start from a certain view of Man, whether it be materialist or spiritual, existentialist or evolutionist, humanist or Christian, or whatever. It is not that other psychologists are neutral, objective, and unbiased, whereas Christian ones are not. The difference is rather that secular psychologists start from a view of Man that has been devised by apostate Man himself, on the basis of his materialist or evolutionist prejudices, whereas Christian psychologists start from a view of Man based on God's Word-revelation. One thing is sure: both start with *faith*.

Before we explore in more detail "all that goes on in Man," which is the aim of the study of psychology, we must devote some attention to the Christian view of Man, to which I have referred now several times. What this means, unfortunately, is that right at the outset, some of the most difficult questions of Christian psychology come up for discussion. I am afraid this cannot be helped. If we do not get some clarity on the *starting points* of Christian psychology, we will not have a solid and durable foundation on which to erect the actual edifice of psychological theory. The starting points, or first principles, may indeed seem more abstract or theoretical than the concrete results of psychological experiments, but the more thorough our discussion of them at this point, the better our chances of interpreting the results of any psychological experiments correctly a little later on.

Aspects of Man

Let us first try to subdivide all of cosmic reality into a number of distinct realms, or whatever you call them. Since ancient times, many thinkers have made the following distinctions in empirical reality:

(a) The *inorganic* (or *inanimate*, or *physical* world) of material, lifeless things (stones, mountains, lakes, hydrogen molecules, gold nuggets, bridges, houses, bicycles, paintings, etc.).

(b) The *organic* (or *vegetative*, or *biotic*) world, or the realm of plants, that is, all living organisms that, as indicated in the word "biotic," possess life but lack any form of consciousness or sensitivity.

(c) The *psychical* world, or the realm of animals. These are the organisms that not only live but also possess some form of consciousness, and possibly also sensitivity or feeling. This is a rather complicated group, and so we must immediately make a further distinction which has often been neglected. I will not discuss the lowest organisms, such as the unicellular animals (such as amoebas or paramecia) and the sponges, which have no nervous system.

1. The *perceptive* group: There are many lower species of animals that have instincts and the ability to develop reflexes and experience sensations because they possess sense organs and a nervous system—no matter how primitive—but have no knowl-

edge of affections or emotions. This category may include most animals with the exception of birds and mammals, and perhaps some other species.

2. The *sensitive* group: Higher animals not only know sensations, reflexes, and instincts, but also have a richly developed life of feeling (affections, emotions, drives). The reason for this is that their brain has certain centers that are lacking in the lower animals.

(d) The *spiritive* world, or the realm of human beings, who not only possess a life of feelings, but a richly developed thought-life as well. Because of their thought-life, they can, for example, amass and reproduce conscious knowledge. Moreover, they possess an abundance of creativity, and are also capable of making conscious, deliberate decisions as acts of the will. (I have coined the word "spiritive" for the world of the mind to avoid the word "spiritual", which often has a religious meaning.)

When we look closely at these four realms, we soon see that each of them includes the previous one. Man is, indeed, a typically "spiritive" being, but his life also has a sensitive aspect, a perceptive aspect, a biotic aspect, and a physical aspect. The word "aspect" (from the Latin) literally means "the act of looking." Thus, an aspect is a particular point of view from which we can look at something. Hence we can look at Man from a spiritive point of view, a sensitive point of view, a perceptive point of view, a biotic point of view, and even a physical point of view, even though the spiritive involves the aspects that most fully characterize Man.

Likewise, we can look at higher animals from a sensitive, perceptive, biotic, or even physical point of view, although it is the sensitive aspect that is most characteristic of these animals. In similar fashion, lower animals can be looked at from either a perceptive, biotic, or physical viewpoint, even though the perceptive aspect is most characteristic of lower animals. In the same way, plants can be looked at from either a biotic or physical viewpoint, even though the biotic aspect is most characteristic of plants. A stone has no biotic aspect because it is inanimate. And an animal is not "typically biotic" because, even though it has organic life, this life is not what most fully characterizes it. An animal is characterized by the perceptive or the sensitive aspect, respectively.

On the basis of the distinctions made above, we can now draw a diagram of five realms using the aspects as a perpendicular division. In horizontal terms we were able to distinguish five realms. Continuing on this basis, we can distinguish five aspects vertically. In order to look more carefully at these aspects, we must first introduce some new terms. Technical terms are necessary in this context because they have one meaning only, whereas words used in everyday life may well have a number of different meanings. Taken together, I shall call the perceptive, sensitive, and spiritive aspects the *mental aspects*.

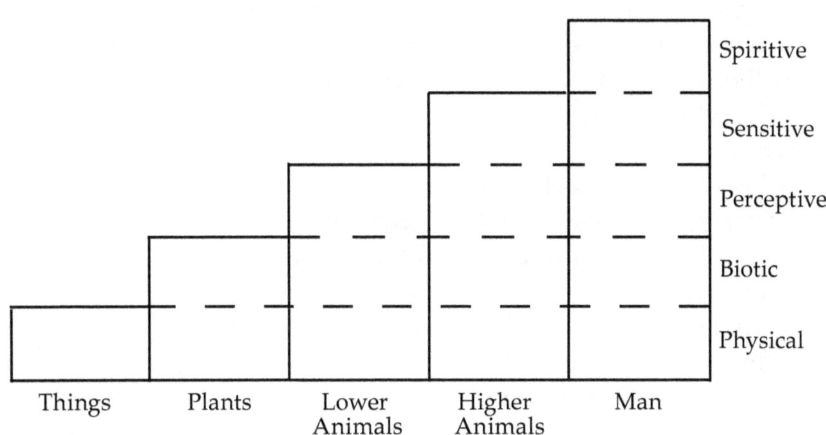

Now let us examine the three mental points of view from which we can look at Man.

1. First we have the *perceptive* aspect, or the aspect of sensation and *perception,* that is, sense perception. Note that this involves not only the physical stimulation of the sensory organ (the light that falls on the retina, etc.)—which is purely physical-biotic—but also the sensory *awareness* of those stimuli through the brain. Such awareness is, in fact, the most fundamental form of consciousness. Please note that it is not the brain that is aware of things; the animal (or Man) is aware of some things, with the help of the brain.

2. The *sensitive* aspect, or the aspect of feeling in the broadest sense. Later on, we will distinguish between affections, drives, and emotions, but without concerning ourselves too much about the differences between them.

3. The *spiritive* aspects (note the plural!). Here I am thinking of what typifies the functioning of the human spirit or mind, which later will be further subdivided into knowing, imagining, and willing. Now, these are not the only ways in which we can view this functioning of the human mind, for Man, as a "spiritive" being, is also one who thinks rationally (*logical* aspect), creates culture (*formative* aspect), and formulates his thoughts in language (*lingual* aspect). Furthermore, he is a social, economic, and aesthetic being (*social, economic* and *aesthetic* aspects). He possesses a sense of justice (*juridical* aspect), as well as a moral sense (*moral* aspect). Finally, he is a believing being, ("believer" is here taken in the most general sense); every Man has basic beliefs of some kind, whether they are expressed as an ideology or a religion (*pistical* aspect).

For a fuller explanation of the theory of the modal aspects, I refer you once again to my book *Wisdom for Thinkers*; you will not find it easy to understand the following arguments without having read this previous volume. In it, you will find that in the Christian philosophy that I present, I actually distinguish *sixteen* different modal aspects. Earlier in this chapter, I have distinguished four lower aspects—the physical, the biotic, the perceptive, the sensitive—and nine different spiritive aspects. Now I add that the physical aspect presupposes a kinematic aspect, the kinematic presupposes a spatial aspect, and the spatial presupposes an arithmetical aspect. That is a total of sixteen modal aspects.

In the meantime, it should be clear to the reader that each higher aspect presupposes every aspect below it. What I mean to say is that we can never conceive of a higher aspect that is completely detached from all the lower ones. Within our empirical cosmic reality, there are no spiritive beings that are not at the same time *also* sensitive *and* perceptive and biotic *and* physical beings. In other words, people—who are the only spiritive beings within empirical reality that we know of—have all the other modal aspects in their makeup as well. That being said, we do know of sensitive beings that are not spiritive, for example, mammals. But we do not know of any sensitive beings that are not at the same time *also* perceptive *and* biotic *and* physical. We know of biotic organisms that are not perceptive or sensitive, namely, plants. But we do not know of any biotic organisms that are not at the same time *also* physical *and* kinematic *and* spatial *and* arithmetical. And I could go on. It all comes down to this: the lower aspects can do without the higher, but (at least in the visible world that we inhabit) the higher do not occur apart from the lower. We can speak here of a *hierarchy* of realms and aspects.

This point is very important for understanding the difference between "feeling" and "thinking," for example. Feeling and thinking are frequently put on a par. Some earlier authors have even argued that the *soul* consists of *reason, feeling,* and *will* (we can still read this in certain Christian writings, e.g., by Watchman Nee); the idea reminds us of Plato's tripartite soul. In reality these three are not on a par at all, since emotion does occur without thinking (as is the case in mammals and even—under certain circumstances—some people). However, thinking is *not* possible apart from feeling; that is to say, in beings that think (i.e., humans), the thinking they do could never be detached from certain drives, affections, or emotions. We see something similar in the case of the *will* (which, psychologically speaking, is a confusing term anyway). Even the lowest impulses in Man or animal could be called a (primitive) form of will, if you like, and this will can certainly get along without any thinking or feeling.

In summary, reason has to do with our spiritive life, more specifically with the logical aspect of it. Feeling has to do with our sensitive life, and the will has to do with our perceptive life (impulses), our sensitive life (drives), and our spiritive life (the will in the sense of deliberate decisions). We conclude from this that it is hardly useful to describe mental life as consisting of feeling, thinking, and will.

The *Ground* of All Things

What makes this theory of the modal aspects of cosmic reality so important? More to the point, is there anything especially Christian about distinguishing in reality the five realms I have listed? Yes, there is. Such a division of reality into five different realms can already be found in the ancient world, both in the Bible and elsewhere. When we read the biblical story of creation as recorded in Genesis 1, we see the various realms of creatures successively appearing from God's hand, just as though a new dimension was being added in each case to the creation taken as a totality:

1. In verse 1 (the first day of creation) we hear about the creation of *material things*. "Heaven and earth" is a common description of the entire cosmic reality (cf., e.g., Ps. 69:34; Jer. 23:24; 33:25; Matt. 24:35; Acts 17:24).

2. In verse 12 (the third day) we see *plant life* appearing.

3. In verse 21 (the fifth day) we are told about the creation of the *lower animals*.

4. In verse 25 (the sixth day) the *higher animals* appear on the scene.

5. In verse 27 (also the sixth day) we witness the creation of *Man*.

However, as I indicated above, the fact that such distinctions also occur in the Scriptures does not make them specifically biblical or Christian. What is of prime importance is the *use* (whether Christian or non-Christian) to which these distinctions are put. In the past, researchers have time and again proven unable to resist the temptation to try to *reduce the different modal aspects to one another.*

This temptation is entirely understandable. Any thinking person would want to get a general overview of the enormous diversity of phenomena. Now, one way to do so would be to introduce a certain order into the cosmic world by claiming that all aspects are in fact specific forms of just one of them. One could say, for example, "While it is true that I see living organisms and even thinking people all around me, I nevertheless maintain that, in the final analysis, it all comes down to *nothing* but matter." This is the claim that even the most complicated spiritive processes can be reduced to the activities of atoms and molecules.

Anyone who makes such a claim has provided himself with a kind of "transparency" by stating that, in the end, everything is just matter. Such a person has not *per se* denied the biotic, the psychical, or the spiritive. He has left room for them, but he is arguing that they can ultimately be *reduced* to the physical aspect. Organic life is a reality, but in the end it is nothing but a specific organizational form of matter. Perception and feeling are realities, they are no illusions, but on closer inspection, these phenomena can be boiled down to specific properties of atoms and molecules.

People who hold such a belief (Marxists, for example) we call *materialists,* for they believe that at bottom everything is "matter." There have also been people who have argued the exact opposite. They can be called *spiritualists* (or, in my terminology, *spiritivists;* they are not to be confused with *spiritists,* people claiming to communicate with the spirits of the dead). They claim, for instance, that matter is compressed energy, and energy is just another word for "mind." At bottom, everything is spiritive, or "mind." They look to the spiritive as the ground of all things, and they argue that, in the final analysis, even matter is spiritive in nature—except that in matter, the spiritive is still strongly "encapsulated," or something like that. In plants, the spiritive, or mind, has reached a somewhat more advanced stage, where it assumes the form of the biotic. When we turn to animals, we see that the development has progressed still further, for there it assumes the form of the perceptive, or even the sensitive. And in Man, the spiritive (consciousness, mind) has come to its fullest development.

Of course, there is a large difference between materialists and spiritualists, but in one respect there is a clear similarity between them. Both locate the ground of all things *within visible reality itself,* that is to say, within matter or within the mind. Thus, the so-called *vitalists* (from the Latin *vita,* meaning "life"), a group including people from Hippocrates (c. 460-c. 370 B.C.) to Hans Driesch (1867-1941), look for this ground within the biotic, while the so-called *psychical monists,* such as Gerardus Heymans (1857-1930), look for it within the "psychical." What is important to understand is that all of them look for it *within created reality.* Supposedly, the principle from which the whole of reality can be explained may be found somewhere within cosmic reality. People who hold this kind of view ("A, B, and C are at bottom nothing but P") are called *reductionists,* because they reduce the entire cosmos to one single basic principle.

Because they do so, we must characterize all the views of reality they develop as fundamentally un-Christian. A Christian view of reality looks for the ground of all created reality not *with-*

in creation, but *outside it*—in the Creator. When we use the word "ground," we mean two things:

(a) God is the *Creator* of all things; he has called them into existence by his word (Rom. 5:17; Heb. 11:3);

(b) God is also the *Preserver* of all things; he constantly upholds the universe by the word of his power (Heb. 1:3), so that created things do not exist in themselves, independently of God, but exist continually and without interruption by virtue of God's sustaining strength.

Only the Bible reveals to us a God who created and preserves the world (the Qur'an has just borrowed this from the Bible). Only Scripture speaks of a God who was there before the world began, who was and is always above and outside the world, while at the same time sustaining the world and remaining most intimately involved with it. Once we have understood that the ground of reality is not to be found within created reality or any of its modal aspects, but in the Creator himself, we will no longer be tempted to try to reduce all the aspects to just one or two of them. Anyone who does carry out such a reduction takes away from what is absolutely unique in the physical, the biotic, the perceptive, the sensitive, and the spiritive as God has constituted them.

Some researchers, having understood this to a certain extent, have tried to reduce everything to *two* aspects rather than just one. For example, they start from a psycho-physical duality, which consists of a physical factor ("matter") and a psychical factor ("mind"), and claim to see instances of this duality everywhere in created reality. Of course, they have thought in particular of Man as a duality of body and soul (or spirit). This idea is still very common, especially among Christians. But those who reason in this way still get stuck. In the first place, it is not possible, on the basis of such a dualism, to do proper justice to the other aspects, especially the biotic aspect and the various spiritive aspects.

In the second place, those who see duality everywhere easily turn this into a true *dualism*, in which the two recognized basic factors stand in a kind of antithesis to one another. Such thinkers do not sufficiently recognize the *unity* of the whole of creation. In our understanding of the world, it is important that, on the one hand, we should leave room for the *diversity* of the created cosmic reality (including all of the sixteen modal aspects I have discussed in my *Wisdom for Thinkers*). On the other hand, we should remain aware of the fact that the whole created reality finds its unity in the one God, who created the different modal aspects, and preserves all of created reality through his power. As a matter of fact, even within Man himself the various aspects come together in a striking way, namely, in what we call the heart. But this is a matter that we will deal with later (see especially chapters 3 and 9).

For the present, it suffices to establish that in a Christian view of Man we do not derive one aspect from another but allow each aspect to stand in its unique sense as given by God. We do not reduce the aspects to one another but relate them to God, the Creator and Preserver, as the ground of all things. In other words, we do not look for the ground of the realities surrounding us within creation itself, because to do so would ultimately be a form of idolatry. After all, idolatry is the worship of part of creation, making it into an absolute, and deifying it as though it were the Creator himself (see Rom. 1:22-23). We do not make an absolute of matter, of life, of the psyche, or of the mind, because all these are but facets of creation. Rather, we relate them all to God, their Creator. As Christians, we regard them as dependent on God, the Preserver, who, as the One-and-Only, is really "absolute." Only God is self-sufficient and independent of everything else. Every part of the creation is dependent on God for its coming into being and for its continuing existence. We do not worship the creation or any part thereof (whether that be the material or the spiritive) by absolutizing it. We worship the Creator.

Christian Theory of Man (Anthropology)

Up to this point, we have talked about five different realms of cosmic reality: the physical, the biotic, the perceptive, the sensitive, and the spiritive realms. At the same time, we have spoken of the physical aspect (dealing with matter, the biotic aspect (dealing with life), the perceptive aspect (dealing with perception), the sensitive aspect (dealing with feeling), and the various spiritive aspects (from the logical to the pistical, the modal aspects of the human mind). Furthermore, we have seen that, except for the aspects of the mind, all other aspects are not limited to Man. All of visible reality is physical (or material); all organisms are biotic (or living); all animals as well as Man are perceptive; all higher animals as well as Man are sensitive in nature.

In this part of the chapter we shall be dealing with Man in particular. The science that undertakes to understand a little more about Man, systematically laying out how Man is put together and what makes him tick, is called *anthropology*. This word is derived from Greek, and means a "logical analysis of Man." We should understand here that we are talking about philosophical anthropology, and not cultural anthropology. The latter (which used to be known as ethnology) is a special science focusing on the history and development of humankind, and its various cultures, nations, and races.

It is easy to see why the study of philosophical anthropology is fascinating to so many people. Anthropology does not study just any creature—no, in anthropology Man confronts the human phenomenon, that is, he studies *himself*. Philosophical anthropology came to the fore about a hundred years ago, at a time when Man had become a mystery to himself, and had begun to ask, "Who am I?" The question is not meant to inquire just about the individual in comparison with other humans, but it refers to every human as such. What kind of peculiar animal, or living organism, am I? What makes me different from all other living beings? By studying such questions, Man indulges one of his own deepest interests, namely, the interest he takes with regard to himself. In this way, anthropology can be called an analytical, abstract, theoretical, systematic form of *self-knowledge*.

According to the Bible, Man is the only creature who has been created in the image of God and after his likeness (Gen. 1:26, 28). As such, Man is the head of creation. Therefore the entire creation, the whole *cosmos*, does not only find its *ground* in God, the Creator and Preserver, but finds its *center* in Man, the being that is its head and *raison d'être* (the very reason for its existence). Christians believe that cosmic reality would make no sense if Man had not been created. Therefore, no phenomenon within the universe is more interesting, more fascinating, more relevant, and more important for analysis, investigation, and study than the human phenomenon.

Idionomies in a Mint

We have already seen that there are sixteen different *aspects* to be distinguished in Man, varying from the arithmetical to the pistical aspects. Now we will go a step further and assert that we can also distinguish five *structures* in Man. In my *Wisdom for Thinkers,* I have called them individuality structures, or identity structures, and also "idionomies," the term I have preferred. Each of the five idionomies we can distinguish in Man's immanent, corporeal existence, functions in all of the sixteen modal aspects we have distinguished. This distinction between modal aspects and idionomies is an important step forward in our argument. To make it easier to understand, we shall begin by looking at a mint plant, and will continue with a midge, a mouse, and finally with Man.

Like a mount, a mint has a physical (material) aspect. In this regard, the mint and the mount have something in common. But at the same time, there is a considerable difference between them, even in their physical respect. On the one hand, the material of a mint is subject to the same physico-chemical laws as the material of the mount. But on the other hand, the material of the mint is also entirely *different* in nature. The difference is that the material of the mint is constituted in such a way as to *anticipate* life. Mint *matter* is not life, but it is put together in such a way as to make life possible; that is to say, it can *carry* life, or provide a *foundation* or *substratum* for physiological (organic, vegetative, "life") processes. The matter we find in a mount cannot do this. In the mount there is only one structural plan to be found—the physico-chemical idionomy. But in the mint we can distinguish two idionomies:

1. The *physical idionomy*: This structural plan includes the chemical elements, physical processes, and chemical reactions that, on the one hand, guarantee the unity of the material structure of the mint and by which, on the other hand, the material components are still able to undergo constant change. In this physical *structure* we distinguish five modal *aspects,* the arithmetical, the spatial, the kinematic, the physical and the biotic aspect. We will now focus on the last two as being the most relevant to our present purpose:

(a) *The physical aspect*: The mint matter is subject to physico-chemical laws.

(b) *The biotic aspect*: The mint matter is not as such subject to biotic laws but it nevertheless anticipates the biotic aspect; that is to say, it is put together in such a way as to carry life, that is, provide a foundation for it. In my book *Wisdom for Thinkers*, I have explained why in radical Christian philosophy we express this as follows: the physical idionomy has *subject functions* in the arithmetical, spatial, kinematic, and physical aspects, but it also has an *internal object function* in the biotic aspect. That is, mint matter as such is not alive, but it functions as an object in the life processes of the mint (we can think of the inanimate molecules in the mint's living cells).

2. *The biotic idionomy*: This includes the cell structure, the tissue structure, the organic structure, and the physiological life processes of a living organism (breathing, digestion, metabolism, reproduction, and hormonal processes). In this biotic idionomy, we can distinguish the same five aspects: the arithmetical, spatial, kinematic, physical, and biotic aspects. Again, we will focus on the last two:

(a) *The physical aspect*: The physiological processes in the mint are carried by the mint's physico-chemical structures and processes, which thereby provide a substratum for these life processes.

(b) *The biotic aspect*: In accordance with their own unique nature, physiological processes are subject to biotic laws of nature. Therefore, we say that this second idionomy is *typified* or *qualified* by this biotic aspect. The biotic idionomy has subject functions in the arithmetical, spatial, kinematic, physical, and biotic aspects. It may also have object functions, but they are of an *external* nature. That is, mint plants may function as objects in the life of animals and humans.

What we encounter here, then, is a hierarchical "piling up" of idionomies, in which the higher idionomy, so to speak, *encloses* (encapsulates) the lower idionomy.

Idionomies in a Midge

In a similar fashion, we can now take a look at the midge, where we encounter a hierarchy of *three* idionomies. Midge matter anticipates (enables, conditions, carries) not only physiological processes but also processes of sensory perception, which we may characterize as a form of awareness or consciousness, no matter how primitive. For that reason, we need to pay attention not just to the first four subject functions and the internal biotic object function of the physical idionomy, but also to the internal perceptive object function when we study the physical idionomy of a midge.

In more common language, what does this involve? Midge matter as such is not subject to perceptive natural laws—atoms and molecules cannot see or hear or smell—but it is of such a nature as to *anticipate* perception. That is, this physico-chemical material in the midge is such that it has the capacity of enabling, conditioning and carrying perceptive processes. Please note that although matter as such is purely physico-chemical, in animals and Man it is unique in that it is capable of something that no other physico-chemical material in the cosmos could ever do: it can carry perceptive processes, thereby enabling some form of awareness or consciousness. Please note, too, that while these perceptive processes cannot be *reduced* to physico-chemical properties, they are not conceivable *without* a physico-chemical substratum.

So it is with the biotic idionomy of a midge, in which we likewise distinguish a perceptive object function inasmuch as the physiological processes in the midge also anticipate perception. What this means, very concretely, is that in the central nervous system of the midge, there are biotic processes that make conscious perception of sensory stimuli possible, condition them, or carry them. But then, in the case of the midge, there is yet a third idionomy, namely, the *perceptive* structure, in which there are again these various modal aspects to be distinguished. That is, the sensory phenomena, which belong to this perceptive idionomy, are supported or carried by physico-chemical structures and processes, as well as biotic processes, but they themselves, as such, are subject to perceptive laws (such as the laws of stimulus and response).

The perceptive idionomy has six subject functions, varying from the arithmetical to the perceptive subject function. This simply means that it is subject to arithmetical, spatial, kinematic, energetic (physical), biotic, and perceptive laws. However, it is *not* subject to any laws ranging from the sensitive to the pistical (laws which take on the nature of *norms*). For instance, the perceptive idionomy does not contain thoughts; that is, it does not have a logical subject function. But it can be thought about, analyzed and investigated by humans; in other words, it has a logical object function in that it can be the object of human thinking.

Idionomies in a Mouse

In a similar fashion, we can distinguish *four* idionomies in the mouse. In addition to the physical, biotic, and perceptive idionomies, the mouse also has a sensitive idionomy. The latter structure has subject functions in the arithmetical, spatial, kinematic, energetic, biotic, perceptive, and sensitive modalities.

As to the energetic (physical idionomy, mouse matter differs from mint matter and midge matter in that it anticipates the sensitive—it has an internal sensitive object function—whereas mint matter and midge matter do not. What this means, concretely speaking, is that in the brain of a mouse we find certain lobes that have a peculiar physico-chemical structure that makes *feelings* possible. That is to say, they enable, condition and carry feelings (affections, drives, emotionsin a purely physico-chemical way. On the one hand, feelings cannot be *reduced* to these physico-chemical processes, but on the other hand, without these processes they would be impossible. A house is more than its foundation, but it could not do without it.

The biotic idionomy of the mouse too has an internal sensitive object function, for the physiological (organic, vegetative) processes in the brain lobes and activities in the autonomic nervous system are specialized in such a way that they too help to make the mouse's life of feeling possible. There can be no feelings without these physiological processes. The same is true for the perceptive structure of a mouse: its perceptions are equally necessary to make its life of feeling possible. Nevertheless, at the same time, its life of feeling cannot be *reduced* to the perceptive aspect or the biotic aspect, much less to the physical aspect. The mouse's affections, drives, and emotions are something entirely new and unique; they have their own characteristics and properties. That is why we postulate a fourth idionomy in the mouse: the *sensitive* one. This sensitive idionomy is typified or qualified by the sensitive aspect, which has its own unique laws.

The Five Human Structures

If you have managed to follow me so far, it will only be one more step to understand the *five* idionomies that we must distinguish when it comes to Man. In addition to those we have already mentioned, Man also has a *spiritive* idionomy. We must note carefully what this means. In the first place, it implies that the lower idionomies—the physical, the biotic, the perceptive, and the sensitive—are essentially different in Man than they are in mints, midges, and mice. That is to say, when it comes to Man, the physical, the biotic, the perceptive, and the sensitive idionomies all have an internal spiritive object function. In a concrete sense, this means that, when we study the human brain, we see clearly that (a) the physico-chemical matter we find there, (b) the physiological ("life") processes, (c) the perceptive processes, and (d) the sensitive processes we find there, are so constituted as to make possible (enable, condition, carry, and form a substratum for) the spiritive life of Man, which includes his thoughts, deliberations, decisions, imagination, etc..

Man's spiritive functioning is proper to this new fifth idionomy, which we call the spiritive idionomy. The special characteristic of this highest idionomy is that it has subject functions in all sixteen modal aspects, from the arithmetical to the pistical aspects. Whereas the lower human idionomies have only internal spiritive object functions, Man's spiritive life functions as a subject in all spiritive modalities. That is, Man's spiritive idionomy is concerned with the fact that he can think, deliberate, make decisions of the will, invent, create, love, believe, etc. However, I repeat that, on the one hand, his thinking, deliberating, etc. cannot be reduced to the physical, the perceptive, or the spiritive, but on the other hand, these spiritive processes would not be possible without the lower idionomies, which carry them.

To put it bluntly, there can be no thinking, no loving your partner, and no believing in God (or the gods), without an exchange of potassium and sodium atoms on either side of the cell membrane (A. E. Wilder-Smith [1915-1995]). You may go wrong here in two ways. Those materialists who claim that thinking, loving, and believing can be *reduced* to such physico-chemical processes are utterly mistaken. Thinking, loving, and believing are carried by these processes, but they go far beyond them. However, those spiritualists (including many Christians) who think that thinking, loving, and believing are activities of some soul, spirit, or mind, which allegedly operate independently of the body, are equally mistaken. There can be no faith without physics.

As I have already explained in my *Wisdom for Thinkers*, the physical, biotic, perceptive, and sensitive idionomies are entirely governed by natural laws. But the spiritive functioning of Man knows functions in accordance with its own specific laws. These laws are not to be considered natural laws but *norms*, which are entirely different in nature. I will come back to this later.

The Mental Human Structures

The five idionomies that together make up Man's immanent corporeal existence may be called *human structures* (German: *Humanstrukturen*; Dutch: *humaanstructuren*), in order to make it clear that Man differs from mints, midges, and mice not only in possessing a spiritive structure, but also in that the four lower human idionomies do in fact differ fundamentally from the corresponding idionomies as found in plants and animals. For instance, the physical idionomy in mints, midges, and mice can carry biotic processes, but not spiritive ones.

Let us now take a closer look at the three highest idionomies of Man, which we shall call the *mental* idionomies:

1. *The perceptive idionomy*: This includes sense perception and a number of phenomena directly based upon it. They are:

(a) *Instincts*: An instinct is a behavior based on an innate response to a particular sensation. (The sucking behavior of a baby may be an example—perhaps the *only* example—of a human instinct; as soon as the baby's lips touch the mother's nipple, it begins to suck.)

(b) *Reflexes*: In the broadest sense of the term, a reflex is any immediate behavioral response that occurs involuntarily and without special thought, especially the learned responses. We immediately step on the brakes of our car when we see a small child suddenly crossing the street; this is an example of such a learned reflex. In Man, perceptive processes are carried by the brain stem, but the cerebellum also plays an important role here.

2. *The sensitive idionomy*: This includes all inner emotions and feelings. Here we can distinguish between the following:

(a) *Affections*: This is feeling disposed to or attracted by something (positive affections) or repelled by something (negative affection), finding something pleasant or unpleasant, desirable or undesirable, pretty or nasty, likable or unlikable.

(b) *Impulses*: These are needs, longings, desires; the experiencing—felt as unpleasant—of a lack of something, or a pressing desire for something that one is not willing, or not able, to do without; often called "urges" or "drives," for instance, the sexual drive.

(c) *Emotions*: Being touched, suddenly being moved inwardly. Some common examples are: joy, pleasure, sorrow, rage, fear, displeasure, disappointment, shame. In Man, the sensitive structure is carried especially by the limbic system (lobes) of the brain.

3. *The spiritive idionomy*: This includes what we call the spiritive functioning, or, if you like, the functioning of the human mind (as long as we do not make the mind a thing which is independent of the body). It is within this idionomy that human deliberations, imaginings, and decisions occur. Such operations of the human mind are sometimes called *acts*. Acts are inner operations of the mind that are directed toward resulting actions, to external behaviors. An animal also performs certain *actions*, but they do not arise out of *acts*, for animals do not have a spiritive or act-life. The actions of an animal follow instead from its perceptively determined instincts and/or sensitively determined urges or drives, not from mental deliberations and free decisions of the will.

Such instincts and drives are not absent in Man, but human deeds are determined primarily by Man's act-life or spiritive life, that is, the free, deliberate functioning of his mind. This is why Man must take responsibility for his deeds, whereas an animal does not have to. Responsibility is *response-ability*: a human being has the ability, and the duty, to give a response to the question as to why he or she did this or that, in other words, from which (mental) *acts* his/her *actions* arose. Man can, and should, *answer* for his deeds.

Spiritive Functioning

People engaged in scientific research sometimes employ strange terms. Their aim is not to appear interesting. Rather, they use such selected terms because they can give them very precise definitions. The words we use in our ordinary, everyday speech are often unsuitable for precise use because they have various undesirable additional meanings and connotations, or perhaps because they are not precise enough to define exactly what is meant. Therefore, in this explanation too, it is inevitable that, on the one hand, the reader will be burdened with a number of new terms that at first might appear strange. On the other hand, he will miss certain other terms that are familiar to him, such as "soul" and "spirit," words that have so many confusing meanings that they are hardly worth using at all in psychology. But the reader should rest assured that technical terms will be used only when necessary. In due course, the technical terms to be introduced here—just a small number—will become quite familiar.

It is now time to take a closer look at the spiritive functioning or "act-life" in Man. First, we may distinguish *three* dimensions in it:

1. *The cognitive dimension*: This involves *knowing* and *coming to know* by means of thinking. Those acts—internal processes within the spiritive idionomy—that deal especially with such thinking and coming to know, with deliberation and reasoning, we call *cognitive* acts.

2. *The creative dimension*: This involves *imagining*, fancying or picturing (visualizing) something, (trying) to devise/invent something. Acts that consist primarily of trying to imagine (picture, visualize) something which already exists (Dutch: *zich indenken*), or of trying to invent something new (Dutch: *uitdenken*), we call *imaginative-creative* acts.

(3) *The conative* (or *volitional*) *dimension*: This has to do with willing or with conscious striving after something, that is, with desiring, choosing, and deciding. Acts that primarily involve an inner choice or a decision we call *conative* (or volitional) acts.

These three dimensions, of course, are always interwoven with one another; they never occur separately. For example, the decision to buy a house is by definition a typically *conative* act, but at the same time, there is a cognitive element to it. One needs to know a great deal about houses in general, and the house under consideration in particular. Furthermore, one needs to have some knowledge of one's own financial prospects, and so forth. And there is also a creative element involved in buying a house. In making the decision, one undoubtedly takes time to imagine what it would be like to live in the house in question, and one has probably spent some time thinking about what one might be able to do with the house.

There are several other ways to look at *acts*. Earlier I indicated briefly that there are as many as nine different spiritive aspects that can be distinguished, varying from the logical to the pistical. We can now further explain that every act is always specifically *typified* or *qualified* by one of those aspects. Here are a couple of examples to make the point clear.

The acts of a scientist are *analytical* in nature; that is to say, they are characterized by the logical modality, that is, by *differentiational thinking*, which is a kind of thought that takes apart or dissects (*analyzes*).

The acts of the man who likes to work with material, and also the acts of the statesman are typified by the *formative* modality. That is to say, they are characterized by the exercise of power, domination, or control of something, whether it be control of a material, like wood, or of people, as in a state.

The acts of a person directed at formulating his thoughts in words and sentences are characterized by the *lingual* modality; that is to say, this person considers which sound symbols (the things we call *words*) to choose in giving expression to his thoughts.

Similarly, the acts of someone whose aim is association with others are *social* in nature; that is to say, they are characterized by interpersonal contact, by social living, by community. The acts of a businessman who takes inventory and makes up a budget are *economically* qualified; that is to say, they are governed by principles of management, saving, and pricing. The acts of an avenger or of a judge, which are aimed at retribution, are *juridical* in nature; that is to say, they are qualified by principles of justice and righteousness (principles that are obeyed *or* disobeyed). The acts of a person in love or of a philanthropist are *ethical* in nature; that is to say, they are characterized by benevolence, by love. Finally, the acts of someone who prays, worships, takes part in the Lord's Supper, or reads the Bible believingly—or worships in a mosque or synagogue, and studies the Qur'an or the Talmud believingly—are *pistical* in nature; that is to say, they are characterized by the certitudes of a certain religious or ideological faith (*pistis* is the Greek word for faith).

Act-Determining Factors

There is still a third way in which we can classify human act-life. Our spiritive life is influenced by a number of *act-determining factors,* which belong to the peculiarities of each individual person, to his or her personal individuality. People who are faced with a similar situation in a similar environment will often respond in very different ways. This is because of their personal, individual disposition or temperament. They respond differently because their makeup is different, as a consequence of hereditary and learned factors. Both nurturing and environment play a role in how people respond to similar stimuli. We can point to at least three kinds of act-determining factors:

1. *Constitutional factors*: A person's constitution is his bodily and mental makeup, his system, his nature, his natural bent, or predisposition. Our acts are determined first of all by our constitutional possibilities. These possibilities can vary from one person to the next and from one moment to the next. People differ from one another in terms of health, physical fitness, level of emotionality, mental ability to cope, temperament, IQ, creativity, and so forth.

2. *Operant factors*: These have to do with differences in aptitude to perform certain operations. Our acts are determined in part by the skills that we have taught ourselves or that others have taught us—and this is true for almost *all* our skills. We can think of our acquisition of numerous *automatic* activities, such as walking, playing the piano, driving a car, or of certain learned emotional reactions, or the ability we acquire to think logically, or

the technical skills we have learned, our mother tongue, the social abilities we have acquired, the sense of justice we have formed for ourselves, and even the capacity to love we have acquired. All such operant factors exert a great influence on our behavior.

3. *Motivational factors*: The term motivation is derived from the verb "to move." Our acts are also determined by our motives, by the incentives that move us to action. Thus, there are a large number of innate or learned *needs*: the need for food, warmth, and sleep, the need for sensory stimulation, the need for things to think about, the need for a certain amount of power, the need for social contact, for success, for an identity of one's own, for fair treatment, for love, and for loving.

Of course, these three kinds of act-determining factors too are closely bound up with one another. For example, much of what we learn is linked to the limitations of our constitution. Therefore, most of us never become good hockey players or artists. Many of our motivations are also closely tied to what we have learned. For example, a man who has lived all his life in the jungle will never succumb to a sudden desire for a hamburger. I am sure the reader can think of many other connections between these three kinds of act-determining factors.

Chapter Three
THE UNITY OF MAN

Earlier we saw that a Christian view of Man must put considerable emphasis on the unity of the cosmos, as well as on the unity of Man himself. But up to this point in our discussion, the unity of Man has hardly been dealt with. Rather, we have talked about no fewer than five different idionomies called *human structures* which can—at least in my view—be distinguished in Man's immanent, corporeal existence. We also saw that in these five human idionomies we can distinguish a number of subject functions: four in the physical idionomy (from the arithmetical to the energetic functions), five in the biotic idionomy (from the arithmetical to the biotic functions), six in the perceptive idionomy (from the arithmetical to the perceptive functions), seven in the sensitive idionomy (from the arithmetical to the sensitive functions), and sixteen in the spiritive idionomy (from the arithmetical to the pistical functions).

Moreover, in the physical human structure we encountered twelve internal object functions (from the biotic to the pistical), in the biotic human structure eleven internal object functions (from the perceptive to the pistical), in the perceptive human structure ten internal object functions (from the sensitive to the pistical), and in the sensitive human structure nine internal object functions (from the logical to the pistical). In total, this means thirty-one subject functions, and forty-two internal object functions, or seventy-three angles or viewpoints from which we can look at Man. So what has become of the unity of Man in all this complicated diversity? How can the unity of Man be understood in the midst of this variability?

Images

Perhaps a few images can help us here. A circle consists of an infinite number of points. But all the points making up the circle have something in common, namely, that they are equidistant from a point we call the center. A lens can transmit an infinite number of light rays, but all of these different rays have something in common, namely, that at a given moment they must all pass through one and the same focal point. Well then, metaphorically speaking, Man also has such a center or focal point; it is here that all the modal aspects and all the human-structures "come together," so to speak. It is here that they find their unity, coherence, fullness, and integrity.

This focal point cannot be physically located in the human body, nor is it susceptible to scientific analysis. The marvelous wonder that we call Man is too great, too profound for this to be possible. We must remember that Man is God's greatest creation, created in his (God's) own image and after his own likeness, in his profoundest being just as transcendent, and therefore just as inscrutable, as God's being itself. Why would we expect God to be inaccessible to scientific scrutiny (for a more detailed discussion, see my *What Then Is Theology?*), whereas Man, in his transcendent fullness as God's image, *could* be laid on the scientific dissection-table?

Only by means of such metaphors as "center," or "focal point," or, if you like, "prism" (through which one single ray of light is separated or dispersed into many different colors), can we find an accessible way to talk about that point of unity in Man. From time immemorial, people have come up with all kinds of descriptions for that point of unity. Among them were: the soul, the spirit, the ego, the personality, the mind, the "I," the self. For my part, I prefer to use the term that the Bible usually uses for this focal point, namely, the *heart*. Of course we must bear in mind that even this term is only a metaphor. The Bible almost never refers to the organ that pumps our blood when it uses the word "heart."

Non-Christian views of Man usually make the unfortunate mistake of locating this *transcendent* "I" or ego in one of the *immanent* human structures. As a result, some have declared the spiritive aspect, the sensitive aspect, biotic life, or even pure matter to be that which is most elementary, most fundamental in Man. But all of these views are gravely in error. The point to grasp is that the ego is *not* one of the "parts," idionomies, or modal aspects of

Man. The ego is no more a part of Man than the center of a circle is one of the points on its circumference. The ego is not a "part" of Man but rather the point at which all of the human parts (aspects, structures, idionomies) come together and find their unity.

Multipartite Theories

In fact, the ego is the point where Man not only finds his unity, but where he *transcends* all his immanent diversity. In his deepest self, Man is a transcendent being, and as such he has—or is—an ego, whereas an animal has—or is—no such thing. And because Man has an ego, a heart, in which he transcends all temporality, he is destined for eternity. I have already quoted elsewhere the verse which says that God has put "eternity" into his heart (Eccl. 3:11). In his ego, Man is oriented toward the higher things, toward eternity, toward God (or, because of sin, possibly a god, an idol). There are many temporal, immanent, transient structures to be distinguished in Man, but in his ego Man transcends all that is temporal, immanent and fleeting.

Precisely because this ego is directed toward eternity, it is beyond normal logical-rational conceptualization, and thus beyond scientific analysis. Therefore, it is difficult to speak clearly and explicitly about it. Hence we must be very careful not to offer a cut-and-dried definition of such concepts as "soul," or "spirit," or "heart," as these occur in the Bible. There are far too many popular books that define these biblical terms too simplistically. They do so by making use of just a few selected Bible texts. One popular evangelical definition is: "I *am* a spirit, I *have* a soul, and I *live* in a body" (which can be found so many times on the Internet), or even worse: "I *am* a soul, that *has* a spirit, who *lives* in a body" (Gary Carpenter). Not one part of these two slogans is correct!

What we should notice is that the Bible uses the terms such as spirit, soul, and body in a great variety of ways, just as we ourselves do in our everyday life. Therefore, we must be extremely wary of wanting to detect in the Bible all sorts of references to "divisions" of Man into several "parts." For instance, Paul says to the Thessalonian believers, "[M]ay your whole spirit and soul and body be kept blameless at the coming of our Lord Jesus Christ" (1

Thess. 5:23). Too many commentators claim something like this: Paul is "teaching" here that Man "consists" of three "parts": spirit, soul, and body. Of course, Paul is "teaching" nothing of the kind: he does not use terms like "consisting of" or "parts." They are read into the text by staunch trichotomists (adherents of *trichotomy,* the theory that Man consists of three parts).

Why then are there no tetratomists (adherents of a theory of four parts)? After all, Jesus says in Luke 10:27, "You shall love the Lord your God with all your *heart* and with all your *soul* and with all your *strength* [i.e., your body] and with all your *mind,* and your neighbor as yourself." So might we not conclude from this that Jesus teaches that Man actually consists of four parts: heart, soul, body, and mind? But why stop at four? Why could we not adopt a five-part theory and call ourselves pentatomists, seeing that David speaks of his "kidneys" (i.e., his conscience), his heart, his "glory" (i.e., his mind), his flesh, and his soul (Ps. 16:7-10)? And so on. Using Bible verses in this biblicist way, anyone, with very little effort, can come up with his own "multipartite" view of Man. In reality, the Bible *never* speaks of certain "parts" of Man (with the exception of *body* parts).

Unity

What the Bible does primarily is to speak of Man as a *unity,* in which the spiritive and the corporeal are totally fused. For instance, Scripture ties the sensitive and the spiritive even to concrete parts of the body, such as the heart, the kidneys ("in the night also my kidneys instruct me," Ps. 16:7b [note], or the bowels ("your law is within my heart [lit., bowel]," Ps. 40:8b). Thus, we find the Bible speaking on the one hand of the "breath" (Hebrew *neshamah*) of God (Job 34:14), and on the other hand of the "spirit" (*ruach*) of the animals (Gen. 6:17; Eccl. 3:21) — just to confound all our cheap, simplistic models. The biblical words for "soul" and "spirit" originally meant nothing more than breath or wind. The soul is not some "part" of Man; on the contrary, in many cases it is the whole Man. Thus, "eight persons" in 1 Peter 3:20 is literally "eight souls." The soul or the spirit is not the specific part of Man that is supposed to be in relation with God because it is the whole

Man who is in this relation with God (or the gods). Even the *body* is dedicated to God (Rom. 12:1), the *flesh* yearns for God (Ps. 63:2), and soul and spirit glorify God (Luke 1:46-47).

That is how the Bible presents Man, not as an amalgam of parts, each of which allegedly has its own specific task, but as a unity. Nor is Man a totality of parts that only secondarily are bound together in some sort of unity, but as primarily a (transcendent) unity, in which, secondarily, we can distinguish a number of facets, aspects, structural plans (idionomies), as a dispersion of Man's unity within the (immanent) world. In addition, this unity is identified as the "image of God," a unity that finds its point of concentration in the human ego, that is, in the heart. Thus Man, in his ego, as a unity, stands before God, and thus the believer serves God with spirit and flesh, with soul and body, with all his heart, spirit, strength, and mind, with his breath, his kidneys, and with his bowels. There is no room for separate parts here.

In this human unity, the heart is the center, the focal point, the innermost depth, the very real and essential inner core of the human personality. In the Bible, the heart is often spoken of as the genuine kernel of Man, which is then placed in contrast with the (often rather inauthentic) exterior of Man. "Keep your heart with all vigilance, for from it flow the springs of life," says Solomon in Proverbs 4:23.

Religion

Viewed in this way, the heart has a tremendous *religious* significance. I define "religion" here as the transcendent relationship of Man, either with God or with the gods (idols, ideologies). Religion in this sense is not just a matter of one particular human structure, or of a "part" of Man, the "spirit" (using the expression suggested by some Christian authors: "With my spirit I am in a relationship with God"). Neither does religion involve only part of Man's time, namely, when he is occupied with pistical activities, that is, activities in the immanent-religious sense, such as praying, praising, and preaching. Religion is a matter of the whole Man, and thus of the kernel of his total existence, his heart. In virtue of his origin, Man, as a creature of God and as the image of God, has an intense bond with his Creator and Sustainer and is totally oriented toward him, *all* the time. Whether he eats or sleeps, buys or sells, drives his car, or washes his laundry, does his daily work, or prays and praises, he is always doing all these things as standing either before God (*coram Deo*) and in relationship with him, or in the case of apostate Man, with the false gods.

Indeed, as a consequence of Man's fall into sin, this bond and orientation were radically disturbed, but through Christ's redemptive work and Man's conversion and rebirth in the power of the Holy Spirit, the bond is restored. Whether Man has been redirected to his God, or remains turned away from him in an apostate attitude, comes to its profoundest expression in his transcendent heart, and from there in all the immanent functions of his daily life. There are many places where the Bible identifies the heart as the "place" where evil is hatched, where false prophecy originates, where Man in his pride sets himself up against God. To take just one example, let us listen to the words of Jesus: "For out of the heart come evil thoughts, murder, adultery, sexual immorality, theft, false witness, slander" (Matt. 15:19). The heart is the center of self-worship, of ungodly self-reliance, and of conscious resistance against God. But it is also the focal point of our sense of guilt, the place where God works in us to bring about repentance and to purify us, so that we have "our hearts sprinkled clean from an evil conscience" (Heb. 10:22).

Focal Point

The heart is the focal point of our existence in which we seek after God as we yearn for communion with him. It is the central place of the fear of the Lord, of the service of God, of our walk with God: "...so that Christ may dwell in your hearts through faith—that you [may be] rooted and grounded in love" (Eph. 4:17; cf. Rom. 5:5; 2 Cor. 1:22; 3:3; 4:6; Gal. 4:6; Phil. 4:7; Col. 3:16; 1 Pet. 3:15). It is the place of sorrow before God and gladness in him. It is the focal point of adoration of God, of looking into and keeping and treasuring his commandments, of praying to God and trusting in him.

When we become aware of all this, we can easily see that the pistical aspect of our spiritive life which I have mentioned above constitutes the basic connection between the *immanent* spiritive idionomy and the *transcendent* heart. The pistical modality has, so to say, a borderline position. But it is the heart which most uniquely characterizes Man in his deepest (transcendent-religious) being.

The heart is inaccessible to psychology in the strict sense, because scientific research is by definition limited to our immanent, empirical world. The true meaning and nature of the human heart can only be known through God's Word-revelation. This Word cannot be known just by means of our feelings, our intuition, or our intellect as such, but only by the heart itself. Only the *heart* can know the *heart*—and this only when it is in the power of God's Word and Spirit.

At the same time, we must realize that the transcendent heart cannot be separated from its many immanent functions, including the sensitive, the logical and all the other spiritive functions. Knowledge of God is definitely associated with, and expressed through, certain sensitive feelings, affections, and drives, as well as spiritive deliberations and decisions. But it cannot be *reduced* to these. It is only in the (reborn) heart as the transcendent focal point of all our immanent functions that we can have true knowledge of that same heart, of God, and of ourselves.

Personality

Because each human being has a heart—in its metaphorical-biblical sense—he or she is what we call a *person*. The whole of Man's spiritive life, including his thinking, his imagination, and his willing is directed, governed, and determined from his heart. In his heart and because of his heart, Man is responsible before God, as I have said before. In the final analysis, he is guided not by drives, instincts, reflexes, affections, and emotions, but by spiritive acts, which are subject to divine norms and have their deepest origin in his heart. Since the way in which this process unfolds differs from person to person, each human being is a unique personality, called to express his responsibility toward God in his own unique manner, that is to say, in an entirely "personal" way.

It is quite remarkable that the *term* "person" does not occur in the Bible, except in certain translations, where the original word rendered as "person" is, for instance, literally "soul" (1 Pet. 3:17). However, we do find the term "person" in the literature of antiquity (Greek *prosôpon,* Latin *persona*). This is especially surprising in view of the fact that the *idea* of "person" as *we* understand it is not a Greek concept at all but very much a biblical one. The ancient Greeks could not have a correct image of the (human) "person" because they did not have a correct image of God. One's view of the person flows directly from one's view of God. If *we* do not understand what it means that *God* is a person, neither can we understand what *we* are as persons. John Calvin has expressed this almost at the beginning of his *Institutes of the Christian Religion* by claiming that knowledge of God and knowledge of oneself go hand in hand.

The gods of ancient India were not even "personal"; they were merely impersonal forces. By contrast, the gods of the Greeks and Romans were personal, but they were not infinite, like the God of the Bible. They were not creators, nor were they morally perfect. The Greeks did not have to feel much responsibility or guilt in relation to those quarreling and immoral gods of Mount Olympus. When it came to sin and penitence, the Greeks preferred to fall back upon the still more ancient nature religion, with its unpredictable, freakish, blind forces of nature to which Man was subject. Death was the fate awaiting everyone, the unavoidable outcome of these blind forces.

The influence of this blind fate was extensively portrayed in the Greek tragedies, where fate played a central role. The actors in these tragedies wore masks, which in Latin were called *personae.* An actor wearing such a mask portrayed a certain *character* or *person* (lit., "sounding through," because the actor spoke through a hole in the mask), but the *persons* being portrayed in this way were playthings totally at the mercy of the blind, arbitrary powers of fate. In actual fact, these persons had no character at all. What happened to them was not the result of their own responsible choices, whether good or bad, nor was it a matter of their own deeds. Their bad luck was not their fault and was not due to their own actions; rather, it was due to freakish forces with which they could in no way interfere. It could hardly have been otherwise since even the greatest gods recognized by the Greeks were unable to resist fate. The Greek gods simply were not "big" enough, and so the Greek *person* was not big enough either.

Today's evolutionism is not very different. It is quite hard to believe in myself as a "who," a "personality," if I am nothing but the eventual product of blind forces, of a process governed by purely natural laws, a process starting with the simplest of living organisms. If my personality has developed from such impersonal origins, then either (a) my personality is a mere illusion, or (b) my personality was already encapsulated within these unicellular organisms in some way or another, or (c) somewhere on the way a mysterious miracle happened; with a variation on Judges 14:14 we could say, "Out of the impersonal came something personal." The Greeks and Romans gave us this useful term *person*, but their person did not have the features that we ascribe to a person today, namely, responsibility, free choice, independent deliberation, guilt and retribution, good works and reward.

The concept of the person with which people in the Western world today are so familiar did not come to us from the peoples of antiquity, much less from modern evolutionists and materialists, but from the Old Testament. The Bible tells us of a personal *and* infinite God, who is the Creator and Sustainer of human beings, and who says to us, as it were, "I have made you, and I am going to tell you how you must live. I am giving you my commandments because I love you and because I want you to do well and prosper. Serve me within the boundaries of these commands, and you will be well."

Handiwork and Manual

A passage which explains this beautifully is Deuteronomy 7:8-11: "[B]ut it is because the Lord loves you and is keeping the oath that he swore to your fathers, that the Lord has brought you out with a mighty hand and redeemed you from the house of slavery, from the hand of Pharaoh king of Egypt. Know therefore that the Lord your God is God, the faithful God who keeps covenant and steadfast love with those who love him and keep his commandments, to a thousand generations, and repays to their face those who hate him, by destroying them. He will not be slack with one who hates him. He will repay him to his face. You shall therefore be careful to do the commandment and the statutes and the rules that I command you today."

Or see Deuteronomy 32:46-47: "Take to heart all the words by which I am warning you today, that you may command them to your children, that they may be careful to do all the words of this law. For it is no empty word for you, but *your very life,* and by this word you shall live long in the land that you are going over the Jordan to possess" (italics added).

What we read about in these passages is not blind fate, against which any endeavor or responsible act a human being might undertake is utterly ineffectual. Rather, these and many other passages talk about *real persons,* whose personality is derived from the personality of God. These persons get a configuration or "rule of conduct" assigned to them by God—God's commandments—which Man has to keep if he is to function at his very best, the way God has intended him to. Man is not a puppet of any kind, nor a robot, but is given all sorts of room for a free walk with God, and all the potential to work out his own responsibility. This must take place within the boundaries of God's institutions, which are there not to burden him but to protect him. We are God's handiwork, and his law is the manual that helps us to deal with this handiwork in the best possible way.

The working out of one's responsibility is, first of all, a strictly individual matter. Here again, *individuality* is a concept that is prominent in the Bible, but in ancient thought it occupied a subordinate place. For the Greeks the individual had value only as a representative of the human race. That is the reason why the Greeks did not have a great deal of respect for the *equality* of persons. To the extent that they respected equality, it was restricted to people of their own nation and elite group (notice the distinction between "Greeks" and "barbarians" in Rom. 1:14). In the Old Testament, however, the fundamental equality of persons is highly regarded, and it is not restricted to Israel only: it also applied to foreigners (cf. Exod. 12:49; Lev. 16:29 etc.). The only thing that really mattered in Israel was this: whoever did God's will and kept his commandments was acceptable to God, whether this person was an Israelite or a foreigner, but whoever was disobedient to

God was rejected by him, whether this person was an Israelite or a foreigner.

In order to formulate the point in a New Testament way of speaking, we could say that a real *person* is someone who is "in Christ," someone who lives out of him in the power of the Holy Spirit, someone who does God's will, someone who meets his responsibilities and fulfills his potentials. In such a person Christ is "formed" (i.e., receives shape; cf. Gal. 4:19). Such a person lives life to the fullest; that is to say, only such a person really *lives*. And to come back to the matter of equality, in Christ there is neither Jew nor Greek, there is neither slave nor free, there is no male and female, for all are one in Christ Jesus (Gal. 3:28; cf. Col. 3:11). Being "in Christ" is what matters, not whether one is American, Canadian, or European, leader or laborer, man or woman, young or old, black or white.

Christianity and Materialism

Earlier I emphasized that we must not allow the ego of Man to become reduced to one of the temporal, immanent, transient human structures. This mistake has been made many times in the past, but I shall not deal with all those episodes here. No doubt the most popular and extreme effort along these lines was to let the "I" or ego of Man be reduced to the matter of which he is composed. As I have said before, such thinking is called materialism; it is the view that Man is ultimately "nothing but matter." Or, more specifically, the view according to which all that we might consider typically human can be explained, or will one day be explained, in terms of atoms and molecules and their behavior.

It is noteworthy that during recent decades science itself has encountered a number of phenomena which can scarcely be explained if we adhere to such a "nothing but" faith. It would be well worth our while to examine a few of these phenomena in order to understand more clearly that the ego of Man transcends matter. Of course, we cannot logically demonstrate this beyond any possible doubt; after all, people believe, and will continue to believe, whatever they wish. But at least we can try to explain this issue of Man transcending matter in a way that will make it more understandable for people who have an open mind.

First of all, we should reflect on the fact that a number of leading brain specialists, such as the American-Canadian neurosurgeon Wilder Penfield (1891-1976) and the Australian-American-Swiss neurophysiologist Sir John C. Eccles (1903-1997), made some very interesting discoveries several decades ago. On the basis of their extensive research, each of them concluded independently that the *mind* of a human being is not identical with his *brain*. Eccles even wrote a book together with the most famous philosopher of science in the twentieth century, Sir Karl R. Popper (1902-1994), called *The Self and Its Brain*. In this book they defend the standpoint that the self and the brain must be distinguished, and that they interact with each other.

Their views were very different from those defended in the recent work by the Dutch neurobiologist Dick Swaab (b. 1944) titled *We Are Our Brains*, according to which the self and the brain are identical. Critics of Swaab have argued that, in the end, this whole subject is not a (neuro-)biological issue at all, nor is it a psychological one. It is a philosophical issue. That amounts to saying that ultimately it is a matter of *belief* whether we wish to reduce everything that is typically human to brain processes, or whether we believe that humans are more than their brains.

In a sense, one might say that Swaab has followed circular reasoning. He is fully convinced that the problem of the human mind can be resolved only by neurobiology, and not, for instance, by psychology or philosophy, much less by theology. Therefore it is no wonder that the only answer he finds is a neurobiological one, because he has no room for any other answers. But neurobiology as such knows *nothing* of the human mind; it is simply not a part of its field of investigation. Swaab only studies brains, so the only thing he finds is brains. In my opinion, it is of his own free will that Swaab has decided that there is no such thing as free will! His free will could also have made a different choice, but he chose not to make it. He tries to sell this as a neurobiological decision, but in reality it is nothing but an ideological decision.

In opposition to Swaab and many other materialists, I maintain that it is worthwhile to pay attention to the arguments of people like Eccles and Penfield, as well as more recent authors, such as the Dutch cardiologist, Pim van Lommel (b. 1943), who has made an extensive study of near-death experiences (NDE). In his book, *Consciousness Beyond Life,* he has come to the conclusion that the human consciousness and the human brain do *not* coincide. Of course, his work has been attacked by Swaab. In his turn, Swaab has been heavily criticized by Bert Keizer (b. 1947), a medical doctor as well as a philosopher, in his book, *Waar blijft de ziel*? ("Where Does the Soul Remain?"). A book by one of the leading neuroscientists, the Italian-American Giulio Tononi (b. 1960), called: *Phi: A Voyage from the Brain to the Soul* (2012), as well as the books he has written together with Nobel prize winning American biologist Gerald Edelman (b. 1929), are worth mentioning.

Arguments (I)

Some of the older arguments by Penfield and Eccles are, in my opinion, still interesting. Apparently, a person's "I" or ego can freely make decisions apart from his automatic brain processes, and can "program" brain mechanisms in various ways, or assess what goes on in those brain mechanisms. During a brain operation in which the patient is fully conscious, a brain surgeon can move the patient's hands by stimulating a particular part of the brain electrically. But when the patient is then asked, "Why did you move your hand?" he invariably answers, "I did not do that—*you* did it." Or when the surgeon stimulates another part of the brain, the patient may say, for example, "Everything is suddenly getting bigger." Yet he does not become afraid that the bigger things he sees will crush him because he is well aware that the surgeon has somehow or other caused this phenomenon. When the surgeon's electrode moves the patient's right hand by means of brain stimulation, the patient never says, "I *wanted* to move my hand." His will is not a property of his brain that can be aroused and stimulated by an electrode; rather, it is a property of his "mind," over which the electrode has no control. Apparently, there is not a single area in the brain where electrical stimulation can make a patient believe or decide something that he does not himself independently believe or decide.

In a certain sense, the experiences which the surgeon's electrode produces in the patient occur outside of him; that is to say, outside of his mind. The patient does not experience them as "his own." In psychology, there are various phenomena that seem to confirm this insight. For example, there is the phenomenon of the so-called *cold emotion,* which is a state of purely biotic excitement in which the person does not *feel* excited. In other words, the biotic idionomy has been touched, but the sensitive and spiritive idionomies have not. Similarly, because of a brain disorder, a person may sometimes break out in uncontrollable laughter without ever feeling in high spirits. Now, according to the materialistic way of thinking, the emotion would have to be the inseparable by-product of biotic excitement, and merriment the inseparable by-product of laughter, even if it should turn out that the person does not know *why* he is happy. However, this does not appear to be the case at all. It appears that more is needed if certain feelings are to be aroused along with certain body states. Many scientists believe that this something extra takes place on another level than the biotic, namely, on what we call the mental level.

Suggestion is another area of psychology that provides us with interesting examples. It might be described as the area of the tremendous influence of the mind on the (physical) body. For example, one scientist, over a period of months, was able to increase the breast size of a number of women. He did so by placing the women under light hypnosis, during which he instructed them to imagine that warm water was streaming over their breasts, or that their breasts were being warmed by a heat lamp. Hypnosis is a special kind of suggestion. If, for example, the suggestion is made to a person under hypnosis that a particular pencil is a red-hot iron bar, and if that person's hand then touches the pencil, a blister will appear on the skin. This means that blisters are not just formed "mechanically" through physical contact with hot objects, but that they can also arise in purely mental ways. This shows us how strong the influence of the mind on the body really is. Medical doctors have even discovered that people who were seriously tortured in the past can, in a moment of intense recall, produce blisters and bleeding welts at exactly the same places on the body where they had originally been inflicted. This shows that the mind can actually make the body ill.

Arguments (II)

Furthermore, every medical doctor also knows that the mind's will to live and to get better is of the greatest importance to patients who are undergoing an operation or recovering from a serious illness (see Prov. 17:22: "A joyful heart is good medicine, but a crushed spirit dries up the bones"). Materialists have no acceptable explanation for the fact that the mind (the ego, the heart) influences even the body's growth or state of health. I am not saying that materialists would not be able to come up with all kinds of ingenious explanations. What I *am* saying is that the assumption of the mental—something that surpasses the physical—yields a more plausible explanation than any form of materialist reductionism.

An entirely different example is the patient who suffers from Parkinson's disease. His main problem is that he is not able to turn his wish to move his leg into an actual *movement* of his leg, even though his nerves and muscles are intact. However, it is remarkable that the patient can sometimes get around this problem in a purely mental way. For example, when he is unable to walk through a door, he can try all kinds of thoughts until he manages to *dance* through the door opening, or he can divert his will to another goal replacing the thought "I want to move my legs" with the thought "I want to get into the other room." Here again it appears that there is a mind, an "I," an ego which can freely—beyond the reach of natural laws!—decide to make use of various brain mechanisms in order to reach the goal the patient has set for himself.

A final example comes from the area of so-called optical illusions. Here I am thinking of figures that can be perceived or interpreted in either of two different ways. For example, look at the cube below.

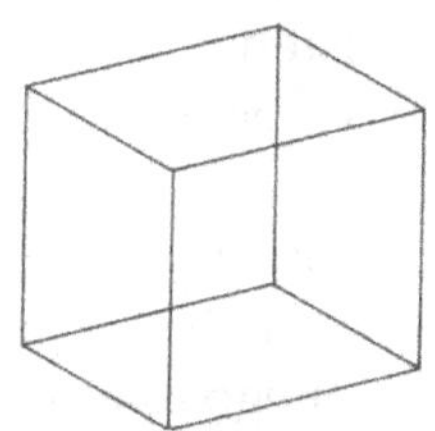

You will soon discover that the square on the lower left can be perceived either as the front or as the back of the cube. If you stare at the figure for a while, you will notice that it switches by itself from one of the two possible interpretations to the other. That is to say, the square which you have been perceiving as the front of the cube suddenly becomes the back of the cube. The interesting thing is that you can also bring about such a switch by means of a conscious act of the will. Apparently, this switch can occur either "automatically" (because of certain properties of the eyes and the brain), or by means of a conscious act of the will. The "I" or ego can "hold on" to one of these interpretations for quite some time. However, in doing so it must exert itself to resist the brain, which has the tendency spontaneously to replace the one interpretation with the other. Here again we see that the consciously choosing, willing "I" or ego stands in opposition to the brain, with its spontaneous physical and biological processes that function in accordance with the natural laws.

Mind and Body

It is very difficult to form an appropriate idea of the relationship between the "I" or ego (the mind, the heart, or whatever you call it), on the one hand, and the human structures, on the other. It is too simple to talk as though Man consists of two separate "things," namely, a mind (or spirit) and a body. In fact, it is downright wrong. The "I" or ego is not a "thing" *inside* another "thing," namely, the body. It is only a "point," the focal point where all the "rays" of our physical, biotic, perceptive, sensitive, and spiritive existence come together. My ego is not corporeal, but neither is it a "thing" that can be distinguished from my body. Thus, my ego cannot think, feel, will, believe, desire, and so forth without my body. (This is true at least of our human existence as we know it here on earth; as to our existence after death, we know next to nothing about it from a biological and psychological point of view.)

The "I" or ego is distinguished from the body just as the center of a circle is distinguished from its circumference. At the same time, without my body my "I" or ego is amputated, just as the center of a circle is nothing but a mere point and no longer the center of anything without the circle's circumference. It would be like a pianist without a piano. He might still be *called* a pianist, but the designation would mean next to nothing if there were no piano to play. Only *with* a piano is a pianist really a pianist. When he plays a piano, he becomes one with it. In itself, the piano is just a mute thing, just as the pianist without a piano is helpless. In neither case is there any music. Well then, we could say that the heart is the pianist of the body. When a believer dies, he is with Christ, which is far better (Phil. 1:23). But it is only in resurrection, when "piano" and "pianist" are reunited, so to say, that perfection is reached and redemption is complete.

In Summary

Thus, our Christian view of Man maintains both the *diversity* and the *unity* of Man. On the one hand, we have highlighted the great differences between physical, biotic, perceptive, sensitive, and spiritive phenomena. They cannot be reduced from one kind of phenomenon to another. Each of them has its own unique God-given laws and distinct features. Therefore, we are not materialists, who seek to reduce everything to the physical. But neither are we spiritualists (or spiritivists), who reduce everything to the spiritive or mental.

We are not "dualists" either, even though a metaphor like the one of the pianist and the piano might suggest this. In true dualism, the two factors have nothing in common and form an antithesis. But Man's heart and his corporeal existence, as I see it, do not form a dualism at all, for the heart *itself* is *nothing but* the transcendent focal point of all Man's immanent modal functions, and the functions are *nothing but* the immanent divergence of the transcendent heart *itself*. Moreover, we can maintain this full diversity of phenomena in human existence precisely because we do not reduce these phenomena to one or two of them but instead relate every one of them to God, who is their Creator and Sustainer.

Considering Man's heart, our Christian anthropology prevents us from viewing Man as the sum of all his different "parts." If we did this, we would lose sight of his unity. We stress the unbreakable unity of the physical, biotic, perceptive, sensitive, and spiritive phenomena in human existence because we find that unity in something that *transcends* all those *immanent* human structures, namely, the human "I" or ego (heart, mind).

Of course, to say this is not the same as *explaining* "the phenomenon of Man." On the contrary, our very view of Man suggests the reason why the human phenomenon *cannot* be fully explained. It is precisely because Man in his ego transcends all his temporal, immanent, and transient structures that his deepest ego cannot be grasped in some concept or by way of some scientific analysis. In the end, Man is a mystery—but a mystery that we try to approximate as closely as possible through our theory of the modal aspects and the various idionomies of animal and human existence, and our view of the human heart.

Chapter Four
PSYCHOLOGICAL KNOWLEDGE

In the previous chapters of this book, I have occupied myself especially with the question: *What* do psychologists really study? The answer I came up with was: psychologists study what happens within a person's perceptive, sensitive, and spiritive idionomies, and what is the resulting human behavior. In other words, they note how sense perceptions, reflexes, impulses, affections, drives, emotions, deliberation, and imagination, etc., lead to certain human actions.

I could also put this in simpler terms and say that psychologists are doing their best to understand what goes on inside people and how what goes on inside them determines their behavior. Psychologists seek to understand why person A or B or C acts in ways P or Q or R, under circumstances X or Y or Z.

However, the question of *what—what* is it the psychologist tries to do?—is immediately followed by questions such as *why—why* does the psychologist carry out his investigations?—and *how*—what are the methods he follows in doing psychology? First, *to what end* does the psychologist collect his psychological facts? What is his purpose? Second, by what methods does the psychologist gather his knowledge? Which methods lead to reliable knowledge, and which do not?

Let us first briefly look at the "why," and then spend some time on the "how."

Conditions of Knowledge

The first reason why psychologists, like scientists in general, wish to attain scientific knowledge is that knowledge implies *power*. The saying, *Scientia potentia* (or, *potestas*) *est*, that is, "knowledge is power," is attributed to the British scientist and statesman, Francis Bacon (1561-1626). When we come to know something, understand it, and begin to grasp how it works, we can also learn to control it. The more knowledge psychologists can assemble about the mental life of human beings, the better they will be able not just to understand people but also to find ways to influence and change them. We see these possibilities realized particularly in advertizing, in politics, in education and social work, and in pastoral counseling and psychotherapy. And sometimes we see them realized in the terrible things dictators are inflicting on their victims.

The second reason is that knowledge provides satisfaction. It gives us joy and grants a sense of accomplishment. More specifically, accurate psychological knowledge is satisfying because it affords us deeper insight into the riches of God's highest work of creation: Man. As David said, "For you formed my inward parts; you knitted me together in my mother's womb. I praise you, for I am fearfully and wonderfully made. Wonderful are your works; my soul knows it very well" (Ps. 139:13-14). On the one hand, as Elihu tells Job, "I too was pinched off from a piece of clay" (Job 33:6b), but on the other hand, as he states just a little earlier, "The Spirit of God has made me, and the breath of the Almighty gives me life" (Job 33:4). As a human, I am basically clay and dust—and at the same time I am a "living soul" of a very special kind through the breath of God himself (Gen. 2:7). I am from below, "woven in the depths of the earth" (Ps. 139:15b), "from the earth, a man of dust" (1 Cor. 15:47), and I am, in a sense, from above, because I originated through the breath of the Lord (cf. Ps. 33:6b; 104:30).

The third and most important reason is that knowledge of God's creation deepens our knowledge both of God himself *and* of Man as standing in a relation to God—Man in his transcendent-religious self. No matter how much the heart of Man may ultimately refuse to be analyzed scientifically, psychological knowledge turns out to enrich our insight into Man as a religious being who is in a relationship with his Creator, and into Man's heart, the site where Man and God meet one another. However, if it is to have such an effect, the psychologist must have a correct biblical view of the nature of the cosmic reality of which his field of investigation forms a part. That field of investigation includes the mental (perceptive, sensitive, and spiritive) human structures. The believing psychologist needs a proper Christian ontology, including a proper Christian anthropology.

Methodology

Moreover, the psychologist will have to be sure that he is gathering his psychological knowledge *in the right way*. In order to obtain this knowledge correctly, he needs to keep three things in mind:

1. *The light of Scripture*: Just as in the case of every other science, psychology must be practiced in the light that shines forth from the Scriptures and illuminates all of created reality. Only in the light of Scripture are we able to see, from the very outset, all the right relationships and connections (cf. Ps. 36:9b). Thus, we obtain the right Christian worldview, and from there an acceptable Christian-philosophical view of reality and knowledge. This furnishes the framework within which our research can be properly done. Anyone who lacks such a framework of reference is ultimately groping about aimlessly in the dark (see the previous chapters).

Thus, a radical Christian philosophy must be in place at the very *beginning* of our research, for it provides us with certain assumptions with which every kind of scientific research must start. Such a Christian philosophy also *accompanies* us *during* our research. It keeps us from being diverted onto false side-roads or getting stuck in dead ends. This Christian philosophy should also be found at the *end* of our research when we seek to put our results to the test in a biblical way within Man's practical life. Just as humans by nature are "groping" for God (Acts 17:27 NKJV), Christian psychology might be described as a way of "groping" for (the essence of) Man.

2. *The central role of the heart*: It is of vital importance to realize that all true knowledge, in the final analysis, is not just a matter of one's intellect, or of one's feelings, but of the *heart*. This statement applies just as much to the everyday knowledge we gain in our ordinary life as it does to our theoretical-scientific knowledge. Just as *all* of our acts and actions ultimately proceed from the heart, in the same way, our scientific acts and actions also proceed from the heart—and to the same extent. Precisely because the heart is never neutral, our scientific activity can never be neutral. Think again of the discussion in chapter 3 about whether Man and his brain coincide, or whether

Man is more than his brain. In the end, this essential question is decided neither by neurobiology, nor by psychology, nor by any other special science (theology included), but by one's philosophy, or one's ideology, or one's worldview, or whatever you choose to call it. The question whether we believe that Man has a free will—and is *therefore* more than his brain—is ultimately decided, not by scientific experiments but *by Man's own free will*, that is, by his heart.

In his heart, a person is always oriented either toward God or toward the gods (idols or ideologies). Therefore, his knowledge, too, in the end is directed either toward God or the gods and is thus basically either true or false. Knowledge is insight into God and into God's creation, but ultimately this insight is not available to any human being who fails to recognize the integral connection of cosmic reality to God the Creator. The man whose heart is not "true" (Heb. 10:22) does not have "knowledge of the truth" (see 2 Tim. 3:7), particularly that truth "which accords with godliness" (Titus 1:1). Nowhere does this become more obvious than in the case of true psychological knowledge that Man has—or does not have—about himself. After all, Man can only understand himself rightly if he does so on the basis of his profoundest being, which lies "outside" him, in his relationship to God, or to the gods.

3. *The goal of the service of God*: If psychological truth can indeed be obtained along the lines just sketched, then the truth we come up with is necessarily truth-unto-God (see again my books *Wisdom for Thinkers* and *What Then Is Theology?*). For example, let us remember what Jesus said: "I am the way, and the truth, and the life. No one comes to the Father except through me" (John 14:6). In the Bible, the full meaning of "knowledge of" is "communion with." As for eternal life, the essence of it is both "knowledge of" and "communion with" the Father and the Son (John 17:3; 1 John 1:2-3). In the Bible, having communion or intimate relations (intercourse) with a woman is freely spoken of as "knowing her" (Gen. 4:1; Matt. 1:25). It is similar when it comes to our knowledge of God. Anyone who has received true knowledge through regeneration and the illumination of the Holy Spirit has intimate communion with God, or has intimate knowledge of God, of Christ, of himself, and thus of all reality.

True knowledge, that is to say, heart-knowledge, can be had

in this present age only in Christ, who is the Truth (1 John 5:20), and through the "Word of truth" (Eph. 1:13) as well as the "Spirit of truth" (John 14:17 ff.). This is the genuine Truth with regard to the whole of empirical *and* non-empirical reality, the old and the new creation, God and Man, Spirit and flesh, the kingdom of the devil and the Kingdom of God. All truth is concentrated in Christ, because in him all things hold together (Col. 1:17). It is *in Christ* that we learn to walk in the truth, and *from him* that we receive light on all parts of reality, through the power of the Holy Spirit. Finally, all our knowledge is *unto him*, in order that we may learn to serve and worship him better.

Psychological Subdisciplines

As we have seen, psychology could be described as the discipline that deals with what goes on in the mental structures. At the same time this field of investigation is so multifaceted and complicated that psychology winds up maintaining close connections with all the other disciplines. Its various subdisciplines can be classified in accordance with our scheme of the five mental idionomies plus the various natural and spiritive modalities that we have distinguished earlier within the whole of Man's immanent functioning.

When this is done, we get the following overview:

Arithmetical and spatial: Mathematical psychology (mathematical modeling of mental processes).

Kinematic and energetic: Psychophysics (especially the study of the relation between sensory stimulation and perception), psychopharmacology (the study of the influence of drugs on our mental life).

Biotic: Neuropsychology (the study of the relation between brain processes and mental processes), physiological psychology (the study of the connection between physiological—especially nervous and brain processes—and mental processes).

Perceptive: Psychology of sensation and perception, psychology of conditioning (the study of learning by means of classical and operant conditioning).

Sensitive: Sensitive psychology (the psychology of our life of feeling, including affections, drives, and emotions).

Analytical: Cognitive psychology (the psychology of thinking, deliberating, insight, knowledge, imagination, creativity, etc.).

Historical: Psychohistory, biographical psychology, developmental psychology (the psychology of the different developmental stages of human life), and educational psychology. The Dutch psychiatrist, Jan Hendrik van den Berg (1914-2012), has even coined the term *metabletics* or historical psychology (the study of the changes in human mental life throughout history).

Lingual: Psycholinguistics (the psychology of the use of language).

Social: Social psychology (the psychology of social life).

Economic: Economic psychology (the psychology of economic life).

Aesthetic: Psychology of the visual art, psychology of music, psychology of literature.

Juridical: Forensic psychology (the psychology of the criminal and of the administration of justice).

Ethical: Psychology of ethical behavior (not to be confused with ethical psychology, i.e., a psychology that meets ethical standards).

Pistical: Psychology of religion.

The Place of Psychology

There is a special reason why psychology occupies such a specific place among all the other disciplines: it is because psychology is situated right in between mathematics and the *natural* sciences (physics, chemistry, biology) on the one hand, and the *cultural* sciences (or the *humanities*) on the other. *Nature* includes those modal aspects of cosmic reality that are governed by *laws of nature* (or *natural laws*). This refers to the arithmetical, the spatial, the kinematic, the energetic (physical), and the biotic aspects. *Culture* includes the domain of that which is not governed by natural laws but by *norms*. This refers to the spiritive modalities (from the logical to the pistical aspects). A natural law tells us how something is (for example, iron expands when heated), but a norm tells us how something *ought* to be: if you want to do something correctly, you must do it in such and such a way.

There are all kinds of norms (which I have described at greater length in my *Wisdom for Thinkers*): logical-analytical, technical and historical, lingual, social, economic, aesthetic, juridical, moral, and pistical (faith norms). These norms tell us what we ought to do, but this implies that they can also be disobeyed. Therefore, we are familiar with both logical and illogical reasoning, historic and ahistorical action, social and asocial behavior, righteous and unrighteous deeds, moral and immoral activities. In the natural modalities, which involve natural laws, such disobedience is impossible: there is no such thing as "unphysical" or "unbiotic" behavior (not to be confused with non-physical and non-biotic). It is one of the tasks of psychology to throw light on the question as to *why* people sometimes behave illogically, make linguistic mistakes, act asocially, uneconomically, or immorally, etc.

The perceptive and the sensitive aspects occupy an intermediate position between nature and culture. The perceptive aspect lies adjacent to nature; the sensitive aspect borders on spiritive life. Just as these two aspects occupy an intermediate position, so too psychology takes up an intermediate position between the natural sciences on the one hand and the cultural or spiritive sciences (the humanities) on the other. We see this intermediate position reflected especially in the sensitive aspect, which is so typical for psychology. Our life of feeling is not predictable in such a manner as to allow us to consider the sensitive aspect to be an aspect of nature. On the other hand, our life of feeling is not sufficiently subject to our will for us to be able to call the sensitive an aspect of spiritive life.

Because the sensitive aspect has this transitional character, psychology differs from both the natural and the cultural (or spiritive) sciences. You can also say this in a positive way: psychology has characteristics in common with both the natural sciences and the cultural sciences. Like the cultural sciences (the humanities), psychology is much less mathematical and exact than the natural sciences, and much more descriptive. It also places much more emphasis on individual and particular characteristics, as opposed to general ones. Thus, there is also more room in psychology for the spontaneous and the fortuitous. Moreover, psychology more often asks what something is *for* than what something is *caused* by.

In these respects, then, psychology is more allied with the cultural sciences, even though it must be admitted that the features we have mentioned are also true—albeit to a lesser extent—for the science of biology when it is contrasted with physics and chemistry. At the same time, psychology is akin to the natural sciences, as we see from the fact that various characteristics of the natural sciences also play a role in psychology. This is a point that we now have to investigate a little further.

Psychological Experiments

Experimentation plays an important role in both the natural sciences and psychology. In the minds of some people, the phrase "psychological experiments," conjures up the frightening mental image of human guinea pigs being subjected to the whims of unscrupulous technocrats. However, this is not what goes on in most psychological experimentation.

To experiment means simply to carry out tests. What it involves is measuring a certain phenomenon, for instance, intelligence, so that it is better understood and becomes more predictable. Even something as simple as a psychological intelligence test is really a form of experiment.

We should bear in mind that *measuring*, as it is done in experimentation, is not just the prerogative of psychologists. In everyday life, we are all constantly busy measuring people in our thoughts or our discussions. The questions we ask during conversations and the observations we make are often nothing but forms of experimentation, attempts to find out who and what the other is and how he thinks, responds and behaves, in order to establish how we ourselves should behave towards him. The real difference between such everyday activities and what psychologists do is, first, that the latter go about their measurements in a more conscious, exact and systematic manner. Second, our everyday testing of one another is always of a *practical* nature: knowing and understanding another person helps me to know how I should behave in relation to that person. However, psychological testing has a *theoretical* purpose: it is carried out in order to collect scientific knowledge of human beings in general (see for this important difference between the practical and the theoretical my books *Wisdom for Thinkers* and *What Then Is Theology?*).

Of course, psychologists are not able to measure things with as much exactness as physicists can. Physicists have very refined instruments that they can use to obtain often extremely precise measurements of temperatures, points of time, speeds, and so forth. But when a psychologist administers an intelligence test, for example, he is quite happy if he is able to conclude that a person's IQ lies somewhere, say, between 115 and 120. In fact, in this regard the psychologist is much like the biologist, who, in many cases, can also do no more than measure a certain phenomenon in an approximate way.

Guinea Pigs

Another point of comparison between psychology and the natural sciences is the creation of what we might call *experimental conditions*. When a physicist undertakes to measure the solubility of a certain substance, he simply dissolves the maximal amount of this substance in water of a certain temperature. He tries things out. But when the psychologist sets out to measure the degree of irascibility or of compliance in the guinea pig of his experiment, he is facing quite a different situation. He could expose this guinea pig to all sorts of irritating situations so as to observe his response. However, this would be both ethically objectionable and very difficult in technical respects. Thus, psychologists face various problems that physicists do not have to deal with.

To get around such problems, psychologists sometimes make use of questionnaires, which ask the subject how he *would* respond to a particular type of irritating situation if he were exposed to it. But an experiment of this kind is not without many problems either. Will the subject *really* tell us what he would do in this situation? Will he be honest about it? Is he in fact in a position to be able to determine such a thing about himself with any degree of certainty? Might he not greatly overestimate, or perhaps underestimate, himself? Indeed, can we be sure that he would always react in the *same* way in a given situation? Would not the answers to these questions depend on many other circumstances external to the experiment, all of which are of such a nature that neither the subject of the experiment nor the psychologists could control them, so that they often seem wholly arbitrary to us?

It is no wonder, then, that psychologists in a great many cases reject the questionnaire approach and would rather expose the subject to a number of experimental conditions. In following chapters we will look at some examples of such conditions. Then we will also see why it is essential for the guinea pig not to know exactly what the experiment is about, that is to say, not to know what the psychologist is really trying to get at. The aim in such a situation, of course, is to get the subject to respond as naturally as possible. What happens in such a case is that the psychologist explains the experiment to the subject in advance, giving him the impression that he wants to measure phenomenon A (e.g., learning ability), whereas in reality the purpose of the experiment is to measure phenomenon B (e.g., responding to dangerous-looking circumstances). The psychologist does not want the subject to know the real purpose of the experiment, for then he would no longer react in a spontaneous or natural way.

However, it is obvious that such experiments run into certain ethical problems as well:

(a) In the first place, there is the issue of misleading the subject. I would maintain that it is totally unacceptable to deceive this subject simply for fear that otherwise he would refuse his cooperation. On the other hand, there is also the kind of misleading I have just described, which is really a kind of stage management. Giving the subject complete information prior to the experiments of a certain sort would indeed make those experiments impossible, and so a certain amount of information must be withheld. What is important to realize is that any good psychologist informs his subjects fully as to the real aim of the experiment immediately after it is finished. Thus the withholding of information lasts for only a short period of time, and it may not extend any further than what is strictly necessary for carrying out the intended investigation.

(b) In some cases, in the course of an experiment subjects are directly or indirectly goaded into engaging in behavior that is in conflict with God's norms, for example, when they are asked to lie, to steal, or to commit fornication or adultery. It should be clear that such experiments are always unacceptable in a Christian psychology.

(c) It is also important to stress that the guinea pig must suffer no lasting psychical damage as a result of the experiment. In itself, it may be difficult to predict in advance what damage might occur. However, we do possess important data to the effect that many of the more radical experiments have been followed up by thorough and lengthy psychiatric investigations, in which no evidence of lasting psychical damage to the subjects was found. It appears that people can take a great deal. It is also worth noting that after the experiment is over and has been explained, the subjects usually state that they were quite happy to have participated in the experiment and that they considered the temporary misleading of only minor importance.

Psychological Prejudices

It stands to reason that whenever the natural scientist engages in counting, measuring, making observations, or undertaking experiments, he tries to eliminate his personal experiences, affections, emotions, prejudices, etc., as much as possible from his research. His personal reaction to the phenomena he is measuring—whether he finds them pleasant or revolting—must not play any role in his explanation of them.

However, when it comes to the psychologist, it is more difficult to eliminate all personal experience. Perhaps it is not even desirable to do so. A psychologist studies a certain human behavior in order to get at the meaning and aim of that behavior. But in his quest to understand the behavior, he cannot ignore his own feelings and preferences. On the contrary, he has to be able to identify with the subject who exhibits the behavior in question. He must have empathy, that is, he must be able to enter into its meaning. Even so, the psychologist must try to eliminate his own person as much as he can from this process. The question for him is not whether or not he would behave in the same way if he were in the same circumstances. Rather, his aim is to understand the meaning of the behavior of his subject. Thus, he must set aside his own psychical qualities and his own ideas as much as he can, and try to approach the subject of his experiment in as unbiased a manner as possible.

However, he will never be able to be as objective as the physicist. Psychology has to do with a much more "human" form of knowledge. Therefore it is much less neutral and value-free. The theoretical prejudices and even the worldview of the psychologist play a much greater role in his theorizing than they would in the theorizing done by a physicist. This is part of the reason why we find among psychologists schools of thought very diverse in their worldviews, whereas among physicists these are rarely found. This also means that it is much easier, and far more important, to work toward a Christian psychology than toward a Christian physics. In principle there should be no difference, since *all* special sciences must be grounded in a Christian-philosophical view of reality and knowledge. In practice, however, it does make a difference, as psychology is far more sensitive than physics to prejudices relating to worldviews.

Psychological Explanation

When a natural scientist tries to explain certain phenomena, he constructs theories with respect to them. He hopes to make his theories so airtight that, in the long run, they acquire the status of *natural laws*. Such laws are fixed rules according to which certain natural phenomena appear to behave; we can think, for example, of the laws of gravity formulated by Isaac Newton (1642-1727). In contrast, the psychologist is less interested in the universal than in what is unique and individual, such as the meaning of a special behavior of a particular person in a specific situation. Even so, the psychologist tries to classify individual behaviors under more general categories, for instance, the average behavioral patterns of the unemployed, of retired citizens, of pre-school children, of soldiers, of truck drivers, of buyers, of neighbors in either big cities or small villages, etc.

Actually, this is not very different from what we do in everyday life. We often talk about strictly unique events, but we do so in general terms. For example, we say: "The doctor became very upset, and took out his aggression on his patient." Without consciously realizing what we are doing, we categorize the event, recognizing that it has certain properties (agitation, aggression, taking it out on a person) that we had previously taken note of as properties of other "unique" events. The psychologist is trying to do the same thing, but in a more exact and systematic manner. He is trying to classify what is unique under more general headings, looking for general regularities; in short, he is trying to formulate *laws*.

We should not understand the word "laws" in too absolute a sense. In science, a law is really nothing more than a theory that has not been disproved as yet. A law describes only how a certain phenomenon has behaved up to this point in time. To declare that there is such a law means that up to the present we have not been able to observe an exception to this rule. Moreover, there are also laws—more common in psychology—which describe not how a phenomenon *always* behaves but how it *usually* behaves. For example, we may say, "In children, intelligence usually increases with age," or, "Neighbors are usually closer in villages than in cities," etc.

There is one other difference between physical and psychological laws that deserves mention here. Physical laws usually indicate a *cause* (iron expands because it is heated), whereas psychological laws are often more likely to indicate a *purpose* or *aim*. Psychologists are greatly interested in the aim of behavior, i.e., in the motives or incentives that induce a person to undertake certain behaviors. In this regard their work is more like that of the cultural sciences (humanities), which also take a great interest in motives and incentives. Thus, we see again that, as it develops its theories and formulates its laws, the science of psychology occupies a unique position between the natural sciences and the cultural sciences.

Chapter Five
THE DEVELOPMENT OF PSYCHOLOGY

Experimental psychology as we know it today is less than a century and a half old. Actually, it *could* not have put in an appearance very much earlier, because it had to wait, so to say, for other developments to take place first. For instance, the idea of the *experiment* first had to be discovered and introduced into the world of science. That was a development that came fairly late in our history. The thinking of Western Man had to go through quite a development before room was found for the idea that it was important to make sensory observations of concrete phenomena and for the realization that one could do experiments with those phenomena.

This change in thinking came about only at the time of the Renaissance (especially the sixteenth century); the experiment as such was invented by Leonardo da Vinci (1452-1519). The empirical attitude was further fostered by the spirit of the Reformation. Under the influence of the latter, Western Man once again became interested in God's creation. People no longer took their own preconceived ideas regarding the creation as their starting point but began modestly and reverently to put "questions" to the creation. That is to say, they began to make observations and do experiments.

First Results

The result was that the creation, little by little, began to yield up its secrets. The experimental method proved to be extremely successful in many different sciences. A number of researchers operating in the general tradition of the Reformation, such as Johannes Kepler (1571-1630), Francis Bacon (1561-1626), Robert Boyle (1627-1691), and Isaac Newton (1643-1727), as well as Catholic scientists such as Galileo Galilei (1564-1642), did pioneer work in this respect. These developments made possible the swift growth of the natural sciences in the seventeenth and eighteenth centuries. The growth of these sciences was also necessary before experimental psychology could make an appearance. A certain amount had to be known about the physical and biotic aspects of Man before it could become feasible to gather knowledge about the mental aspects. Thus it should not surprise us that the first psychologists in the nineteenth century were originally physicists, physiologists, and physicians.

Here I could mention such famous names as Johannes P. Müller (1801-1858), who discovered the *reflex* (see below), and his pupil Hermann L.F. von Helmholtz (1821-1894), who occupied himself with the question of nerve-stimulation and motor reactions, among other things. Other important pioneers were Ernst H. Weber (1795-1878), and Gustav T. Fechner (1801-1887), who was appointed professor of physics at Leipzig in 1834. Both of these men did interesting research work in the area of the physiology of the sense organs (in order to answer the question "How do the senses work?").

In 1860 Fechner wrote his *Elemente der Psychophysik* (translated into English as *Elements of Psychophysics*), which exercised a tremendous influence on the early history of psychology. This work might well be called the first textbook in experimental psychology. Fechner's book breathed the spirit of Charles Darwin's *On the Origin of Species*, which had been published the previous year. Thus, evolutionist notions were to influence the young science of psychology for a long time to come, as we shall see in due course. Simply put, what happened is that the evolutionist psychologists claimed that the human psyche could be explained in purely physical or physiological terms, as a consequence of its development from the animal kingdom.

Fechner launched the method of experimental psychology, but it was another investigator who managed to base a whole science on the foundation of that method. That second investigator was a pupil of Johannes P. Müller, the physician Wilhelm M. Wundt (1832-1920). In 1873-74, after making a thorough study of the work of Helmholtz, Weber, and Fechner, Wundt published his two-volume epoch-making work *Grundzüge der physiologischen Psychologie*, translated into English as *Principles of Physiological Psychology* (1904). Through this work, Wundt became the first psychologist. Yet the very term "physiological psychology" already indicates that Wundt, as a Darwinist, proposed to explain the human psyche in a purely physiological way. In other words, he intended to explain it in terms of the human mind's far-removed animal origins. In our terms this means he attempted to reduce the perceptive and sensitive modalities to the biotic modality.

Structuralism

In 1875, Wundt became a professor at Leipzig, where he opened the world's first psychological laboratory. Before long this laboratory became a world-renowned center where research workers from far and wide were brought together to undertake psychological study modeled on Wundt's. Once these visiting investigators returned to their home bases, they proceeded to establish similar laboratories themselves. Thus, by this means, a whole network of centers for psychological research quickly sprang up, both in Europe and in North America. In the United States it was the great philosopher and psychologist William James (1842-1910) who set up a psychological laboratory at Harvard University in Cambridge (Mass.), thereby becoming the pioneer of psychology in that country.

By about the year 1900, psychology had in this way become an independent and established science throughout the entire Western world. Therefore, we can say that psychology is still quite a young science—so young that the majority of all psychologists who have ever lived are still alive today.

Just how truly psychology was still in its infancy is evident from the fact that around the year 1900 there were different schools of psychology that combated one another vehemently. Because there were as yet relatively few experimental data, these new researchers were driven back to the prejudices embedded in their various worldviews and philosophies—and those prejudices can differ quite a bit. The first psychologists agreed that the primary task of psychology should be to study *consciousness*. For them, psychology was the theory of consciousness or of the phenomena exhibited by Man's consciousness. But there were various matters on which their opinions differed, such as what really mattered when it came to consciousness, and how one could make observations of consciousness.

Wundt and his followers were advocates of what was called *structuralism*. According to them, the idea was to look for the *structure*, contents, and various elements of consciousness. Included among such elements were, for example, tones, colors, tastes, smells (in our terms purely perceptive phenomena). Moreover, among these elements there were all sorts of relations to be distinguished. For instance, certain colors, sounds, smells, forms, and temperatures are associated with the concept "fire," and were thus coupled to one another. In such a manner, consciousness was "filled" with elements, relations, concepts, images, feelings, etc. *Introspection*, as it was called, was the method recommended by Wundt to investigate the structure of consciousness. This term literally means to look inside oneself. Human subjects were assigned the task of observing changes of consciousness within themselves as the person in charge of the experiment administered all kinds of sensory stimuli.

Functionalism

However, there were other researchers who did not think very highly of introspection. It soon became evident just how subjective this method was: different investigators using this method would obtain totally divergent results. Moreover, introspection could only be used in the case of adults; it was useless when dealing with animals, the mentally challenged, or children. In this way, one could not learn anything about the *development* of consciousness, whether about the individual development from baby to adult, or about the (alleged) evolutionary development from animal to human being. Yet these were precisely the things that many Darwinist psychologists wanted to find out about. Just as biologists concerned themselves with the changing functions of the organs during this (supposed) evolution, so there were psychologists who wanted to find how the actual *functions* of consciousness had developed during the continual struggle for survival in the evolutionary process.

Psychologists of this kind could be called *functionalists.* William James, whom I have mentioned earlier, was the leader of this school. Although the functionalists did not altogether brush introspection aside, they were the first psychologists to introduce other kinds of experiments as well, such as observation of *behavior* in children and in animals. By not asking their experimental subjects what they were experiencing "within themselves" but observing how their subjects responded—even though they realized that one could only observe the subject's exterior—these functionalists felt they could construct a psychology that would be more objective than that of the structuralists.

Depth Psychology

In complete independence of the developments I have just sketched, there arose in Europe, at about the same time, a different psychological school, which was associated with the famous Austrian physician and psychiatrist, Sigmund Freud (1856-1939), and afterwards with the Austrian Alfred W. Adler (1870-1937) and the Swiss Carl G. Jung (1875-1961). I limit myself to Freud here, just to give a general impression of this school.

In one important respect, Freud was in agreement with the thinkers I have mentioned above, in that he was a convinced and consistent Darwinist. Freud introduced into psychology the revolution that Darwin had brought about in biology. He arrived at his psychoanalytic theory not by means of experiments but by observing neurotic patients. He took the radical position that psychology was not at all concerned in the first place with consciousness. It was allegedly concerned rather with a *deeper* and much more influential layer or stratum in the human personality, namely, the *unconscious* (German: *das Unbewusste*)—hence the term *depth psychology.*

Freud's first investigations focused on the phenomenon of *hysteria,* which was quite widespread at the time. People with hysteria suffer from genuine (not feigned) bodily disorders of such a sort that there does not appear to be any physical cause. Such disorders apparently have purely mental causes. Freud developed a method by which his hysterical patients—almost all of whom were women—were able to recall all sorts of emotional experiences of the past. He came to the conclusion that those emotional occurrences could be attributed to conflicts between passionate (especially sexual) desires on the one hand and the taboos of the environment on the other. He theorized that because those conflicts were unpleasant, they were repressed to the unconscious, where they were stored up without the patient's being aware of it. Nevertheless, the conflicts did come to expression, but then in a roundabout way: they were disguised or camouflaged by means of the hysterical symptoms. If the patient could just bring the repressed emotions back to the surface, by making them a part of his or her consciousness, he or she could get rid of them and be healed of his or her disorders.

Before long, Freud added to these initial theories a number of new ones, which were just as original —and in many cases, incidentally, just as dubious. One of these new ideas was the *Oedipus complex*. According to Freud, every little boy was supposed to have the unconscious desire to get rid of his father so that he could have the love of his mother entirely for himself (including sexual intercourse with her!). Freud used the term "Oedipus" because the mythical Greek king Oedipus had unintentionally done that very thing: he had killed his father and married his mother. With advancing age, this hatred toward the father was supposed to give way to *identification*: the boy would then take his father, and later also some other great and admired figures, as his models. Freud theorized that in the case of people who are mentally ill, this process did not unfold in the proper way. Instead, it developed into an unhealthy attitude of revolt against persons in authority.

Gradually, sexuality began to occupy an ever larger place in Freud's theories. Thus, he taught that, in our dreams, all sorts of unfulfilled and even forbidden desires, especially of a sexual and perverse nature, made themselves known. Freud maintained that even the very small child already has sexual drives, which are directed toward the parents. He believed that the sexual behavior of the child bears a strong resemblance to certain perverse kinds of behavior occurring in adults. Persons who experienced abnormal development, he thought, could remain stuck in certain stages (*phases*) of childish sexuality. As a result, they would develop all sorts of mental aberrations.

In later years Freud came to distinguish between the *Id* (German: *Es*; the unconscious instincts or drives), the *Ego* (German: *Ich*; the I-consciousness), and the *Super-Ego* (German: *Über-Ich*; the largely unconscious *conscience*, which is allegedly imposed upon us by norms and taboos that stem from our environment, especially during our upbringing).

For Freud, this body of ideas formed an almost unassailable worldview or ideology, which was indissolubly connected with his materialist and evolutionist thinking. Scientifically speaking, Freud deserves credit for placing great emphasis on the significance of unconscious emotions and of the experiences of early youth. But for the rest, his views tell us more about the Victorian morals of his time than about the nature of Man. Even so, these views have had an enormous effect on Western thinking, and as such are comparable to the influence of the British naturalist and evolutionist Charles Darwin (1809-1882) and the German philosopher and communist Karl Marx (1818-1883). Terms like *repression, inhibition, frustration, "Freudian slip,"* and the *unconscious* have become household words among modern Western people. Moreover, Freud's arrogant writings on religion, which he viewed as a mental aberration, have contributed in a marked way to the de-Christianizing of the Western world.

It should also be noted that Freud is the psychologist perhaps most responsible for the fact that in our Western world we have come to place much less value on ideas of genuine moral guilt and personal responsibility. Man is now represented as being, on the inside, the plaything of unconscious forces, and on the outside, the victim of the environment's strong taboos; moreover, he is not personally responsible for anything that happens to him as a result of these influences. Freudianism has taught us to shift the blame from the person to his parents and society. In opposition to all such thinking, Christian psychology emphasizes that every individual is personally responsible to God and to all who are in authority over him, even though unconscious forces do play a certain role in our lives, as we shall see.

Reflexology

We have now taken a brief look at the initial period of development of the science of psychology, focusing on Western Europe and the United States. At this point we will shift our attention to Russia and look at the work of Ivan Pavlov (1849-1936). About 1900, Pavlov began his famous experiments with dogs, studying their *reflexes*. We speak of a reflex action when a stimulus is directly and immediately followed by a particular reaction, which psychologists call a *response*. The response is uniquely correlated with the stimulus. The brain and consciousness seem to be excluded in all of this. A standard example is the salivating reflex. When good food is placed before a hungry dog, or even before a hungry person, the salivary glands *automatically* begin to secrete saliva. This is an example of an innate reflex: under normal circumstances, the stimulus leads *unconditionally* to the response. Psychologists speak here of an unconditioned stimulus and an unconditioned reflex.

What Pavlov did was to investigate this salivating reflex. The *stimulus* was the sight of food, and the *response* was drooling. In the course of his investigation, he combined the stimulus with, for example, the ringing of a bell. After he had done this on a number of occasions, he proceeded to ring the bell *without* showing any food. Lo and behold, the dog began to drool. This indicated that the reflex was *coupled* to a new, conditioned stimulus and therefore had become a conditional or *conditioned* reflex. The dog had learned a new reflex. This particular form of learning is called *conditioning*.

It is important to understand that the dog does not start to drool because he *knows* that food is on the way whenever he hears the bell ring. Conditioning has little to do with knowing. This is apparent from the fact that conditioned reflexes can be produced even in very primitive animals. Such reflexes occurring apart from any knowledge can also be produced in human beings. An example is the eyelid reflex. The eyelid closes automatically without the person being aware of it when it is subject to a stimulus, such as a gust of wind. If you combine the gust of wind with a weak flash of light, you will find that after a while the reflex occurs after the flash of light unaccompanied by anything else and without the person realizing it.

The experiments performed by Pavlov, for which he ultimately received the Nobel Prize, did not just have an effect in scientific terms. Pavlov placed his results within the framework of a particular worldview, and thereby managed to exert great influence. He declared triumphantly that there was no need whatsoever to appeal to any sort of consciousness in order to explain the results he had obtained. He maintained that, if anything along the lines of conscious phenomena existed, they were at most side effects which should not be allowed to play any further role in psychological explanations. Since Pavlov was a convinced Darwinist, this point was of great importance to him. The great emphasis he placed on animal experiments also arose from his Darwinist convictions.

When his experiments became known in America, they inspired admirers to emulate them there. Earlier we saw that the functionalists gradually devoted themselves increasingly to performing experiments on animals, claiming that in this way they would be able to understand Man better. This is a typically Darwinist strategy. One such important functionalist was Edward Thorndike (1874-1949). Working completely independently of Pavlov, Thorndike conducted experiments in which he explored the learning process in animals. He wanted to know in what way animals learned how to free themselves from cages called *puzzle boxes,* which he had constructed specifically for the purpose of his experiments. When a hungry cat is placed in the puzzle box, it sees food lying outside the puzzle box and is eager to get out. It is able to escape if it pulls on a loop. Gradually the cat catches on, and learns how to free itself more and more quickly as the situation is repeated again and again.

Thorndike called this kind of learning behavior *trial and error.* It was his conviction that behaviors that resulted in satisfying specific needs lead to the formation of specific nerve connections in the brain. As those behaviors are repeated and yield the same positive result on each occasion, they are continually strengthened. This idea of strengthening or *reinforcement* would soon begin to play a major role in psychological investigations, especially in the study of learning processes.

Behaviorism

The experiments of Pavlov and Thorndike eventually led to the rise of a particularly influential movement in psychology that came to be known as *behaviorism*. The founder of this school was John Broadus Watson (1878-1958). In 1913, Watson announced that psychologists would finally have to make a radical break with any and every form of a theory of consciousness. The reason was that psychology, as he saw it, was a purely objective, experimental branch of the natural sciences. Introspection was fundamentally misconceived; instead, psychologists should concern themselves only with observing human *behavior*. Hence, the name that came to be associated with his way of thinking was behaviorism.

As for such things as consciousness, mental states of affairs, the will, mental images, etc., Watson claimed that they simply could not be described scientifically. Behavior, however, *could* be observed and described. Appealing to the experiments done by Thorndike and Pavlov, Watson maintained that it is clear that behavior can be *explained*, and in purely physiological terms at that. Watson believed that, if he could simply disallow all mental concepts and get rid of them, he could purge psychology of all prejudices derived from any sort of worldview, ideology, or philosophy. Apparently, he did not realize that he himself was simply introducing a worldview or philosophy of his own—a materialist and evolutionist one.

In the method he applied, Watson was quite consistent. For him, thinking did not imply anything mental: it was nothing more than a form of inaudible talking, accompanied by tiny movements of muscles in the larynx, the tongue and the lips. He thought that emotions could be completely reduced to secretions of various sorts of glands and activities of the autonomic nervous system. Human beings are essentially nothing more than robots or puppets. According to Watson, even the noblest human reactions to feelings arise from nothing other than conditioned reflexes.

In the 1920s, Watson's school dominated all of American psychology, but in the 1930s people began to see that his view was simply too extreme and too limited. A number of psychologists renounced their radical behaviorism, while others developed a more moderate form that came to be known as *neo-behaviorism.* The most famous of the neo-behaviorists was B. F. Skinner (1904-1990), who was known especially for his experiments with rats and pigeons. His experiments involved the *operant conditioning chamber,* commonly known as the *Skinner box,* which was a successor to Thorndike's puzzle box. In the Skinner box is a small lever that the rat presses, or a small plate that the pigeon can peck. When either of these actions is performed, a little pellet of food rolls directly into a pan inside the cage. In this situation, the animal gradually learns to recognize the connection between pressing a lever and the food appearing in the cage. By means of this simple apparatus, numerous clever experiments were carried out to investigate what it takes to establish conditioned reflexes, as well as what it takes to break them down.

If we speak here of conditioning and reflexes as Skinner himself did, it is important to point out that, of course, there is quite a difference between the conditioning experiments of Pavlov and those performed by Skinner. What Pavlov did was to start from *existing,* unconditioned reflexes such as the salivating reflex. In such an experiment, the animal subject always remains passive. However, in the conditioning as carried out by Skinner, the animal subject itself actively learns how to perform certain operations by which it can itself introduce into its surroundings certain changes that are pleasing to it. Or, in the case of some other experiments, the animal can escape or avoid unpleasant changes in its surroundings.

Pavlov's conditioning is called *classical* (or *respondent*) conditioning, and Skinner's is called *instrumental* (or *operant*) conditioning. It is very important to understand that both forms of conditioning also occur in human beings, as we shall see later. This is a truth which needs to be faced just as much as the truth that all human learning cannot be *reduced* to conditioning, in spite of all the assertions of the extreme behaviorists to the contrary. Though human beings do indeed undergo a certain amount of conditioning, they also experience higher forms of learning, which are of quite a different order.

Humanistic Psychology

In the 1950s, an entirely new school of psychology appeared on the scene. The leadership for this new school came from the American psychologist Abraham Maslow (1908-1970). This school presented itself as a *third force*, professing strong opposition to psychoanalysis on the one hand, and behaviorism on the other. Maslow reproached the behaviorists for acting as if rats and pigeons could serve as simplified stand-ins for human subjects. According to Maslow, much human behavior is totally unique and definitely cannot be reduced to the behavior of rats or pigeons, or even of apes. Examples he mentioned were the making of fire, the construction of tools, speech, abstract thinking, creative social behavior, the arts, science, morals, and religion.

Maslow also had a bone to pick with the psychoanalysts. He argued that there is no proof whatsoever that *all* human conduct can be reduced to unreasoned drives or childhood conflicts. In opposition to what Freud tried to do, he maintained that one cannot possibly understand the behavior of healthy persons on the basis of the psychiatric observation of mentally disturbed people. The behaviorist thinks in terms of animals, the psychoanalyst thinks in terms of patients. In opposition to both these approaches, Maslow proposed thinking in terms of *healthy persons*. It was time for psychology to become a genuine *human psychology*. Therefore, the somewhat confusing name *humanistic psychology* was adopted.

How do we define a "healthy person"? According to Maslow, it is a human who has realized all his inner possibilities. Being (mentally) healthy depends on the degree of *self-actualization* or *self-fulfillment* of the person. To achieve such actualization or fulfillment, according to Maslow, a substantial quantity of life-experience is necessary, along with favorable social circumstances (good social opportunities, possibilities for the development of spontaneity, creativity, and so forth). It follows from this that Maslow was not much interested in experiments. Another thing that follows is that, as other psychologists have done before him, he inevitably presents us with another worldview or philosophy on which psychology was to be built.

In order to attain self-actualization or self-realization, according to Maslow, a person must attain the satisfaction of his needs. Moreover, the needs must be satisfied in a distinct order (Maslow's *hierarchy of needs*, often depicted in the form of a pyramid). First of all, the physical needs must be satisfied (thirst, hunger, sleep, and so forth); if this is not done, one will never get around to the higher needs. But once the physical needs have been satisfied to some extent, certain higher needs present themselves: the need for safety, the need for security, settledness, and stability (settled surroundings, regular income, and a well-ordered existence). In addition, when these needs have been met to a reasonable extent, the person feels the need for love and *belongingness*. Beyond those needs, he feels the need for esteem and respect; this includes self-respect as well as respect for others. And when those needs have been reasonably met in turn, the highest needs of all are felt: the need for self-actualization, that is, the need for the highest development and highest use of all one's abilities and qualities. Only when all of this has been achieved can a person really be said to be mentally healthy.

When we consider the strong emphasis on *needs*, we see that Maslow has not really gotten beyond Darwinism either. He has not really succeeded, any more than the other psychologists discussed above, in putting his finger on what makes Man typically human, and by this I mean not his (mainly) sensitive needs, but his spiritive qualities. Certainly Maslow has not pinpointed what is most fundamental in Man, that is, his transcendent-religious *heart* and his relation to God (or to the gods). Thinking along typically humanistic lines, Maslow maintains that in Man, the satisfaction of needs (directed at *himself*) and *self*-actualization are central. In Christianity, however, what lies at the heart of Man's life is the actualization and development of his relation to God and of the new life in Christ.

In the Christian's life, the highest need is exactly this: the development of communion with the Father and the Son (1 John 1:3-4), with all the resulting implications for the believer's practical daily life. It is on the very basis of a Christian way of thinking that we can come to understand all sorts of phenomena for which there is no place in Maslow's understanding of things. An example of this is how (spiritive) norms transcend (sensitive) needs. For example, we can think of the person in a concentration camp who, in spite of his own gnawing hunger, shares his meager rations with someone else. In such a situation, the highest values play a role, whereas an elementary need such as hunger remains largely unsatisfied.

Cognitive Psychology

When Hitler came to power in Germany, many German speaking psychologists fled to North America. The result in North America was that a thorough exchange of standpoints between psychoanalysts and behaviorists took place, and the exchange had a very fruitful effect on the development of psychology. One of the results was that more and more behaviorists abandoned the old simplistic scheme: S → R. That is to say, a certain stimulus S leads to a specific response R, but what happens between S and R was regarded as being of no significance or interest whatsoever. But gradually, more and more psychologists *did* begin to regard the "in between" as intriguing. They wondered whether the response was really conditional on the stimulus only, or whether there might be something going on in the organism itself that partially determined the response.

Let us consider an example. In the case of the cat escaping from the puzzle box, is it really just a question of a purely automatic trial and error, or are such things as *insight, intentionality,* and *goal-directedness* involved? More and more, psychologists began to insist that there was something more going on, which meant that we would indeed have to assume in both animals and human beings things which are known as *cognitive factors.*

Let us take the instance of *perception.* Seeing, hearing, smelling, and so forth are not to be understood simply as particular physiological conditions of the brain. There is much more to perception because some form of awareness or consciousness is involved. Moreover, our perception is a determining factor in our behavior. Therefore, it becomes necessary to place at least a P (for perception) between the S and the R: S → P → R. Or we could consider the active learning process in Man, as reflected in the learning of a language. Conditioning has very little to do with learning a language. There is much more to it, and the extra dimension can only be explained if we assume not just perceptive factors but also sensitive and especially spiritive factors (see chapter 2). I will have more to say about this matter in chapters 6 and 7.

Many more examples could be given of human actions that can only be understood if we assume that such higher factors are involved. In our Christian anthropology, which we have taken as the starting point for Christian psychology, this was a perfectly obvious first principle. But in secular psychology, which has suffered for so long under the tyranny of materialist and evolutionist first principles, psychologists have only slowly and reluctantly come to the point where they are willing to accept the presence of such cognitive factors. In this regard they were ill served by the prejudices built into their worldview.

An example of such a cognitive psychologist is the neo-behaviorist C. Edward Tolman (1886-1959), who placed great emphasis on goal-directedness (intentionality) in animal behavior. For example, a rat that must learn to find its way in a maze by walking and searching learns to avoid all sorts of blind alleys and in the end finds the shortest way to the food that beckons enticingly. Its successful performance indicates that it is not merely conditioned to carry out a series of individual movements; it learns the route to follow, or a procedure, or, as psychologists like to say in such a case, a *cognitive map*. That which determines the animal's eventual responses, according to Tolman, is not the stimuli in themselves but the cognitive map.

Now, I am not happy with the use of the term "cognitive" in this context, for I would rather reserve it for Man (see chapter 2). But my objection to the terminology does not take away from the thrust of the argument, insofar as we see that even in the behavior of mammals there is more involved than simply conditioned reflexes.

Gestalt Psychology

Cognitive psychology was also influenced by a school that assumed a rather special place within the history of psychology.

The founder of this school was the Berlin psychologist Max Wertheimer (1880-1943). Whereas the structuralists of a previous generation had sought to carve consciousness up into *elements*, Wertheimer totally rejected the idea of separate elements. He stressed that in perception, people do not perceive separate elements, but rather coherent wholes, each of which possesses its own structure. In the German language, such a whole is called a *Gestalt*, and because this word is difficult to translate, it has been borrowed by several other languages and used to designate this psychological concept. An example of such a Gestalt is a melody. A melody may be played on a number of different instruments, at various tempos and in various different keys, but it is always recognizable as the same melody. It is obvious that the melody retains its own quality, structure, form, and figure (in brief, its *Gestalt*) in all these different circumstances.

We often encounter another example of a Gestalt when we are driving in traffic. If we see two red warning lights, the one just above the other, and they are alternately going on and off, we perceive what is before us as though one single light is moving up and down. We do not perceive the two lights going on and off as separate stimuli; rather, we regard them as parts of a whole, a Gestalt.

Consider the example of the two sketches of a face below. In the one case we have a laughing mouth, and in the other we see a sad mouth. It is very striking that the eyes, which are drawn in exactly the same way in both figures, make a very different impression. In the one figure we see happy eyes, while in the other we see sad ones. Here we have a fine example of a Gestalt: the faces as wholes. All the parts within each face are dependent on one another. Or to put the point in a slightly different way, we could say that the way we perceive the eyes is not just dependent on how those eyes look by themselves but is influenced by how the eyes are connected with all the other subordinate parts in the total *stimulus field*.

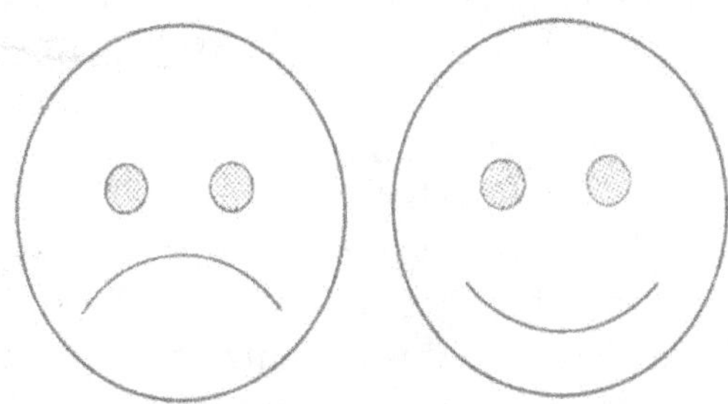

Newer Gestalt Experiments

Wolfgang Köhler (1887-1967), a noted pupil of Wertheimer, performed a series of now celebrated experiments on chimpanzees. From those experiments, it became apparent that higher animals are able to solve problems by relying on a certain kind of insight. By the way in which they go about it, it is obvious that their behavior is dependent on the way they experience their entire stimulus field, that is, the surroundings they perceive. Because the animal's perception of the field suddenly becomes focused so to speak, in a different way, the animal suddenly sees the solution of a problem. For example, the chimpanzee may see how it can reach a banana that appears to be beyond reach by making use of a stick or a box.

A fellow-thinker of Köhler's, Karl Bühler (1879-1963), spoke of the *Aha-Erlebnis* ("aha-experience"). On the basis of this kind of experimentation and explanation, Köhler enlarged the theory of perception of the Gestalt psychologists and made it into a complete psychological theory.

A similar expansion of the theory was undertaken by another student of Wertheimer, Kurt Lewin (1890-1947), who came to the United States before the Second World War, just as Wertheimer and Köhler did. Lewin began with experiments in the area of motivation psychology, which examines the question of what it is that activates a person. He concerned himself with the *dynamic forces* in people that help to determine their behavior. In the course of his investigations, he made the stimulus field into a complete *dynamic field* influencing human actions. The total *psy-*

chological field which determines Man's behavior thus consists of the motivational factors *in* him *and* the environmental factors all *around* him.

Lewin sought to express all of this in a formula that has become famous: B = *f* (P,S). That is, behavior (B) is a function of personal factors (P) on the one hand and situational factors (S) on the other. It is remarkable that Lewin leaves the life history of the person out of the picture in this formula. In his attempt to explain a person's behavior, he does not, like a psychoanalyst, appeal to the person's *earlier* youth conflicts or, like the behaviorist, appeal to his *earlier* conditioning(s). Rather, he asks what forces in the psychological field play a role here and now.

Thus it became much more important how the person experiences and views his situation *right now.* Because he thought along such lines, Lewin could make much more room for cognitive factors than the psychoanalysts and behaviorists did. What a person *knows,* or thinks he knows, about his environment and about himself now became a primary factor in human behavior. This conclusion represented an important advance, even though this view had little resemblance to a Christian psychology in other respects.

Existentialist Psychology

There are still materialist behaviorists around today, but they constitute a minority. What happens in practice is that many psychologists no longer pay much attention to their view of Man (German: *Menschanschauung;* Dutch: *mensbeschouwing*). They accept that there are two kinds of phenomena, (i.e. physical and psychical), and they sometimes take some trouble to try to reduce one kind to the other. But for the rest, they do not bother much about the connection between these two kinds of phenomena. They no longer cling to such simplistic formulas as S → R. For convenience, some *black box* or an unknown X, may be placed between S and R, giving us the formula S → X → R. But on the whole, such psychologists do not concern themselves with the question of the nature of Man.

A major exception to this pattern was a group of thinkers which we will now examine, namely, the existentialists. They included such figures as Karl Jaspers (1883-1969), Martin Heidegger (1889-1976), and Jean-Paul Sartre (1905-1980), whose worldview did in fact inquire into the nature of Man. They placed great emphasis on the total, concrete person, on his uniqueness and his authenticity, on his true, full "existence" in the midst of an incomprehensible, absurd world in which he must learn to make choices. These thinkers were somewhat like the humanistic psychologists I have discussed above, in that the views they offered bore more resemblance to a life-and-worldview than to an experimental-psychological theory. Nevertheless, their thinking exercised considerable influence in contemporaneous psychology.

In opposition to psychoanalysis and behaviorism, the existentialists emphasized that Man's consciousness cannot be reduced to physical-chemical processes; instead, the mind is merely *conditioned* by such processes. Christians can agree with this claim, but now come some differences that need to be noted. According to the existentialists, consciousness (or the mind) is completely *free.* Human behavior is not determined by our molecules but by our free choices. Indeed, existentialists affirmed that a human being really lives or *exists* only if his freedom is not curtailed in any way whatsoever. But by taking this stance, they created problems for themselves on two fronts. On the one hand, on a purely materialist and evolutionist basis, any concept of a free will is simply out of the question. On the other hand, a Christian psychology cannot accept a "free will" defined as being free from the ordinances that were given by our Creator in the creation and by His Word—ordinances that are not simply a duty, a burden, but a blessing, a source of life.

The existentialist exalted the freely developing, evolving mind of Man. Whereas the psychoanalyst had talked about a life of drives, and the behaviorist about a completely conditioned existence, the existentialist spoke instead about the mental creative impulse to development. However, this approach is not the solution we are looking for either. On the one hand, Man's spiritive life cannot be reduced to drives (as the psychoanalysts would say) or to reflexes (as the behaviorists would have it). But on the other hand, Man's spiritive life should not be exalted and made into a free mind that hovers fearlessly and voluntarily above matter. The life of the mind happens to be subjected not to drives or reflexes but to the *heart*. And in his heart, Man is directed either toward God and his commandments—in which case he is truly free!—or toward idols and ideologies that enslave him, whether they be false gods within Man (for example, his drives), his open "free" mind, or the idols of his environment, whether material or spiritual.

In summary, in contrast to psychoanalysts and behaviorists, Christians believe in true human freedom (cf., e.g., John 8:32-36; Gal. 4 and 5). But in opposition to humanistic and existentialist psychologists, they maintain that true freedom is placed under God's norms. A mentally healthy person is not the person who is declared to be totally free—because this leads to debauchery (cf., e.g., 1 Pet. 4:4)—but the person who walks in the ways of God (cf. Rom. 6:17-22).

Many more great psychologists, or intellectuals connected to psychology, might be mentioned in this chapter (leaving aside the psychotherapists and the biologists), such as the Swiss Jean Piaget (1896-1980), a trailblazer in the cognitive psychology of children; the American Gordon W. Allport (1897-1967), a pioneer in the psychology of religion; the Danish-German-American Erik H. Erikson (1902-1994), who worked on developmental psychoanalysis; the American Neal E. Miller (1909-2002), the first psychologist to win the National Medal of Science; the American Jerome S. Bruner (b. 1915) and the British-American Hazel Rose Markus (b. 1949), pioneers of "cultural psychology"; the German-British Hans J. Eysenck (1916-1997), who researched intelligence and personality; the Canadian Albert Bandura (b. 1925), who originated social-cognitive learning theory; the American Noam Chomsky (b. 1928), linguist and cognitive scientist; the American Stanley Milgram (1933-1984), famous for his obedience experiments; the American Paul Vitz (b. 1935), the founder of "transmodern" psychology; the Canadian-American Steven A. Pinker (b. 1954), who has made contributions in linguistics, cognitive science, and experimental psychology, etc.

Lessons to Be Drawn

We as human beings are subject to divine *norms*—logical, technical, lingual, social, economic, aesthetic, juridical, ethical, and pistical (faith) norms. These norms have not been invented by humans; rather, they have been laid down by God in his creation order. As I said, true freedom consists not of being independent of these norms but of living in subjection to them. All the schools of psychology that we have discussed up to this point, whether psychoanalytical, behaviorist, humanistic, existentialist, cultural, or "transmodern," have failed, and continue to fail, to appreciate this "vertical" relation of Man to God. All psychologists seek to gain some understanding of Man. But it is essential to realize that the *nature* of Man is concealed in the human heart, which can only be understood in terms of Man's relationship to God (*or* to the idols). Thus Christian psychology would begin with the biblical wisdom that only God can give us with respect to the relationship in which he has placed Man. Making grateful use of that wisdom, the Christian psychologist can then move on to critically deepen and enrich his insights by goal-directed observations and experiments.

The Christian psychologist is like Kurt Lewin in that he is alert to two groups of factors determining behavior: personal (P) and situational (= environmental) factors (S). Nevertheless, in front of both he places the R factor—the religious condition of the human heart. Thus our psychological formula is as follows:

$$B = f\,(R, P, S)$$

The reader is reminded once again that when it comes to these personal factors (P), we can distinguish between biotic (b), perceptive (p), sensitive (feeling) (f), and spiritive (s) factors. Furthermore, there is a division along perpendicular lines to be made between constitutional (c), operant (o), and motivational (m) factors. These additional distinctions now make it possible to present the following two formulas:

$$P = f\,1\,(R, b, p, f, s, S)$$

$$P = f\,2\,(R, c, o, m, S)$$

The R factor (the religious condition of the heart) is itself in turn partially dependent on P and S; yet it is determined first of all by that on which religion focuses, namely, God or the idols. And neither God nor the idols are accessible via experimental investigation. As we saw earlier, the heart, too, in its innermost being, cannot be analyzed in scientific terms. When it comes to the heart, we are dependent on the light of God's truth as it is known to us from Holy Scripture, through the power of the Holy Spirit.

Chapter Six
THE LOWER MENTAL IDIONOMIES

Now it is time to offer a brief survey of the psychological knowledge we currently possess about the mental idionomies. In preparing this survey, I am making grateful use of the psychological information that non-Christian psychologists have assembled. But at the same time, I am presenting this information in an entirely new way—by drawing on the help of the Christian anthropology that I have explained.

If we are to have any understanding of the mental idionomies, we must first study their biotic basis. In human beings, all mental processes are rooted in, or *carried* by, physico-chemical processes. And these processes occur in the central nervous system. When I am suffering from a pain in my foot, it is true that my sore foot is the *cause* of my pain. However, my foot is not the *carrier* of my pain in the sense in which we are using the term here. My sore foot causes a certain physico-chemical state in a certain part of my brain, and it is that state which I perceive as pain. It is not the sore foot but the physico-chemical state in my brain that is the carrier or *ground* of my pain sensation. Therefore, I will deal first of all with brain processes.

The Brain

The brain is part of the *nervous system,* which in turn consists of two parts:

1. The *central nervous system,* which includes the brain and spinal cord.

2. The *peripheral nervous system,* which contains the nerve connections between the sense organs and the central nervous system, and also between the central nervous system and the muscles.

The brain is usually subdivided in the following manner:

1. The *cerebrum*: This is the upper and most important mass of the brain.

2. *The limbic system*: This consists of a number of brain lobes that are positioned between the cerebrum and the brainstem and thus surround the brainstem like a border (Latin: limbus).

3. The *brainstem*: This almost vertical bar-like part of the brain supports the cerebrum as a stem and connects at the bottom with the spinal cord.

4. The *cerebellum*: This is a separate part of the brain behind the brainstem and beneath the cerebrum (in the lower, rear part of the head).

The cerebrum consists of two *hemispheres* (= half-spheres), each of which is the mirror *callosum*. The exterior layer of the two hemispheres is called the *cerebral cortex*. This cortex is heavily folded and thus possesses an unusually large surface area. The cortex is the place where the sensory stimuli ultimately arrive, are brought to consciousness, and are recognized and judged. It is here that decisions are made as to which impulses are to be sent out to the muscles. Hence we could say that the cerebral cortex is the foundation, the carrier *par excellence*, of the *spiritive idionomy*. For example, it appears that there is a connection between the electrical brainwaves in the cortex and such a typically spiritive attribute as intelligence. Different parts of the cerebral cortex appear to be specialized for the spiritive interpretation of certain sensory stimuli originating in sensory nerves that are located in various parts of the body, such as the face, the ear, and so forth.

The limbic system plays a major role in our life of feeling. If parts of this system are damaged, the result will be all sorts of animal-like emotions and instinctive behaviors. Thus, we could say that the limbic system is the foundation or carrier *par excellence* of the *sensitive idionomy*. For example, it regulates the balance between all sorts of mood states, such as rage or anxiety, aggression or withdrawal, pleasant or unpleasant feelings, stress or relaxation.

As for the brainstem, I must make special mention of the *pons* (from the Latin for bridge). This part of the brain contains an unusual network of nerve cells, which has been given the complicated name *reticular* (i.e. having the form of a net) *activating system* (RAS).

According to many researchers, it is this brain system that switches our consciousness on and off. The RAS sends impulses to all parts of the cerebral cortex, and without the RAS such stimuli or impulses could never be brought to consciousness. During sleep, the RAS is inhibited, with the result that sensory stimuli are no longer brought to consciousness. Thus, the pons is very important for the *perceptive idionomy*. The same could be said for the cerebellum, where many learned behaviors (walking, talking, knitting, playing the piano, tying one's shoelaces) that we are able to perform *automatically* appear to be programmed.

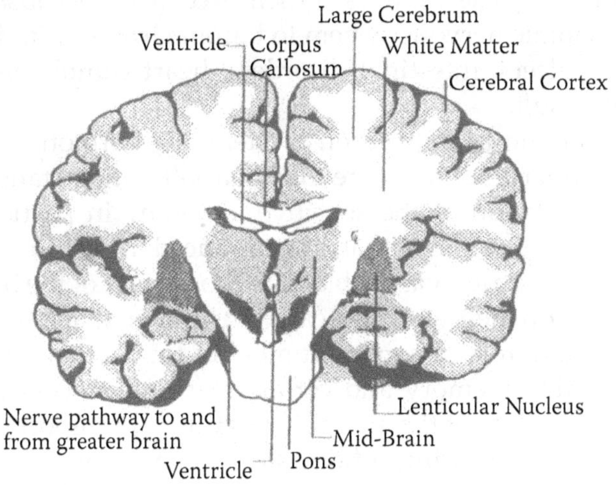

The Autonomic Nervous System and the Hormones

Parts of the limbic system and the brainstem form the center of what is known as the *autonomic* nervous system, which also contains many of the nerve tracks of the peripheral nervous system. This system governs the *smooth muscles*, which are operative in numerous bodily functions that are not normally subject to voluntary control, such as digestion, respiration, metabolism, growth, and circulation of the blood. Thus this system is very important for the *biotic idionomy*, but also for the *perceptive* and the *sensitive idionomies*. In addition there is the *somatic* or *animal nervous system*, which governs the movement of the head, trunk, and limbs. This system can be said to regulate the relation between the individual and his environment. Hence it is of great importance for the *sensitive idionomy*, and even more so for the *spiritive idionomy*.

In what way is the autonomic nervous system of special importance for the *sensitive idionomy*? To understand the answer to this question, one must realize that emotions are closely linked to the workings of the autonomic nervous system. Some examples are a dry mouth, a sudden catching of one's breath, not being able to eat because of nerves, urinating because of nervousness, palpitations of the heart, blushing and growing pale, nervous sweat, and getting goose pimples. When excessive nervousness leads the autonomic nervous system to become irregular in its actions, stomach ulcers, intestinal disorders, heart complaints, and the like can result.

In addition to the nervous system, the hormones are also of special importance if we are to gain a solid understanding of the biotic foundation of the sensitive idionomy in particular. Hormones are substances that are produced in certain endocrine glands, and carried via the blood to those parts of the body where they are to do their work. Research has shown that hormones play an important role in a great number of things that go on within us, including memory and certain learning processes. In addition, the medulla of the adrenal glands is very important because it produces adrenaline, a hormone whose action is very similar to the action of the autonomic nervous system. When a person is under mental or bodily stress, the level of adrenaline in the blood rises. Ill-defined complaints about weakness, total fatigue, listlessness, excessive irritability, depression, and irascibility are sometimes the result of faulty functioning on the part of the thyroid gland, the parathyroid, the ovaries, or the testicles.

Relations between Various Parts of the Brain

Of course, numerous researchers have been intrigued by questions surrounding the functioning of the brain. For instance, it was discovered that, when the *corpus callosum* is severed in the case of certain patients suffering from epilepsy, all sorts of unusual mental phenomena result. The experiments through which this was discovered have taught scientists a great deal more about the functioning of the two hemispheres. The left hemisphere specializes in analytical thinking, the forming of judgments and the solving of mathematical problems. It can express itself in words and has an awareness of time. The right hemisphere, by contrast, thinks in *wholes,* that is to say, synthetically, and could hardly express itself in words. It has very little awareness of time but specializes in the recognition of faces and patterns. The right hemisphere probably contains the center for musical giftedness. (In about half of all left-handed people, the right and left hemisphere are reversed.) The "division of labor" between the two hemispheres has led to all sorts of unwarranted speculation about the existence of two different "psyches," one resident in each hemisphere.

A great deal of research has been done on the relationship between the cerebrum and the limbic system. All stimuli that enter the brain from the outside pass through the limbic system on their way to the cerebral cortex, and in the limbic system they are "emotionally colored." This extremely important fact alone sounds the death-knell for all kinds of speculations about a so-called neutral, objective science. In the limbic system, our perceptions are *charged* with certain positive or negative affections. I will have more to say about this important matter in due course.

Studies about the relationship between the cerebrum and the limbic system have, as a matter of fact, led to all sorts of wild evolutionistic ideas about an allegedly imperfect accumulation of brains, namely, the "reptile brain" (the brainstem), the "mammal brain" (the limbic system), and the "primate brain" (the cerebrum); in this theory, first developed in the 1960s and dubbed "the triune brain," the primates include apes as well as human beings. Because of the imperfect connection between these brains, Man is alleged to have a "limbic psyche," which is separate from his "cortical psyche." None of these speculations has any scientific foundation.

There are somewhat more substantial studies that have been done with regard to the connections between the RAS and the cerebral cortex on the one hand, and the RAS and the autonomic nervous system on the other. As I said earlier, the RAS regulates the excitability of the cerebral cortex. The RAS also exercises a regulating influence on the autonomic nervous system, which in turn either mobilizes the body (via the *sympathetic* part of it) or relaxes it (via the *parasympathetic* part of it). Depending on one's inherited constitution, the RAS will function either to lower or to raise the level of excitability of the cortex, thereby making a person more of an *introvert* (turned in upon himself) or an *extrovert* (turned toward the outside world). Similarly, depending on one's inherited constitution, the RAS can tilt the balance between the sympathetic and parasympathetic systems toward either the one or the other, with the result that the person is either more or less emotional in nature, depending on the balance (Hans J. Eysenck). Thanks to these hereditary differences, we can distinguish four *temperaments* (the theory of which was developed by the Greek physician Hippocrates, 460-370 B.C.):

(a) The verbally fluent, confident, but also somewhat quarrelsome *sanguine* person is the non-emotional extrovert;

(b) The efficient worker who is also sometimes sluggish and self-centered is the *phlegmatic* person, the non-emotional introvert;

(c) The original, creative, but sometimes also depressed and vindictive, *melancholic* person, is the emotional introvert;

(d) The one who is independent and gives good leadership but has tendencies to irascibility, and sometimes even toward criminality is the *choleric* person, the emotional extrovert.

It is obvious that each of these four temperaments has its strong side as well as its weak side; none of them is better or worse than the others. When the heart is turned away from God and yields to sin, the weak sides of a specific temperament make themselves felt. But when the heart is directed to God and surrenders to the leading of the Holy Spirit, the strong side of a personality can be fostered, and then a more Christ-centered development (Gal. 4:19; 5:22) can be seen in the cordiality, the sincerity, the cheerfulness, the friendliness, and the optimism of the *sanguine* person. Likewise, we see it in the leadership, the strength of purpose, the team spirit, and the resoluteness and zest for enterprise of the *choleric* person. Further, we see it in the true friendship, the creativity, and sacrificial spirit of the *melancholic* person. Finally, we see it in the quiet calm, good humor, readiness to listen, tidiness, and thoughtfulness of the *phlegmatic* person.

Thus, we see that our temperament is only the *nucleus* of our character; even though the regeneration of a person does not change his temperament, his *character* can change drastically under the influence of his "new heart." Totally different operant and motivational factors will then begin to play a role in his life, and thus a new knowledge and a new way of thinking will come about, a new *cognition,* and a new direction for his will. In this way the renewed person, within the wide constitutional boundaries of his temperament, can receive an entirely new character in which the image of Christ (cf. Rom. 8:29; 2 Cor. 3:18) takes shape in a completely unique way.

The Perceptive Structure

Up to this point we have been dealing with the biotic idionomy insofar as it forms the phsyiological *ground, foundation,* or *substratum,* for the mental idionomies. Now it is time to take a closer look at the perceptive idionomy, which is the lowest of the three mental idionomies. We already know that characteristics of the perceptive idionomy include:

(a) *Sensation* (meaning: sensory awareness), which we might regard as the most basic form of consciousness (based upon this, there is *perception,* that is, sensitively and spiritively colored sensation).

(b) Moreover, there are the simplest *behavioral responses* (instincts, reflexes), in which no feelings or reflections (that is, conscious deliberations or considerations) are involved, but which in Man are embedded in his sensitive-spiritive behavior. That is, there are also behavioral responses that are sensitively qualified, which means that feelings are involved, but not necessarily reflections (conscious deliberations or considerations), as well as behavioral responses that are spiritively qualified, that is, in which feelings as well as reflections are involved.

We must be careful to distinguish the latter three kinds of phenomena sharply from one another, namely, we must distinguish the non-felt and non-conscious responses—the purely perceptive reflexes—from the felt and conscious responses: the sensitively, or even spiritively "loaded" responses. This distinction is necessary, even though the three hardly ever occur separately in everyday life. It is a characteristic feature of scientific research to *analyze* (or *dissect*) things that in everyday life are completely interwoven; in other words, it takes them apart in order to understand them better.

Sensation and Perception

The biotic idionomy is the first idionomy to develop in the fetus (what the Bible calls "the fruit of the womb"), that is, right from conception Man is a *living* organism. Then comes the perceptive idionomy (everything from the first sensations to the first reflexes), in turn quickly followed by the sensitive idionomy (the first emotions). The newborn infant already has a wide variety of sensory capacities at its disposal, but of course these must be further developed. On the one hand, perception lies at the very foundation of all that takes place in the mental idionomies (feeling, thinking, willing), but on the other hand perception also depends on *how* we *learn* to perceive. There are no two people who perceive the world in exactly the same way: "objective perception" does not exist. *How* a person perceives his environment depends on his bodily makeup (constitution), and on all sorts of operant and motivational factors. Thus we find a strong interaction: our perception influences our thinking and willing, but our thinking and willing influence our perception.

As for the operant factors, our perception is enormously influenced by all that we have *learned*. We live in a society in which, from a very early age, we learn to pay attention to all kinds of "signs." We need only think of social gestures ("Does he want to shake my hand?"), of directory signs ("Is this where I have to be?"), of traffic signs ("How fast can I drive here?"). If a person who had been raised somewhere in the primeval forest were suddenly to find himself in a big city, he in principle would receive the same numerous *sensations* (colors, shapes) as we, but he would perceive almost nothing of them because he has not learned to interpret these sensations. Conversely, if the city person were to walk through that primeval forest, he would notice only a small fraction of what the inhabitants of the forest perceive. The people accustomed to the forest would find it easy to track down food and to detect the presence of dangerous animals, whereas the city people, without resources, would soon perish from hunger or from animal attacks.

A person's *sensation* is loaded with constant experiences, memories, recognitions, which are dependent on one's upbringing and on the environment in which one was raised. Thus, it can even be stated without fear of contradiction that a convinced Christian *sees* (observes, perceives) his environment, his fellow human beings and the things around him, differently than a non-Christian. Not only does he have different convictions, but he literally *sees* everything differently; he wears different "glasses."

This difference becomes much clearer when we add the influence of *feelings* on sensation. All our sensations are deeply *colored* by sensitive factors, that is to say, all kinds of *learned* (= operant) affections (positive or negative), impulses, and emotions, to which we may add (pleasant or unpleasant) memories, prejudices, and, on the spiritive level, logical and social deliberations, moral assessments, etc. Some sensations repel us, whereas others give us a good feeling. Still others make us sad, and it is next to impossible to think of a wholly *neutral sensation*. As we saw earlier, the way in which we give sensitive and spiritive responses to sensations has been learned or acquired. The culture and society of which we are a part play a great role here; we call this the *macro-situation*. Furthermore, we must also consider the dominant values and views of our own social groups, such as our family, our church, our political party, and our scientific school of thought, all of which we refer to as the *meso-situation*. Finally, there is the influence of the concrete situation of the moment, i.e., the *micro-situation*.

Christians in particular may feel the responsibility of recognizing the operant and motivational influences at work in our perception. Not all our perceptions are equally "Christian." We interpret all kinds of stimuli as either pleasant or unpleasant, depending on our attitude toward the source of those stimuli. We tend to like a sermon more when it is being delivered by a preacher we greatly appreciate than when it is being preached by someone we do not know. And when we dislike something or someone, we tend to notice those things about it or about him that serve to strengthen our dislike, while at the same time overlooking positive things that might perhaps change our mind. Of course, sympathy produces just the opposite result.

The sensations passed on by the RAS to the cortex move through the limbic system where they are colored by positive or negative affections. But none of this makes us any less responsible for our feelings. Ultimately, everything that occurs in the mental idionomies is under the control of our intellect and our will, which in turn are governed by our heart—and what is the attitude of our *heart* towards our fellow human beings? We are fully responsible for our sympathies as well as for our antipathies, although psychology has helped us tremendously to acknowledge that much of this occurs at a semi-conscious or unconscious level. On the one hand, it is true that we are not aware of the gigantic load of sensitive factors we are carrying with us, which were formed by our upbringing and our culture, and which do indeed color our sensations. On the other hand, the ultimate *result* of this coloring, that is, the ultimate perceptions, become conscious in our cortex or within our spiritive idionomy.

We humans are able to take our perceptions and feelings into consideration and, where necessary, condemn and confess them. What crops up within them is not always under our control, but the central question is: What do we *do* about this? As Luther reportedly said, "I cannot help it if a bird drops something on my hair, but I *can* help it if it builds a nest in my hair."

Lower-Level Learning

Because we are able to perceive, we can also *learn*. Learning in its most basic forms means developing a certain response or reaction to a certain stimulus. We see this first of all in the case of *lower-level* learning, which has been called *conditioning*. In our terminology, we speak of it as *perceptive* learning. It needs to be distinguished from both *sensitive* learning (the learning of affections, dispositions, and emotional responses) and *spiritive* learning (for example, the learning of language, abstract concepts and norms, and learning how to solve intellectual problems).

Human beings have their perceptive idionomy in common

with the animals, and so the learning of *automatic* actions is something that occurs among human beings just as it does among animals. We should be thankful that this is the case, for our Creator has used it to provide for us in at least three kinds of situations. First of all, such learning occurs in even the smallest child that is as yet undeveloped in sensitive, and particularly in spiritive respects. Second, even seriously mentally challenged persons can still learn quite a bit perceptively. Third, by means of this perceptive learning, normal people can learn hundreds of behaviors which they are called upon to perform very frequently and which they can carry out without having to stop and think. This is a very good thing. Just imagine what it would be like if you had to concentrate on what you were doing each time you bent over to tie your shoelaces, just as if it were the first time! It took some effort to learn that skill, but since then, we have reached the point where we can tie our shoelaces quickly and without thinking about it.

I indicated that Man has his perceptive idionomy in common with the animals, but we have also seen that at the same time there is a big difference between human beings and animals in this respect. In the perceptive idionomy of Man, the perceptive aspect *anticipates* the sensitive and spiritive aspects. This type of anticipation—especially as it relates to the spiritive aspect—is not found in the case of any animal. To focus for the moment on the sensitive, because the perceptive anticipates the sensitive, we learn all kinds of emotional automatic motor responses (and in particular, we learn the emotional types more strongly than non-emotional types). Think of such motor responses as flaring up, clutching at your head or heart, all sorts of nervous tics, nail biting, and so forth.

As for the anticipation of the spiritive, learning one's mother tongue, playing the violin, or driving a car consists to a large extent of automatic actions, which we have learned laboriously by instrumental conditioning. Nevertheless, there is no animal that speaks a language, plays the violin, or drives a car. Even though animals also have a perceptive idionomy, they would not be *able* to learn those actions. The more clearly our actions are spiritively *loaded*, the more *human* they are. These, then, are automatic actions that we have had to learn in a very conscious way. Thought precedes such learning, for one must also *want* to learn to play a musical instrument, or to ski, and must consciously persist in the process in order to obtain the desired result. To be sure, the learning is perceptive, but it is done under the guidance of the spiritive aspect.

Thus we see how relative the resemblances between humans and animals are. It was very naïve of the behaviorists to want to reduce all human learning to conditioning. Their approach was entirely mistaken for at least two reasons. In the first place, in Man the most characteristic learning is not conditioning, but spiritive learning—the learning of one's native tongue, of concepts, and of how to solve mental problems. In the second place, in Man even conditioning itself is something different in principle than it is in the animal, for in most cases this perceptive learning in Man occurs under the guidance of the sensitive modality and especially the spiritive modality.

An example of *pure* perceptive learning in human adults is learning how to use all sorts of simple gadgets, such as the special doorknob of a particular make of car or of a particular room, which is something a dog could learn just as easily.

Affections and Impulses

Let us now turn our attention to the sensitive idionomy. In this idionomy we distinguish three kinds of feelings, between which there is a considerable degree of overlap: affections (inclinations), impulses (objective needs, desires), and emotions. When we discussed the perceptive idionomy above, we observed that sensations are invariably loaded with, or colored by, certain positive or negative affections. Sugar molecules stimulate the taste buds, which thereupon send impulses to the *taste center* in the brain. There, taste originates, as the conscious perception of the stimulus. But in this perception of taste an effective evaluation is immediately involved, for most people find the sweetness of the sugar to be "tasty," whereas other things they perceive to taste "bad."

This affective valuation has a very important practical use. For example, when we perceive the smell of something burning, when we hear screaming and running back and forth in the house, when we see blood or feel pain, or when we eat something that does not taste quite right, we are immediately alarmed. These are all stimuli that, for us, are charged with a negative affection.

In all such cases, our sense of alarm is a *learned* response. It is a conditioned reflex based on an affective reaction to stimuli. The question can be raised whether *all* of our affections are learned, that is to say, whether innate affections can be said to exist at all. For example, there have been quite a number of experiments and discussions concerning the question whether a *maternal instinct* really exists. It is conceivable that what is commonly called the maternal instinct is also something based upon learned behavior, which would then mean that mothers could only give love if they themselves had received it when they were babies. In our "civilized" Western world, thousands of children are abused by their mothers every day. It appears that many of the mothers who perpetrate this abuse had not experienced loving relationships with their own mothers in childhood, and perhaps they themselves had been abused.

Thus, even love, to quite some extent, is something that has to be *learned*. Affections do not belong to the spiritive idionomy but to the sensitive idionomy. Yet, at the same time they ought to be under the *guidance* of spiritive life; in this case, of love in the deep ethical sense, as governed by the heart. The Christian in particular ought to understand that he is responsible for everything that takes place in his life of feeling. Thus we would do well to be more vigilant against all sorts of unreasonable negative affections that could be called *prejudices*, for example, against Native or Afro-Americans, against Catholics or Muslims, against men with long hair or piercings.

Some Christians are only too happy to attribute such affections to a kind of spiritual intuition; for example, they claim they can "feel" that artists or politicians are "no good." The truth of the matter is that such supposed intuition is really based on learned negative affections that are completely without foundation. Thus, our spiritive life also has its moral side, as we have seen. Under the guidance of a heart, oriented toward God and his commandments, we learn that we are able to judge our affections in a critical way, and, if necessary, condemn and unlearn them. Likewise, under the guidance of the heart we also learn to judge our *positive* affections critically and—if they are morally good—to foster them.

As for impulses (or drives, if you will) what was said about the affections also applies to them. Since they fall within the sensitive idionomy, they ought to be under the *guidance* of the spiritive idionomy. It is true that both men and animals have urges or drives (desires, longings, inclinations), which drive us and which precede sober-minded judgment. But the noteworthy difference is that in the case of human beings, those drives are, so to speak, *embedded* in our spiritive deliberations and decisions. This is the reason why Man is also responsible for what he does with his drives. The most important drives are hunger, thirst, and sexual desire. It has proven very difficult to determine exactly how many drives there are and whether we may speak of separate drives as opposed to variants of the same drive. There is no need to go any further into these questions at this point.

No matter how animal-like our drives might appear to be, the manner in which we deal with them, as noted above, is spiritive, and therefore thoroughly human—or in any case, it *ought* to be spiritive. Naturally, we have a strong desire to validate our drives, but on the other hand, it can also be very pleasurable for us to heighten our drives. Thus (spiritively!) we have devised all kinds of ways to *increase* our appetites. Even our sexual behavior does not aim at immediate gratification of our sex drive, for that would leave us acting just like animals. Rather, Man is first of all directed toward increasing the sexual stimuli (sexual stimulation). Because of his spiritive idionomy, Man has the capacity to increase and refine the pleasure of gratification by strengthening these internal stimuli before satisfying them.

Thus, for this reason we know something very striking, namely, that sexuality in Man does not solely—or even primarily—have a biological function. Rather, it is intended by God to be an expression of married love between a husband and his wife (see Gen. 2, or the Song of Solomon, where sexual intercourse between husband and wife is described as a matter of joy, without any reference to offspring). This is why it is even possible, for example, for a husband to be willing to abstain from sexual intercourse with his wife if she has become an invalid or is temporarily ill, while he devotes himself to caring for her. Or to take another example, one may abstain entirely from sex and remain unmarried in order to become a missionary. In Man, then, the drives are on an infinitely higher plane than in the case of animals, because they are embedded in Man's spiritive life. And what is especially important to note is that Man's drives are under the guidance of the *heart*, which serves either God or the idols.

Emotional Life

It is natural for affections and impulses to be accompanied very often by strong emotions, which may vary from merriment to rage or fright. The emotions can also occur by themselves, as happens when we feel afraid or excited but are not aware of the cause of these emotions or their meaning. Such emotions could be the result of disturbances within the biotic idionomy, for we have seen that the autonomic nervous system has a great influence on our emotional life, as do certain hormones. Such vague fears and feelings of excitement can also find their cause in the sensitive idionomy itself, for example, when we are unconsciously afraid of something. This is quite an important point in counseling, as we shall see in the final chapters.

There have been many efforts to categorize the emotions. There are some psychologists who distinguish between (a) "positive expectation" (*hope*), which might be followed by *disappointment*, and (b) "negative expectation" (*fear*), which might be followed by *relief*. Some psychologists believe that all the emotions can be categorized under these two headings. But there are other psychologists who have developed much more complicated schemes, in which they distinguish, for example, between anger, ecstasy, loathing, grief, horror, bewilderment, affection, attachment (devotion), hope, and the like. Again, each of these emotions can occur in varying degrees of intensity. For example, at its lowest degree of intensity, anger may be expressed as irritation, and at its highest degree of intensity as rage or frenzy.

It should also be noted that, on the one hand, our emotions are embedded in the whole of our sensitive life, as well as in our spiritive acts, and even in the operation of our heart. But on the other hand, our emotions are foundationally embedded in physico-chemical processes (physical idionomy) and physiological (organic, vegetative) processes (biotic idionomy). An example will make this clearer. Let us suppose, for instance, that somewhere I unexpectedly run into an acquaintance who has done me some wrong in the past, or perhaps I meet someone whom I have treated rather badly. In the first case, I might well become angry right away, or at least irritated. In the second case, I become somewhat embarrassed or even afraid. Perhaps, by way of defense, I assume an attitude of either indifference or aggressiveness. In this situation, several *elements* can be distinguished:

1. *Biotic*: The immediate activation of the sympathetic nervous system and the secretion of the hormone adrenaline for the medulla of the adrenal gland.

2. *Perceptive*: My perception of the acquaintance and my spontaneous startle reflexes.

3. *Sensitive*: The excitement, anger, fear, indifference, or aggressiveness.

4. *Spiritive*: The memory of what the other person did to me, or of what I did to him, the rational evaluation of that memory, and the resulting interpretation of my emotion, as well as the deliberations and decisions as to what I am going to do with that memory and that emotion.

5. The *heart*—which is my *self*—ultimately determines what I will do with my emotions, in the light of my relationship with God (or, the gods). I can give unbridled expression to these emotions, or I can condemn them and bring them under my control and act in the proper biblical way. If I choose the second path, I will, in the first scenario where I have been wronged, try to win back my brother (cf. Matt. 18:15); in the second scenario where I have wronged my brother, I will confess my guilt to him (cf. Matt. 5:23-24).

Spiritive Facets

Let us focus for a moment on the fourth point I have just mentioned, namely, the interaction between the sensitive and spiritive idionomies regarding the emotion. Biologically speaking, all emotions are similar: they are all caused by the same activity of the autonomic nervous system, and are all accompanied by the same characteristics of *physiological excitement*. However, the question how we (spiritively) deal with this excitement will depend on our situation and our assessment of it.

For example, when someone has been given a placebo that he *believes* is a medication causing physiological excitement, he will *feel* much less emotional when he is in an emotional situation than some other experimental subject will. The reason for this is obvious: the person simply attributes whatever excitement he is experiencing to the placebo, and accordingly does not think that he *feels* excited. Thus, there is a considerable difference between purely biotic and sensitive excitement. One can interpret the same biotic excitement as "*no* excitement" ("I do not *feel* excited"), or as fear, anger, affection, and so forth, depending on the situation.

This is one reason why Christians must be very careful when they interpret their life of feeling. To take a rather extreme example, it is clear that a man should not propose marriage to a woman when he is under stress conditions. Psychologists have demonstrated that people who share an experience of great danger sometimes interpret their physiological excitement as affection toward one another; they may even imagine that they are in love. Such a situation is hardly a reliable basis for taking such an important step as making a marriage proposal. Some have learned this the hard way: they began a relationship, but later, when the danger was over, they found out that in fact they did not have enough of a basis for a relationship.

Chapter Seven
THE SPIRITIVE IDIONOMY

We now come to the spiritive idionomy, the highest of the three mental idionomies as well as the highest of the five human structures, the idionomies which together constitute Man's immanent, corporeal existence. The spiritive idionomy largely corresponds with what we call the *mind*.

Apart from the heart—the human Ego—the spiritive idionomy is characteristic of Man. The lower idionomies he shares with lower living beings, but his spiritive idionomy is unique in cosmic reality.

The Cognitive Dimension

First, we will look at what I have called the *cognitive dimension* of the spiritive idionomy, which has to do with thinking, deliberation, investigation, and knowledge. The first thing I note is that the development of language is of great importance when it comes to the development of our thinking. However, it appears that the child, at a very early age, even before language has begun to develop (as we can see especially from the case of a child who is deaf), begins to learn concepts like "table," "chair," and "bed." Little by little, it learns concepts which are more and more complicated, until it reaches abstract ones.

The progress made by the child in this regard depends upon his or her *intelligence*. Now, intelligence is itself quite a difficult concept. It has been defined as "the ability to solve problems," or even as "the ability to keep up with one's class in school," or "the ability to follow a certain kind of instructions." It must be admitted that these definitions are quite vague, but this is only because the concept is so complex. The various factors that contribute to what we call intelligence are one's language skills (stock of words or vocabulary, distinguishing of concepts, and the like), arithmetical skills, observation, reasoning, memory, spatial insight, and so forth. Thus, intelligence is not only determined by one's heredity ("constitution"), it also depends to some extent on the environment. Does the child find itself in an environment that is rich or poor in language resources? Does it receive little or much support from the adults in the environment? Does the environment offer the child a good amount of stimulation (by providing, for example, the right kind of toys to stimulate its fantasy and creativity), or not enough?

The development of intelligence in the child might well be described in terms of the ability to solve increasingly difficult problems. This line of thought has to do with another, even more difficult question: What is *thinking*? It, too, might be described as "the mental activity of problem-solving." Psychologists have done all kinds of experiments and tests to try to determine just how thinking works. In the discipline of *logic* people try to figure out how we *ought* to think if we are to be regarded as thinking clearly, correctly, and efficiently. But in *psychology* we investigate how people often really do think—in jerks, circuitously, going off on tangents that lead to dead ends, suddenly having something come clearly to mind by intuition or by subconscious processes, and so forth. In most cases it all works out for us, but we definitely do not always follow the shortest or most logical path to our destination. The way we actually think in a great many cases brings the influence of the sensitive idionomy especially to light, and the sensitive idionomy is something we have in common with the animals. Because they possess it, animals can indeed get sudden insights and in this way solve certain simple problems.

In chapter 5, we saw that the Gestalt psychologists speak of *aha-experiences* in this connection. Such experiences also occur in people. Yet this should not necessarily lead us to conclude that thinking actually occurs in animals. In the thinking of human beings, the sensitive does indeed play a major role much of the time, but thinking as such is nevertheless substantially much greater than, and very different from, the sensitive—it is spiritive. What this means is that Man, but not the animal, has the capacity in the spiritive idionomy to consciously put a series of representations in a sequence, selecting them, debating in his mind, comparing, putting in order, pondering them, weighing them. He does all this in order to find connections, to draw conclusions. Not until these things are occurring can we properly speak of thinking.

Importance of Rationality

Throughout the history of our Western culture, much emphasis has been placed on the *importance* of this matter of logical thinking. A number of thinkers in the past have even supposed that thinking was *the* distinguishing mark of the human mind, and thus *the* most essential difference between Man and the animal (in spite of what Ps. 73:22 says: "I was brutish and ignorant; I was like a beast toward you"). After all, Man was—above all else—called a *rational* being! Even of Jesus Christ we can read in the Athanasian Creed: "... Perfect God, perfect Man, having a *rational* soul and human flesh"—just as though the most characteristic feature of the soul or spirit of Christ, or of any human, was *rationality* or *thinking*! This was a typical result of the power of rationalism for more than two thousand years in the Western world.

Now, thought is no doubt a typical characteristic of Man but, in my view, it is by no means *the* characteristic feature, nor is it the most important difference between Man and animals. In the East—and also in Holy Scripture, which originated in the East—much more emphasis is placed on a kind of thinking which has a much broader definition, namely, a thinking that visualizes and meditates, a thinking in which there is much more sensitivity, affection, and involvement, and much less abstraction and theorizing. It is thinking in a particularly religious sense: "...when I remember you upon my bed, and meditate on you in the watches of the night" (Ps. 63:6). "I said, 'Let me remember my song in the night; let me meditate in my heart.' Then my spirit made a diligent search" (Ps. 77:6; cf. v. 12). "I remember the days of old; I meditate on all that you have done; I ponder the work of your hands" (Ps. 143:5). "On the glorious splendor of your majesty, and on your wondrous works, I will meditate" (Ps. 145:5).

When the Psalmist lies on his bed at night thinking and pondering (as in some of the psalms I have just quoted), his activity has little to do with what our Western world calls "rational thought." Ultimately, while thinking *is* a side of our spiritive act-life—the logical is a modality of cosmic reality—it is nonetheless still controlled by the *heart*. The highest kind of "thinking" is to be found not in our life of feeling or in the understanding; rather, it is that which is directly governed by the heart. Our logical thought stands—or falls, if you will—with what goes on in the heart. "The heart has its own reasons, which reason does not know," declared the great Christian thinker Blaise Pascal (1623-1662).

Proverbs 23:7 (NKJV) says of a certain person, "As he thinks in his heart, so is he." The thoughts of his heart show what kind of person he is, as these thoughts become manifest in his behavior (words, gestures, deeds). Thinking (knowing, deliberating, meditating, pondering, deciding) is one of the "springs of life" that flow from the human heart, as we have seen (Prov. 4:23). "Thinking in your heart" is a common matter in the Bible (Deut. 9:4; 2 Sam. 13:33; Esther 4:13; Isa. 10:7; Zech. 8:17; Matt. 9:4). Let us think again of the difference between *structure* and *direction*. In the sense of structure, "good" thoughts follow the laws of logic. In the sense of direction, "good" thoughts follow the "laws" of a heart directed toward God.

The Creative Dimension

In addition to *cognitive*, logical, rational thought, there is a different kind of *thinking* to be distinguished, namely, *creative* thinking. This kind of thinking has directly to do with the *imagination*, which is the *compartment* of our mind where on the one hand we can imagine or visualize things that already exist (Dutch: *zich indenken*), and on the other hand we can *invent* new things (Dutch: *uitdenken*). I will first illustrate what I mean by the former (imagining, visualizing). I call my wife on the telephone, and in my thoughts I see her at home walking around in the living room. Or I recall our vacation and "smell" the sea once more, or I remember the scares I had in the high mountains of Switzerland. As for the latter aspect of imagination (creative invention), let us say that I want to invent a new detergent, construct a new psychological theory, or think up a new recipe. So then I try to imagine how I can achieve the goal I have set for myself in a good way and as soon as possible. In every sphere of our spiritive life, this creativity is useful and necessary in several ways:

(a) *Logically-analytically*: No scientific investigator can do without creativity when it comes to thinking up new experiments or new theories.

(b) *Formatively*: The technician ("How can I make this?") and the statesman ("How can I get the support necessary for my plans?") both need creativity.

(c) *Lingually*: The instructor who, for example, is called upon to explain some difficult subject-matter ("How shall I put this?").

(d) *Socially*: Someone who is applying for a job, for example ("How shall I write an original letter of application?" or "What shall I wear for my job interview?").

(e) *Economically*: The advertising person, for example ("How can I get the attention of the public, and persuade them to buy my product or service?").

(f) *Aesthetically*: The artist, of course, is the creative person *par excellence*, who expresses his deep feelings and deliberations in the visual arts, in music, or in literature.

(g) *Juridically*: The creative criminal ("How can I sneak into this house or this shop-window without getting caught?").

(h) *Ethically*: The young man who is in love can be very creative as he tries to see or please his beloved.

(i) *Pistically*: The believer who tries to imagine what God will think of his deeds, looks for ways of serving God, and (assuming he uses the proper approach) does so by the light of Scripture.

The Creative Eye

Often creative persons can "see" possibilities that other, non-creative persons do not see. For the latter, orange crates are simply intended to contain oranges. But the creative person sees another possibility—that he could make a bookcase out of them. Or perhaps he sees the possibility of turning a garbage can into a flowerbox. Seeing such potential is characteristic of creativity: it involves reaching a projected goal by seeing new possibilities that until that moment had not been thought of. Moreover, this usually occurs unexpectedly, without any preparation or warning, when people are doing something else entirely.

To be capable of all of this, a person must be open to new experiences and impressions; he must have a flexible attitude, not a conventional one. Here is a simple example. Take six matches of length *p*, and make *four* non-overlapping equilateral triangles out of them, each triangle having sides of length *p*. It looks more difficult than it is, but you will be able to solve the problem as soon as you leave the obvious pathways.

Furthermore, the creative person needs a high level of energy and prolonged productivity (because it "does not come easily"), and what is of crucial importance is that he must free himself from the fear of making mistakes, from lack of assurance, from lack of motivation, and also from conformism. Many Christians are conservative in the bad sense of the word in that they only know how to follow well-trodden paths. And they are always afraid of what others, or the church, will say of them. All they know to do is to emphasize working hard and unimaginatively. As a result, their faith life is just as lacking in creativity as their daily work and their marriage. So let us have three cheers for creative Christians!

When it comes to this matter of creativity, surprising things often happen in the creative Christian life as well. Let us assume that you have been taking a good look at a certain problem. You turn the matter over in your mind, and review the whole thing within your spiritive idionomy. At that point the thing to do may be to just let it stand, sometimes for a few minutes, sometimes for several years. And then there are those occasions where you have to "sleep on it." The information has to sink down somehow into the mind. All of a sudden, there is a sense of "relief" or "enlightenment." Creative insight has emerged—sometimes at the craziest places, or during the weirdest hours of the day. Sometimes it happens in a dream, as in 1865 when August Kekulé discovered the ring structure of benzene in a day-dream).

According to legend, Archimedes (287-212 B.C.) was in his bath when his "happy thought" (now known as the *law of Archimedes*) struck him, and he was so excited about his discovery that he ran out into the street stark naked, shouting, "*Eureka*!" ("I have found it!"). This story shows us just how excited a new idea can make a creative person. All of a sudden, the scientific researcher has the explanation for all of his experimental results. All of a sudden, the chef has that new recipe in his head. All of a sudden, the shopkeeper gets an idea for his new shop-window. And all at once, the believer gets a clear insight into what he has to do—and he thanks God for it. Believers who place themselves intensely under the guidance of the Holy Spirit often have a special charisma of creativity (which is not always appreciated by more conservative brothers and sisters).

The Conative Dimension

It may be well to remind ourselves that the word *conative* has to do with the *will,* and the will, too, is a typically spiritive and *human* matter. There is quite a difference between the (perceptive) instincts, the (sensitive) drives, and the (spiritive, conscious, deliberating, and choosing) will of Man. In current psychology, the latter two are classified all too loosely under "motivation," just as though there was nothing by which we can basically distinguish them.

We have already seen a very obvious *spiritive* element even in the way we handle our (sensitive) drives: we can deliberately decide to give in to them, or not. The mind rules over our drives. Conversely, the spiritive decisions of our wills are sometimes determined entirely by our feelings. All too often, emotional people allow themselves to be too strongly swayed by their sentiments and emotions, or by their impulsiveness, when they make important decisions. Behavior of this sort does not become a Christian (or any person, for that matter). What we should do instead is to let ourselves be guided by considerations that proceed from a heart that is directed toward God and his commandments.

In practice, of course, we allow ourselves to be guided in this area by all sorts of *operant factors,* that is to say, by everything we have been taught. We need only think of the rules and norms of our culture, our society, our parental home, and our faith community. This is not just a question of all sorts of customs having to do with clothing and manners. Some much more important features of our (traditionally Christian) society come to the fore. We can think, for instance, of the exaggerated emphasis on rational thought, the exaggerated focus on success, on getting ahead, on making progress, on earning money, and on accumulating countless unnecessary luxury articles, and so forth.

We only rarely encounter people who are truly independent, and thus are able to rise above all of these fashions and hypes, by showing that they are neither mindless cattle nor reactionary obstructionists. Moreover, the question could be raised whether such totally unconventional, independent people are actually very easy to get along with, socially speaking. Still, it is very important to consider whether we come to our decisions of will under the influence—or even the pressure—of the environment (society, family, friends, church) as opposed to making our own personal choice in dependence on the Lord, his Word, and his Spirit.

Christians sometimes wrestle with the notion of *free will*, which was denied by both Luther (in his famous debate with Erasmus) and Calvin. To my mind, this whole theological discussion is based upon a philosophical confusion of *structure* and *direction*. As regards structure, the free will is one of *the* differences between animals and humans. As regards direction, the will of natural Man has been corrupted by sin. Even regenerated Man, if he does not live by the Spirit, says, "I know that nothing good dwells in me, that is, in my flesh. For I have the desire to do what is right, but not the ability to carry it out. For I do not do the good I want, but the evil I do not want is what I keep on doing. Now if I do what I do not want, it is no longer I who do it, but sin that dwells within me" (Rom. 7:18-20).

Attribution

To the extent that our decisions are also determined by our environment, it is very important to realize that people are not motivated by the environment as it actually is (objective) but by the environment as they *think* it is (subjective). Since our perception is *colored* by both positive and negative affections—among many other things—the environment also appears to us to be colored; in other words, we come to our experience of it with all kinds of preconceived opinions. And, even *apart from* prejudices, we still often make mistakes in the way we interpret appearances and the behavior of our fellow human beings. Psychologists have a deep interest in what one person attributes—rightly or wrongly—to another or to a situation; here they speak of *attribution*.

It seems that it is very much a part of our nature as human beings constantly to ascribe to our fellow Man certain intentions, opinions, and motives. Of course, this is quite understandable; we wish to comprehend the meaning of our environment so that we can figure out how to respond to it. But there is also a dangerous aspect to this dilemma, as we realize from the warning of Jesus: "Judge not, that you be not judged" (Matt. 7:1); even so, we can hardly refrain from judging. For example, sometimes we may think that someone is being unfriendly toward us; in other words, we *attribute* unfriendliness to that person. As a result, we are reserved toward him. What then happens is that the other person starts to behave in an unfriendly way toward *us*. And the unfriendliness we then perceive leads us to say: "See? I was right! I knew it all along!" Meanwhile, we fail to realize that we ourselves were inadvertently the cause of the unfriendliness.

Also noteworthy is the fact that we attribute certain *responsibilities* to our fellow humans, and make our decisions on that basis. Investigations have shown that we are inclined to attribute a greater degree of responsibility—and *therefore* nobler motives as well—to people of higher social standing, people who have more power and resources at their command. For example, if an earnest request is made to donate blood, and a simple, uneducated, and slovenly person comes forward to volunteer, we are inclined to think that he has agreed to donate his blood because a great deal of pressure was placed upon him. But if a person of "higher" social standing agrees to give blood, we are inclined to think that in his case noble motives played quite a role.

Moreover, we practice *attribution* not only with respect to other people but even with respect to ourselves. Our will is strongly guided by our (positive or negative) self-image—the image we have of our capabilities, qualities, and achievements. Things get still more complicated because—in addition to all that I have mentioned above—we attribute to our fellow humans certain opinions about *ourselves*, that is, we assume that they think this or that about us. This attribution in turn influences the self-esteem that we have of ourselves: we attempt to see—or imagine seeing—ourselves through the eyes of others.

We even appear to be masters in altering the image we think others have of us to make it extra positive or extra negative, depending on what we—in large measure unconsciously—are after. Both the need to achieve success and the need to avoid failure—and these two things should not be confused with one another—are strongly influenced by this kind of attribution. As a matter of fact, even constitutional and operant factors play a role here; some people, when it comes to their natural bent, are just more determined or more timid than others. And then there are some people who have simply had a more stimulating, or more discouraging, environment to deal with than others.

The two needs I just mentioned—the need to achieve success, and the need to avoid failure—have to do with what psychologists call *achievement motivation*, which is an important element in the conative dimension. In some Christian circles, words like *power* and *success* are weighed down with strongly negative affections. This is understandable, for just being out to achieve success, to have power over others, and to receive honor from others is tantamount to pride. On the other hand, fear of failure, or of looking silly in the eyes of others, can be just as much an indication of pride. Perhaps it is for this reason that many people are so passive, indolent, and apathetic. It might not be obvious, but in reality there might be an element of pride in this indolence and apathy.

Generally speaking, the abilities God gives us involve a mandate to look for a place of work and for tasks that are in line with those abilities. If we win the appreciation of our fellow human beings as we carry out our task, we need not be ashamed of the esteem we receive. It becomes a matter of concern only when praise from others becomes an end in itself, which means that it would replace praise from God. Achievement motivation too, is in the final analysis a matter of the human *heart*, so that the honor of God rather than the honor of Man is, or ought to be, the thing that comes first in our lives (see John 12:26, 43). Thus we can well understand that the satisfaction we get from the completion of a difficult task is at the same time a gift from God. This gift never comes to the person who, out of a fear of failure which is symptomatic of pride, works below the level of his ability.

Language

Now that I have dealt with the three dimensions of the spiritive idionomy, I want to pause to discuss briefly two very important spiritive phenomena, namely, language and social life. These two phenomena, as a matter of fact, are closely connected. Here I am using the term *language* in a broad sense. Falling under this heading are *all* means by which people *communicate* with one another, including spoken and written words, gestures, facial expressions, numbers, musical notes, traffic signs, flags, and pictures. Language always makes use of *communication-signs*. What I mean by the latter term is that *this* (a sign or symbol) stands for (points to, means, symbolizes) *that*. *This* word stands for *that* concept; *this* numeral stands for *that* numerical value; *this* traffic sign indicates *that* order or prohibition, and so forth.

Linguists (i.e., students of language) are concerned with phonetic laws, inflection, syntax, and the like, or with the question of how we *ought* to speak if our use of language is to be considered correct. Psychologists, on the other hand, want to know just how we *actually do* talk. They want to know how language functions as a means of communication between persons, how languages are learned, from what kinds of psychical backgrounds new concepts and words might emerge, where slips of the tongue come from, what the emotional value of words is, and so forth.

Anyone who *speaks* or writes, has *encoded* his thoughts, and, to a degree, also his feelings, in language symbols, especially *words*, but also gestures, facial expressions, smoke signals, drumbeats, dots and dashes, and the like. These symbols then need to be perceived by the listener, or reader, and *decoded* in his brain, which is to say that the symbols have to be *translated* back into thoughts and feelings. Communication of this (spiritive) order is, as far as we can assess, unknown among the animals.

Of course animals, too, are able to communicate with one another in countless ways: movements, grimaces, sounds, odors, touch. Yet, when it comes to the animals, this communication is strictly confined to the psychical idionomies. We see evidence of this when we ponder the fact that this so-called "language" of animals cannot be modified or extended by means of thought and creativity; in our terminology, the animal has no spiritive idionomy to be used in such a way. This is the reason why animals are never aware of any such thing as *culture*. Extensive experiments with chimpanzees, which concerned the learning either of spoken words or sign language, have confirmed that these animals cannot learn any language at all in the human sense of the word.

Language Acquisition

How is it, then, that children can learn their native language so easily and so well? Within a matter of a year and a half to two years, toddlers learn the basic structure of even the most complicated languages. Moreover, they accomplish this feat almost without any conscious, systematic instruction. How do children learn how to catch separate words from the stream of sound? How do they learn how to put the words they have acquired together into new sentences on their own, and to connect words with concepts?

Psychologists have supplied us with what I think is the only possible answer: human beings possess a special *aptitude for language*, or, to use an even stronger expression, a *language acquisition system*, whereas chimpanzees or other animals possess nothing of the sort. Now, this answer smacks of overstating the obvious. Even so, it is quite remarkable that non-Christian psychologists, when they offer this answer, have in fact acknowledged in this way that there is, in this respect, a *fundamental difference between humans and animals*. In addition, they have made a real effort to give the term *aptitude for language* a meaningful content.

Noam Chomsky (b. 1928), the famous psychologist of language, has suggested that there is a common basic structure to be found in all languages in the world, and that the child's aptitude for language is a kind of "skeleton key" that serves to unlock the basic structure of its native language, and enables it to discover what words are, how they are joined together, what the grammatical rules are, and so forth. In this way, every normal person, all the way down to someone with a barely minimal intellectual capacity, can "decipher" the basic structure of his native language without any real exertion, and can also deal with the special peculiarities of his own language, the points where it differs from other languages. For the rest of his life, a person is then able to apply the unlimited possibilities built into his own language in endless variations. He continually produces new sentences that have never before been expressed but may still be understood by others with the greatest of ease.

It is exactly this creative element that is so characteristic of human language. According to our model, this element of creativity is rooted in the spiritive idionomy, which in turn is typical of the human phenomenon. In this latter condition we can see the cognitive importance of language. What I mean by this is that our thinking and knowing consist, for the most part, of *concepts* which we can express in words. It may be that animals do not talk simply because they have "nothing to say" to each other. That is to say, they do not talk because they are unable to think in a scale of refined concepts. It is very much a question of whether their communicative signals are ever *symbols* for concepts that are also able to exist *within* the animal independently of the process of communication. Yet this is precisely what makes language so typically human: people can *think* in concepts *and* give those concepts lingual expression.

Social Life

What applies to language in connection with animals applies also to their *social life:* it is strictly confined to the psychical idionomies, that is to say, to instincts and reflexes. Hence, it is to be understood as fundamentally different from the social interaction and communication that takes place between human beings. This is a type of fellowship that can be cognitively considered, creatively modified and conatively (i.e. by means of the will) controlled. This is because human socialization is not governed by instinct. For this reason, we have to learn socialization at a tender age, just as we learn language. This has been demonstrated by research. When an infant smiles for the very first time, it is offering its first *social response* to its surroundings.

The family, the kindergarten, and especially the elementary school are *the* important training grounds for the social development of the young child. It must learn to listen and reply and to adjust to others. It discovers that doing so is easier or more pleasant in one case than in another. It develops its first friendships and finds itself a member of a group. It is especially during the secondary school years that the need of belonging and the sense of solidarity and popularity begin to play an important role in the child's life. Furthermore, during this period of his life the young person must learn how to reconsider his social relationship with his parents. He begins to reevaluate it, and the first closer social contacts with the opposite sex are made.

In addition to all of this, the young person also begins to consider his future social position as he chooses an area of further study with a view to his eventual career. Once he has become part of the work-force, of *socio-economic life*, he is faced with his most intense social contacts: marriage, family, working environment, a club, church, the state. He also begins to encounter strong *social supervision*: "What will the neighbors, or my colleagues, or my fellow club and church-members think of me?" At a later stage in life, social contact falls off somewhat, but still remains important. Without (adequate) social contacts, any person will wither away.

Within a person's social environment there are various elements to be distinguished. First, there is lifestyle: that of the entire society on the one hand, and that of one's own group (family, church, class) on the other. Second, the structure of the society of which one is a part, (for example, the political system) must also be considered. Naturally, the form of the society and the lifestyle of the people are closely connected.

Third, the groups to which a person belongs during his lifetime are very important. Some of these groups are not chosen by ourselves (family, school class, state), but there are others which we do choose, whether because of love, like-mindedness (marriage, church, club, political party), or perhaps common interest (factory, army, group sport, labor union, political party). Beyond all such groups, there are also various kinds of interpersonal relationships. Such relationships are ordinarily based on the *function* of one or both of the participants, so that the individuals themselves do not really matter. We can think, for example, of the shopkeeper and the customer, the policeman and the traffic violator, the person purchasing a ticket and the person behind the ticket-window, the employer and the employee, the teacher and the pupil, the elder and the common church member.

Social and Human Responsibility

Social psychologists are very interested in how people behave with their fellow human beings and with respect to groups. We have already seen a number of examples of such contacts. Think of the significance of prejudices (positive and negative affections) and of attributions. The *first impression* we get of a certain person, often quite accidentally, proves to be very important. It appears that when we form an idea of someone on the basis of that very first impression, it is quite difficult to get rid of that idea later. One is inclined to explain away any later information that conflicts with it.

Sad to say, this even happens among Christians. Thus, if we, figuratively speaking, turn our back on someone on the basis of the first impression, what we are doing may be quite understandable in psychological terms, but from a social and an ethical viewpoint it is inexcusable behavior, if not downright un-Christian. Here again we see that, when it comes to our spiritively governed behavior, sensitive factors have a role to play, even though it is true that we remain fully responsible for that behavior, since it proceeds from the heart. We cannot blame the psychical idionomies for any failures in our conscious behavioral patterns.

We can work out our responsibilities more effectively if we become more *aware* of the presence and influence of these perceptive, sensitive, and social factors that influence our behavior. Thus we have seen that Man is by nature a *social* being through and through, and that we can never abstract him from the (many) groups to which he belongs. The most interesting groups are those in which the members share a strong sense of unity, often holding the same values and norms—a *belief-system* or *ideology*—and interacting in a robust manner with one another. We can think, for example, of a family, a close-knit club, a small church congregation, a small business, a circle of friends, a work group, a group of people who share sleeping quarters in a barracks, or a group of students sharing the same floor in university housing. These are called *primary groups*.

Just being part of such a group has a strongly stimulating influence on a person, no matter what combination of motivating factors there may be within the group. For instance, one might join a certain church congregation because one feels that one can serve the Lord best in that particular faith-community, that is to say, in a way that best accords with Scripture, but it is also conceivable that one might join simply because one feels most at home with the Christians there, and with the way they run their services.

Not all the motives that might lead a person to join a particular congregation are equally spiritual. There are quite a number of very human—sensitive or spiritive—motives that may be at work, whether consciously or unconsciously, in such a decision. Here it is a matter especially of satisfying definite needs, and those needs find expression in one's interaction with a particular congregation, or in some other group. For instance, one might experience safety and certainty there. Unfortunately, the point on which certainty is sought is often far from the question: "Is this the closest there is to the Scriptural idea of a congregation?" but is more likely to be: "Does this congregation confirm my own views about faith?" People are also looking for security, understanding, sympathy, and assistance—and a Christian church provides those things too (at least, if it is what it should be). But we must recognize that these are not the most important things with which a congregation should concern itself.

The "group" satisfies the deep need of "belongingness" we all have, and thus helps to provide an "identity" for the individual. You may find a person saying, "I work for the railroad," or "I belong to the Reformed Church," or "I am a member of the Society for the Prevention of Cruelty to Animals," thereby expressing part of his identity as a person. In some such way, the group has an extremely strong influence on the formation of one's personality. Therefore we find people saying how obvious it is that a certain person is (or used to be) Reformed, that he went to a private academy, that he has served in the Army, that he is an educator, that he studied at Harvard, and so forth. In our Western culture, what we *are* is to a large extent determined by the groups to which we belong, or have belonged.

Chapter Eight
THE NORMAL PERSONALITY

In previous chapters, we saw that language is qualified by the lingual modality, and that social life is typified by the social modality of our spiritive or act-life. I went into these matters in somewhat greater depth at the end of chapter 7. But we have also seen that these are definitely not the highest aspects of our spiritive life. The three highest modalities are the juridical, the ethical, and the pistical.

When we begin to deal with these higher aspects, we are coming very close to the actual being, the deepest inner life, of Man, which we have referred to above as the *heart*. Although we maintain that the juridical, the ethical, and the pistical belong to our *immanent* functioning as human beings, whereas the heart is of a *transcendent* nature, we can still say that the juridical, the ethical, and especially the pistical modality, *border* on the transcendent life of the heart.

The juridical, ethical, and pistical modalities have to do with the *ethos*, the immanent religious-ethical condition (*mentality*) of the transcendent heart. Now it is time to examine this matter of the ethos in a little more detail. Once this has been done, I will raise the question whether there is anything we can say about the stirrings of the heart (chapter 9).

Development of the Ethos

Various researchers have investigated how the ethos, that is, a person's religious-ethical attitude, develops in the young person. They have tried to do this especially by studying the *moral reasoning* of children of various ages, as well as that of grown-ups. Of course, moral values and norms differ greatly from culture to culture and from one social class to another. Curiously enough, however, it still appeared possible to speak of a certain *basic pattern* in all moral reasoning. In other words, it became apparent that people everywhere come to a moral assessment of human behavior in roughly the same way. Despite the enormous influence of sin when it comes to these matters, it appears that we can nevertheless speak of a kind of common *moral aptitude* among very diverse groups of people.

Speaking about sin, I ask you to remember what I wrote in all the previous volumes of this series—as well as in some of the earlier chapters of this book—about the difference between *structure* and *direction*. Sin has to do with the direction of our heart: whether it is reborn or not, and in the believer, whether it is under the power of the Spirit or under that of the flesh (Rom. 8; Gal. 5). Theologians are of course very interested in this matter, but psychologists are more occupied with the *structure* of our mental life, i.e., the perceptive, sensitive, and spiritive factors that affect our behavior. On the one hand, we will see many forms of intertwinement between mental factors and the workings of the flesh. On the other hand, we will always have to distinguish between them in the same way as we do between structure and direction. We are always responsible for our sins—but in our mental makeup there are many factors at work for which we are *not* responsible, and which will help us to understand our behavior.

Coming back to the ethos, please note that I am not yet speaking of the moral motives for one's *own* behavior, but of the moral arguments people use to judge the behavior of *others*. Because of the presence of sin in our lives, these two may be vastly different from one another. Here we should recall what Christ had to say in Matthew 7:3-5: "Why do you see the speck that is in your brother's eye, but do not notice the log that is in your own eye? Or how can you say to your brother, 'Let me take the speck out of your eye,' when there is the log in your own eye? You hypocrite, first take the log out of your own eye, and then you will see clearly to take the speck out of your brother's eye."

What I find especially interesting is that people stop developing at very different *stages* in moral development. Many people reach a kind of *conventional level* where they judge behavior simply by the good intentions of the person involved, or they just ask themselves whether that person is complying with the established rules of the social order. But there are some people who do not even get as far as that: they get bogged down at a *pre-conventional level,* which is very normal in the case of small children. They judge a particular action simply by the material consequences, so that, for example, breaking ten cups accidentally is worse than breaking one cup intentionally. Or they may judge to what degree specific actions satisfy their own wants: "You scratch my back, and I'll scratch yours."

However, there are other people who reach a higher, *post-conventional level.* They recognize a certain relativity in the laws and rules that are in force, and have come to realize that those laws and rules might conflict with higher spiritual values. What is at issue is not a set of specific concrete commands and prohibitions, as at the lower levels, but one's higher values. Often these are even such *universal* values as freedom, justice, equal value, and mutual respect.

The Highest Level

It should be obvious that this final *level,* if we can be satisfied with such a formulation, may be attained just as easily by humanists as by Christians. Indeed, there are humanists who have a much higher moral awareness than a great many conventional Christians (or those who pass for such). Accordingly, it will be necessary to formulate a *still* higher level, namely, a religious stage that transcends all ethics. For why would a person adhere to "universal principles" of truth and justice in the midst of a world that is full of falsehood and *un*righteousness? The humanist is in bad shape indeed if he has to somehow base his position on untrue and unjust Man. On the other hand, the Christian is rich, basing his life on the perfect truth and righteousness of God: "For the kingdom of God is not a matter of [trivialities] but of righteousness and peace and joy in the Holy Spirit" (Rom. 14:17).

Whoever has come to such a realization will also recognize the relative character of all this talk about levels and stages of moral development. This highest religious stage is not to be understood as a phase that, at a given time, follows after the highest ethical stage. In the vast majority of cases, the development of the religious person takes place in the micro-environment, namely, the family, where religion has been predominant, guiding the lives of the young from their earliest beginnings. I need to make this point more strongly by insisting that regeneration (rebirth) and the illumination of the Holy Spirit are necessary for a person to attain this high-level religious judgment of actions. Indeed, it is necessary for a person to come *of his own accord,* inspired by his relation to God and in his power, to the performing of actions that are pleasing to God.

The so-called Christian, who keeps God's commandments just to gain the approval of others, or out of submission to the authority of church and tradition, is only a "conventional Christian." And the one who keeps them on the basis of a specific notion of personal or universal ethical values is just a *post*-conventional Christian. However, the one who keeps them out of a genuine love for God, in intimate fellowship with him, in utter devotion to him, in reverent association with him, and in submission to his Word—that person is truly a Christian. "Whoever has my commandments and keeps them, he it is who loves me... If anyone loves me, he will keep my word, and my Father will love him, and we will come to him and make our home with him." (John 14:21,23).

The biblical truth of the deceitfulness of our natural heart (see Jer. 17:9) should help us to understand how it is that people sometimes hold forth in a highly moral tone while at the same time acting in a way that testifies to a low standard of morality. Perhaps the point should be expressed in stronger terms: social psychologists have found abundant proof that supposedly respectable people who have a highly developed form of moral reasoning are capable, under certain circumstances, of deceitful accommodation to the masses, of quite immoral actions under the cover of some such motto as *Befehl ist Befehl* ("Orders are orders"), and of a gross indifference with respect to the lives of other people, and even of unexpected aggression and vandalism. We should have known these things all along from the Bible, of course, but in the end secular psychologists spotted the connection as well.

If someone believes that he is respectable and law-abiding, how does it come about that he sometimes lowers himself to actions of the basest sort? Christians know the answer: no matter how highly we think of ourselves, our sinful nature will often show through in a painful way, provided the circumstances are suitable. That this is indeed the case will become even clearer from the paragraphs that follow. Before moving on, I will recall the advice of the Apostle Paul, "I say, walk by the Spirit, and you will not gratify the desires of the flesh. For the desires of the flesh are against the Spirit, and the desires of the Spirit are against the flesh, for these are opposed to each other, to keep you from doing the things you want to do" (Gal. 5:16-17).

The Ethos and I

We have seen that it is necessary to distinguish between our (objective) *needs* (what we objectively need, whether we desire it or not), and our (subjective) *drives* (what we desire, whether we need it or not). At this point we can compare our needs and drives with a third entity: our ethos or, as we might call it, our *values*. All three of these entities are governed by sensitive and spiritive factors, with the heart as the deepest and most important influence. However, it is by no means the case that they are always in harmony with one another. Our desires are far from agreeing at all times with our objective needs, the needs which God has put in us as his creatures. And *our* values are not always in agreement with *God's* norms—not by a long shot. Bearing all of this in mind, we see that it is possible to distinguish three kinds of people:

1. A *harmonious* person is one in whom needs, desires, and values (almost) completely coincide, for his drives are attuned to his real needs and therefore also to God's norms. Furthermore, his values also harmonize with the divine norms that have been revealed by God in his Word.

2. A *pseudo-harmonious* person is one who manages to sear his conscience so badly that his values are of the very lowest kind and therefore can coincide with his low desires. When Satan gets his slaves entirely in his power, they have "peace" (Luke 11:21 NKJV). But in actual fact, of course, such a person is quite inharmonious, for while his values and desires do coincide, they do not coincide with his actual needs.

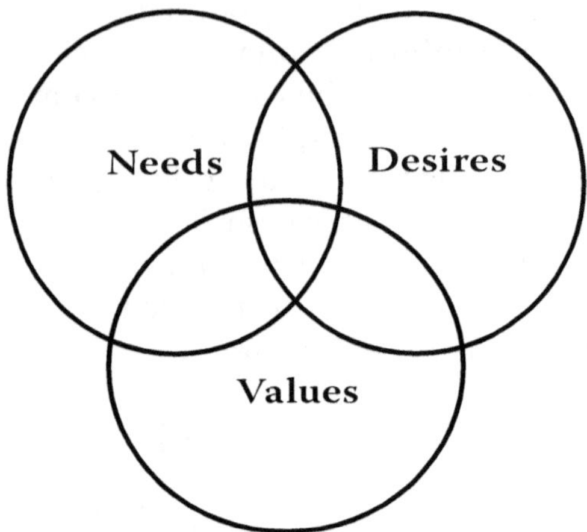

Caption: The connection between the (objective) needs (N), the (subjective) desires (D) and the values one stands for (V). Between N and D and V there are all kinds of possible relations (see text).

3. A completely *inharmonious* person is one in whom no two of the three elements coincide to any significant degree. His low desires deviate significantly from his needs but are also in conflict with his values, which are not yet wholly degenerate, even though they have actually deviated quite sharply from God's norms. Such a person is a slave to sin (cf. Rom. 6:16-22), and in addition to this, he has a bad conscience. Still, for such a person there is considerably more hope than for the pseudo-harmonious person, precisely because his conscience is still at work.

Cognitive Dissonance

To complicate matters, we must now take note of the fact that one of a person's (objective) *needs* is the urge to bring his desires into harmony as much as possible with his *values,* no matter how high or low they may be. After all, every person would like to be a harmonious, or at least a pseudo-harmonious person. Or, to put the point a different way, people generally have an urgent need for *self-justification* (cf. Luke 10:29). In this connection, psychologists like to speak of *cognitive dissonance.* What they mean by this is that, when a person, for example, does certain things that he himself does not believe in, or that are not in agreement with his norms, he feels ill at ease. There is *dissonance* between what he is *doing* and what he thinks he *ought* to be doing, or what he *ought* to have done. Therefore he will attempt to eliminate the dissonance, either by changing his actions, which often proves too difficult, or by adjusting his values, so that he will once again have rest in his soul.

The cognitive dissonance is thus resolved by means of self-justification. We experience this sort of thing every day of our lives. For example, a person may be of two minds—whether to go to church or stay home and watch the football game on television. He chooses the latter and now experiences cognitive dissonance, because he feels that he really should have gone to church, but he did not. He now will try to resolve this dissonance by convincing himself that he really does not feel all that well, so that, even if there had not been a football game on television, he probably would have stayed home from church anyway. Strictly speaking, he does not *change* his norm, because he still thinks that Christians ought to go to church on Sunday afternoon, but he has simply declared that the norm is not applicable in this particular case.

This is one way to preserve harmony between one's values and one's desires. A second method is to justify one's conduct with the help of other, less obvious values. In the present case, for instance, he could say to himself: "Everybody has to relax now and then," or, "If I watch this important football game, I will have an easier time talking with others (for example, my colleagues on Monday morning)," or, "Even in the beauty of human play and the movements of the human body, there is something of the greatness of our Creator to be seen." (The third one is a blatantly sanctimonious cop-out!)

To be quite clear about it, this unethical excusing of oneself is a sin in the fullest biblical sense of the word. Yet cognitive dissonance does not occur on the ethical level alone. We also encounter it in the purchase of all sorts of articles. A housewife buys more expensive detergent because she thinks her laundry will turn out whiter if she uses it. Having made the purchase, she is now strongly inclined to believe it too, even though there is no objective difference to be noted. A person who has transferred to a different church denomination may delude himself into believing that he is indeed much better off there, in this way justifying to himself the step he has taken, even if it has not really improved the situation at all. Or we might consider that the more expensive the medicine, the more the patient is inclined to believe that his treatment is helping him. These forms of (largely semi-conscious or even unconscious) self-deception are not concrete sins, although by and large they may be called consequences of the sinful brokenness of our lives.

Cognitive Dissonance and Education

The theory of cognitive dissonance can also be applied to the upbringing of children. Whenever a child is under severe pressure and therefore refrains from doing something it would like to do, cognitive dissonance develops. Now the child can resolve it by reasoning: "I really want to keep on doing it, but I am stopping because I am being forced to stop." In a stronger case, the severe pressure being applied by the parents can even have a negative effect, for the thing that is forbidden now becomes more and more attractive for the child, who unconsciously says: "If I want this so badly even though it is forbidden, then it certainly must be awfully attractive to me," or, more objectively, "... then it certainly must be very good." The result is that any time children wriggle out from under the authority and direct influence of such strict, authoritarian (not to be confused with authoritative!) parents, they often go and indulge themselves to their heart's content, doing whatever was forbidden to them for so long.

It is quite possible that parents who exercise authority, but try to reach their objective by using milder threats and gentler pressure, and especially persuasion, have more success. Here too cognitive dissonance develops, but studies have revealed that in such cases the child resolves the dissonance in an entirely different way. It reasons: "Oh well, actually I didn't find it nearly as much fun to do this or that as I thought it would be." And where a child receives a good upbringing—especially a Christian upbringing—in which the parents do their best to make it clear to the child *why* this or that is not good, according to God's commandments, the child also learns to see the reasonableness of what his parents are asking of them, and as a result the child has no *need* whatsoever of self-justification, which is actually self-deception. Such children will learn to do a thing, not because their parents command them to, but because they say: "I really want to do this of my own free will."

Also of great importance when it comes to cognitive dissonance is the support that like-minded people give one another. The more people there are who believe something, the more others are inclined to believe it too. People argue that if there are so many sensible, informed people who believe it, it could hardly be untrue. We see this sort of thing occurring among non-believers and Muslims, as well as among Bible-believing Christians. Even in Christian circles there are only a few people with a completely independent judgment that is based solely on the Scriptures.

In making this observation, I am not laying blame on anyone, for many people simply cannot do much more than consciously or unconsciously rely on the judgment of informed people in the group, or on the judgment of the crowd. If they happen to be thrown into contact with another crowd, which turns out to be equally large and equally convincing, cognitive dissonance will develop. Ordinarily this is not resolved by an objective investigation, because such an investigation could force a person to modify his or her convictions, or even exchange them for something else. Usually, one does not wish beforehand to do either of these things, even if one has formed a vague (semi-conscious) impression that others might just be right. Without doing any basic investigating, sometimes without even having a good understanding of the other person's conviction, one simply trots out arguments, which are actually intended more to set one's *own* mind at ease than to convince others.

Even though there are many people who clearly *cannot* come up with any more than this kind of response, it is nevertheless a consequence of the sinful brokenness of our lives. That is why acknowledging this cognitive dissonance and self-justification can be so beneficial. "The heart is deceitful above all things, and desperately sick [NKJV: wicked; ASV: corrupt]; who can understand it?" (Jer. 17: 9). How very difficult it is to be truly honest with yourself—or better yet, honest with God! "Who can discern his errors?

Declare me innocent from hidden faults" (Ps. 19:12). "As for [the seed] in the good soil, they are those who, hearing the word, hold it fast in an *honest* and good heart" (Luke 8:15). One day I will know myself fully, "even as I have been fully known" (1 Cor. 13:12).

The Ethos and the Other

If it is so difficult for a person to know *himself,* as we have seen, just imagine how much harder it would be to know *others,* see into them, know them for what they are. We have already observed how much we allow ourselves to be guided by prejudices and first impressions when it comes to knowing others. Likes and dislikes often play a major role in our behavior, so that our (ethical) *love* of our neighbor can easily become subordinated to our (sensitive) *sympathy* with our neighbor. Still, it remains a very interesting question what it is that causes us to find some people so likeable, whereas certain other people do not come across to us as likeable. Do we go first of all by a person's character, his personality, his emotional balance?

If you think of one of these three possibilities, you are wrong. Psychologists have shown that the *physical attractiveness* or *unattractiveness* of our fellow human beings plays a much greater role in our judgment of them than we generally realize. This certainly holds true for marriage, and so, in the book of Proverbs, we find king Lemuel (perhaps a pseudonym for Solomon?) saying: "Charm is deceitful, and beauty is vain, but a woman who fears the LORD is to be praised" (Prov. 31:30). This pattern also applies to the way in which adults judge children. Studies have shown that the more attractive the child is in appearance, the less inclined adults are to blame him or her for bad actions. From this fact we see just how *un*ethical our judgment of others can often be. There are also some indications that the physical attractiveness of suspects in a criminal case plays a role in the administration of justice, although (thankfully!) the more serious the offense, the less true this is.

Another factor that plays a role in our sympathy (or liking) is the presence of an unusual talent. The area to which the talent belongs does not really make much difference. Things become more complicated here, for people show great sympathy for others who are very gifted in an area of particular interest, for example, sports or science, but there are indications that many people have *less* liking for persons who come across as much too "perfect." Moreover, the feeling of self-esteem that people themselves have seems to make a real difference. A person who is highly talented and uncannily perfect makes the greatest impression on people who are at the top (that is, people with a strong feeling of self-esteem) *or* at the bottom, belonging to the uninteresting class of common folk (that is, the people with low self-esteem).

To make an impression on the large middle group, the people with average self-esteem, the highly gifted person needs to display somewhat more "human" qualities, for example, by making a blunder every now and then. Imperfect as we ourselves are, we do not easily tolerate the superior person—unless we are also superior (or at least think we are) *or* unless we are weighed down by a strong feeling of inferiority. But since most people possess neither of these characteristics, they feel more at home with those who display the same failings as they themselves do. In all of this, we see a clear ethical element: in general, it is hard for us to tolerate a person who is clearly better than we ourselves are. Sinners feel more comfortable amongst themselves.

Helping Your Neighbor

It is obvious that our love for our neighbor is easily "disrupted" by all sorts of perceptive and sensitive factors. Let us say that, at a given moment, we *know* that we must help out a fellow human being, and yet we do not do it. Our failing here may be due to dislike or laziness, but sometimes there are very different factors at work. This becomes obvious when we consider what psychologists have called the *bystander problem*: someone is in distress and many bystanders clearly see it, yet no one extends a helping hand. Why not? Of course, we may say that it is simply the "sin" in our life, but let us not confuse structure and direction! Right now we do not want to judge the bystanders' attitude ethically but psychologically.

What psychical factors are involved in this inertia of the bystanders? If there is just one bystander, it appears that he is much more ready to help his neighbor in distress than when there are many. This may not surprise you, but it is still useful to have psychologists sort out what goes on here and bring some precision to our understanding of such situations. They have pointed to two causes of this pattern, which are actually a little curious. It seems that having a great number of bystanders around works to the disadvantage of the person in need.

The first cause is that people unconsciously judge the passivity of the other bystanders to mean that the situation is not nearly as serious as it may look. If clouds of smoke or a cry for help should suddenly break into a waiting room, the chance of someone's going out to investigate is much greater if that person is alone than if he is with a number of other people. If two people are sitting in a waiting room facing each other, their passiveness is greater than if they sit back-to-back, for in the latter case they cannot judge each other's reactions.

The second cause of the passivity that is found where there are a larger number of bystanders is that the responsibility for helping—and also the shame in case no help is offered!—is *spread* over more persons, with the result that the responsibility per person is experienced as far less than if one had been alone or with just a few others. Even if it becomes abundantly clear that there is a real emergency, in which case the first cause is no longer a factor, bystanders may still remain passive because of this second cause. Research has shown that bystanders in such a situation do not necessarily remain apathetic or indifferent; they may be extremely worried about the situation. Thus, it is not that they have decided not to offer any help. Rather, they have not yet gotten to the point of actually offering their assistance because they are waiting to see whether anyone else will do it.

In situations where it is abundantly clear that there is an emergency, *and* in which no one can convince himself for very long that "someone else will help"—for example, when someone becomes ill in a train—people appear to offer assistance speedily. If neither of the causes explained above is a factor in the situation, bystanders appear not to be such wicked people as one might first think from hearing about their passivity. The evidence points in a more positive direction: in such a situation, once someone rushes forward to help, several others also come forward promptly to offer their assistance. So in some cases, bystanders appear to have a negative effect, but under other circumstances precisely the opposite is true, because the bystanders seem to motivate and activate one another. Thus, people who know they are being observed by others who themselves cannot help—for instance, because they are sitting behind glass—are quicker to offer help than people who are alone.

Thus, it appears that there is always an ethical undertone present in our readiness to assist. Either we shove the responsibility on to others and remain passive, or—because we do not wish to make a bad impression on others—we offer our help. However, the ethical explanation is not sufficient. In the first place, we have to take the psychical factors into account.

Generally speaking, in many cases it is not easy to know what is the right thing to do. Here again, ethics and psychology may collide. People have in the back of their heads the idea that one should not meddle too much in other people's business. They seem to remember what Solomon said: "Whoever meddles in a quarrel not his own is like one who takes a passing dog by the ears" (Prov. 26:17). We should also remember the advice of the Apostle Peter: "Let none of you suffer... as a meddler in other men's matters" (1 Pet. 4:15 ASV). So sometimes it really seems to be better not to offer any help.

Aggression

Finally, when it comes to the ethos and our fellow human being, special mention must be made of *aggressiveness*. What we are facing here is a very complex problem in which many factors play a part. We can think of the following:

(a) *Biotic* factors: We are familiar with all kinds of drugs capable of suppressing aggression in Man *or* substances exacerbating aggression, such as alcohol.

(b) *Perceptive* factors: People can teach themselves or others all sorts of aggressive reflexes. One's upbringing plays quite a role here.

(c) *Sensitive* factors: Violent emotions accompany aggression. We have seen earlier that the highest percentage of criminal behavior is associated with the choleric temperament.

(d) *Spiritive* factors: Sometimes aggression takes place very purposefully, not against someone's better judgment but as a deliberate decision of the will.

There is a place in human life for moderate aggression, that is to say, for justified anger, but there are great dangers here. Consider Psalm 4:4 in the Septuagint: "In your anger do not sin," and the way Paul quotes this verse: "'In your anger do not sin': Do not let the sun go down while you are still angry" (Eph. 4:26 NIV). Do not feed your aggression; control it; that is, let your sensitive idionomy be governed by your spiritive idionomy, under the central guidance of the heart. An aggression that intimidates, extorts, uses force, or is thought to be necessary to provide relief is out of the question in a Christian ethos.

These things can be made still clearer now that it has become apparent psychologically that aggression should not be considered such a good "escape valve" as was often thought by earlier psychologists. Eating stills the urge to eat, but aggressive behavior ordinarily does not still the urge to engage in aggression. It is similar to the urge toward sex; it is well known that sexual activity increases rather than decreases the strength of the urge. And aggression only evokes more aggression as Cain, the first murderer, already realized when he said: "I shall be a fugitive and a wanderer on the earth, and whoever finds me will kill me" (Gen. 4:14). It would be well for parents who, out of laziness or ignorance, allow their children to watch a great deal of aggressive television to be aware of this.

Notorious in this connection is a psychological experiment in which human subjects—assigned to the role of either jailers or prisoners—had to act in an imitation prison. To the horror of the people conducting the experiment, the process released totally unsuspected aggressions among the pretend jailors, even in mild-tempered subjects. What was made clear is that even in honorable people a devil is always potentially present, a devil that can be made to manifest itself under certain circumstances. Again, it is not the theological or ethical explanation—"Man's sinful heart"—

which interests us right now, but the psychical aspects involved in the aggressions that have been brought out in such ways.

The Ethos and God

We will now take a look at such questions as responsibility and obeying God rather than men (as the Apostle Peter puts it in Acts 5:29; cf. 4:19). Ultimately, human beings are completely accountable to *God,* and so they may never go against their consciences (insofar, of course, as their consciences have really been formed in accordance with the norms of Scripture). Therefore we may never take refuge behind what others have told us. People have always tried to excuse themselves by making such pronouncements as, "The woman whom you gave to be with me, she gave me fruit of the tree" (Gen. 3:12), or, "These people ... said to me, 'Make us gods.' . . . they gave [their gold] to me, and I threw it into the fire, and out came this calf" (Exod. 32:22-24). We are responsible for *our own* actions, no matter how understandable it is that people sometimes allow themselves to be led by others, or even to be totally misled: "For we are each responsible for our own conduct" (Gal. 6:5 NLT).

It is remarkable indeed that there are so many people who believe in evolutionism or in Marxism—just as it is remarkable that there are a great many people who accept the body of Christian ideas—without ever really thinking about these things very deeply. But then it is worth asking how many of our ideas are really entirely *our own*. Is it not true that much of the time we parrot others without looking into matters ourselves? Is it not true that we are very susceptible to the opinion of the crowd? Is there not in all of us something of the *conformist,* the person who, without thinking, sticks with current opinions? However, the Bible gives us this warning: "Do not follow the crowd in doing wrong" (Exod. 23:2 NIV).

Quite a bit of psychological testing has been done to establish how far this conformity goes even in very sensible, intelligent people, and the results are shocking. Even in matters that are very obvious, where people can be one hundred percent certain that they themselves are right, there are still some who would rather fit in with the manifestly wrong view held by the crowd. What is it that moves them to think along such lines? Perhaps they have thoughts such as "The others must be right—I've got to be mistaken!" or even "Something has got to be wrong with me ..."

Here we are talking about the testing of students, among whom you may surely expect a certain amount of firmness of character and power of judgment. However, consider how many more people there are in actual, everyday life who go along with the majority when it comes to political, moral, scientific, and religious questions. It is also a remarkable fact that the students who did have the courage to take a stand against the majority sometimes gave their (correct!) answers with a "bad" conscience: "Am I not the one who is wrong?" Thus, people can delude themselves so badly that they consciously do something bad with a good conscience and do something good with a bad conscience!

False Obedience

All this becomes even more striking when tests are performed to find out how far people are willing to go when it comes to obeying an authoritarian, deeply respected person, even if such obedience involves going against one's own conscience and sense of responsibility. In a series of experiments that have since become notorious, Stanley Milgram proved that about two-thirds of the human subjects were willing to inflict unbearable pain on a fellow human being out of obedience to the person conducting the experiment. The subjects inflicting the pain presumably thought they had no other choice, even if—as they were made to believe—they were endangering the life of the person they were dealing with. These experiments involved tests in which experimental subjects were instructed to administer increasingly severe electric shocks as punishment to other subjects whenever they gave a wrong answer to a question. (In fact no severe shocks were ever administered, and all the pain that was apparent in the situation was faked by actors pretending to be victims.)

It is noteworthy that before the experiments were carried out, a group of psychiatrists had predicted that at most one subject in a thousand would persist to the almost lethal level of 450 volts.

The actual number turned out to be 620 times as high—62%! Yet the people who served as subjects in these experiments were not sadists. Rather, they pressed the button inflicting the pain with tortured consciences, under stress, and sometimes almost underwent nervous collapse. Nevertheless, they did continue to obey the person conducting the experiment right to the bitter end. One cause of their action was that they resolved their cognitive dissonance by casting all their responsibility on the person conducting the experiment, or in some cases even by placing the blame on the supposed victims for giving such stupid answers.

We should not be too hard on the two-thirds of the experimental subjects who were guilty. Again, this is not the time for an ethical judgment but for psychological questions, i.e., what factors determine a subject's behavior under such circumstances? Many situations in life are so complicated that it is very difficult to take a proper distance and get a good, comprehensive, and integrated view of the whole, so as to be able to make the proper choice between two moral principles that are equally valid and important. The two principles in this case would be, first, not to inflict pain on your fellow human beings, and second, to render faithful allegiance to a good cause, such as a scientific investigation.

We are all so accustomed to rendering obedience on a continual basis—to the physician, the policeman, the income tax authorities, our employer—that it is often very difficult to know exactly when we are supposed to obey our own conscience (or better, God) rather than Man. Therefore, we may not nonchalantly place this famous experiment on the same level as the *Befehl ist Befehl* mentality of many Nazis in Hitler's Germany. The subjects in the psychological experiments I have mentioned above obeyed because they thought that useful, high level scientific research was the goal, whereas in Nazi Germany anyone involved in reprehensible activities was aware that the most malevolent and disgraceful of aims were involved. The men of the SS and the Gestapo ordinarily did their work in a very vicious way, and definitely did not need much encouragement from their superiors to continue their cruelty. However, as with the subjects in the experiment, they usually obeyed only under great pressure and with tremendous emotional antipathy.

For all who observe these tests from the outside, it is clear what the subjects *ought* to have done. But before you make such an ethical judgment, you should imagine yourself in a situation where you hold a smart professor in his white lab coat in very high esteem, and think to yourself that you are engaged in useful, highly scientific work, while at the same time being aware that you cannot really grasp fully what your actions are doing to your victim. The truth is that only a few of us are sadists, but we are *all* sinners. However, I repeat that sin is too simplistic an answer. First, if we are all sinners, why are only some of us sadists? Second, if most of us are *not* sadists, what are the *psychical* factors that make subjects willing to inflict pain on other subjects? One is that it is often difficult for us to clearly distinguish situations where we know we must *not* obey those who have been placed over us, such as, in this case, the leader of the investigation.

The Criminal

The themes on which I have just touched, which revolve around Man's responsibility to God, bring us to the subject of crime. If it is true that all men are sinners—and that is indeed true—how then does it happen that only a comparatively small percentage of the human race falls into actual criminal behavior? Of course, I am using the word *criminal* here in the juridical sense of delinquent behavior. People fall into such delinquent behavior as a result of situational and personal as well as religious causes. On this point we should recall the formula given at the end of chapter 5:

$$B = f\ (R, P, S).$$

First of all, the environment can have a highly unfavorable influence (the S-factor), as a result of which people fall into crime. On the *macro-level*, we can think of the society to which we belong, which takes a far too tolerant position toward aggression and what is known as "petty crime," toward the (low) values which are sometimes prevalent in certain social classes, or toward bad social contacts: "Bad company ruins good morals" (1 Cor. 15:33). On the *meso-level*, we should think especially of the consequences of a bad upbringing. Children need to acquire social skills of all sorts as they are growing up at home, for they are not born with them. Parents have to deal with their children consistently, especially when it comes to punishment. Otherwise the children will not know what is expected of them. Children can be damaged especially when they are rejected by their parents and do not receive enough love, care, and attention. And on the *micro-level,* it is still true, sad to say, that "Opportunity makes a thief."

As for the *personal* factors (P), there are, first of all, the *biotic* causes. Research has demonstrated that hereditary factors undeniably play a role. Please note, we should not conclude that certain hereditary factors *automatically* make a person into a criminal, but they do increase the inclination to delinquency. Other factors that can increase this tendency are certain brain abnormalities, such as epilepsy, brain tumors, inflammation of the brain, and certain conditions affecting metabolism (e.g., lead-poisoning, lack of calcium), and certain hormonal abnormalities.

In addition to biotic factors, there are all sorts of *sensitive* factors, such as the need for status, the need to project self-assuredness in one's behavior, a certain over-active, anti-social, impulsiveness or aggressiveness, or even a neurotic tendency. The latter appears to occur especially in choleric temperaments (see chapter 6). Researchers have tried to explain these matters in terms of both the emotionality and the extroversion of the choleric person. On the one hand, his emotions (anger, fear) increase his inclination to criminal behavior, while on the other hand it has been demonstrated that extroverts are somewhat less susceptible to conditioning and also are not as quick to learn social behavior during their upbringing. What I am saying here only applies in a general way, of course: on the one hand a person with the opposite kind of temperament, the phlegmatic, can also become a criminal, while on the other hand most cholerics are not criminals.

As a matter of fact, even when P and S are taken into consideration, everything has not yet been said. The R-factor (the religious condition of the heart) is of the greatest (though not exclusive!) significance. Of course, it is true that Christians, too, can fall into crime. However, there are clear indications that among committed Christians the number of delinquents is significantly lower than it is among unbelievers, and also that conversion to Christ is one of the most effective means of putting an end to delinquent behavior. It is when you start to bring *religion* and the *heart* into the picture that you begin to see that more is involved in delinquency than just *social behavior* and *degree of conditionability*, which were discussed above. In fact, social learning extends far beyond (perceptive) conditioning, as we have already seen. Moreover, delinquency is not just a matter of bad social behavior, but of bad juridical, ethical, and pistical behavior.

In an earlier section, we saw that the small child has a moral disposition, which, since people are prone by nature to anti-social and anti-moral behavior, needs to be developed during the years of his upbringing. It is not true to say that a good upbringing completely removes this proneness to evil; otherwise it would be possible to prevent a person's ever falling into delinquency. Favorable circumstances (upbringing, refinement, stable surroundings) can at best block the eruptions of the filthy wellspring that lies concealed in every one of us, and such circumstances are therefore a great practical benefit. But God, who knows and judges even our deepest thoughts (Ps. 139:1-4), sees through the good behavior of the respectable citizen who keeps his lusts in decent check but in fact could not care less about his Creator's authority over him. Both the criminal and the worthy citizen are in need of radical conversion, for in both, the heart is good for nothing, no matter how dissimilar their actions may be.

Chapter Nine

THE HUMAN HEART

We are now coming closer to the inmost depths of the human person, insofar as we have access to them. For the scientific researcher, these depths will ultimately always remain a mystery unless the Word of God throws its light on them. "Who knows a person's thoughts except the spirit of that person, which is in him?" (1 Cor. 2:11a). Only with our hearts can we know our hearts. But I would add: this applies most, or even exclusively, for the person whose heart is enlightened by the Spirit of God: "...having the eyes of your hearts enlightened, that you may know..." (Eph. 1:18).

Heart and Conscience

On a number of occasions, I have already mentioned the *conscience,* which, if I deduce correctly from the Bible, is a function of the heart. The Old Testament does not even have a word for "conscience"; when it talks about the conscience the word it uses is "heart." See, for example, 1 Samuel 25:37 and 2 Samuel 24:10, where the NKJV in both cases gives a literal reading of "heart," whereas the NIV has "conscience." Also compare 1 Kings 2:44; 8:38; Psalm 24:4; 73:1. Precisely because the conscience is a function of the heart, it is always directly related to God. Therefore, a conscience that is functioning properly accuses us whenever we have been disobedient to God and his Word (cf. Psalm 139:23-24). A conscience functions properly only "in [NKJV: through] the Holy Spirit" (Rom. 9:1).

The conscience is not to be understood as some religio-ethical subordinate part of the person, nor is it something like the voice of God in the person's heart; it is the person *himself.* That is to say, it is the individual person in his inmost depth (the heart), in his profoundest self-awareness, willing and doing, which either is or is not directed to God and his Word. In "conscience" (from the Latin *conscientia*), we recognize the root word *scientia,* meaning "knowledge" (it is the same in the Greek equivalent, *syneidèsis*);

this indicates that our conscience is a form of knowledge, insight, and consciousness (a related term) that we possess in regard to ourselves and to the ethical contents of our words and deeds.

All of this is very clear from the New Testament, where the word "conscience" occurs many times. There is a "weak conscience" (1 Cor. 8:7), that is, a conscience that is easily offended, which is broadly similar to a "weak faith" in God in the sense of Romans 14:1. The conscience of the "weak person," which we find in 1 Corinthians 8:9-12, refers in fact always to the person himself in his responsibility toward God. In Romans 13:5, too, the "conscience" is clearly the inner expression of the will of God in our lives. All of this perhaps is most clearly expressed in 1 Peter 2:19, where we find an expression which the NKJV translates as "conscience toward God," but which the NIV translates as "conscious (ESV: mindful) of God." There is not a great deal of difference between the two. The conscience is a consciousness (awareness) of God, as well as our reckoning with God, who knows and judges our inmost depths.

When God has nothing to find fault with in us, we have a "clear conscience" (2 Tim. 1:3), which hardly differs from a "pure heart" (2 Tim. 2:22). But when God, in accordance with his Word, condemns our inner feelings and our outer actions, we have an "evil" or "defiled conscience" (cf. Heb. 10:22, "our hearts sprinkled clean from an evil conscience"; Titus 1:15). Please note that the opposite is not always true, for we may be guilty with a "clear conscience," because our conscience has not been properly educated, or because it may have been "seared" (1 Tim. 4:2; NIV adds, "as with a hot iron"). It is very important to bear in mind that God's Word and the Holy Spirit constitute a perfect standard, whereas our conscience in and of itself does not. Therefore Paul writes: "I am not aware of anything against myself [NIV: My conscience is clear], but I am not thereby acquitted. It is the Lord who judges me" (1 Cor. 4:4). Therefore, it is possible that even though our *conscience* does not accuse us, the *Lord* must still reprove us. The conscience is like an alarm clock, which sometimes does not function properly.

The opposite could happen as well: if our heart (which in this case seems to mean, the conscience) "condemns" us, we may still hand everything over to the Lord in the awareness that he is "acquainted with all my ways" (Ps. 139:3), and will make it clear to us whether there is something amiss, so that we can then get rid of it. I believe this is the sense of 1 John 3:19-21, we "reassure our heart before him; for whenever our heart condemns us, God is greater than our heart, and he knows everything. Beloved, if our heart does not condemn us, we have confidence before God." It can be a warning but also a consolation that God knows our hearts; as Peter told Jesus, "Lord, you know all things; you know that I love you" (John 21:17).

In summary, the conscience is not always a *precise* awareness of the will of God—but it should never be ignored either! We ought not to go against our conscience, even if our conscience has not been properly trained. Therefore, the Apostle Paul can appeal to the conscience of the pagans, even though they do not know the Word of God and their conscience may therefore be expected to function only defectively (Rom. 2:15). Every person is born with a vague awareness of God hidden deep in his heart (see Rom. 1:18-21, 32); because of this, he also has a faint awareness of the will of God, and of good and evil. This flawed natural moral consciousness is further formed—or, in the case of non-believers or apostate and carnal Christians, malformed—by upbringing and the entire cultural environment in which one lives.

Conscience and Conditioning

Although the conscience is a function of the heart, sensitive and spiritive factors play a major role in its development. Even (perceptive) conditioning is involved in it. As a result, some psychologists, influenced by behaviorism and related schools of thought, inevitably view the conscience as *nothing but* a bundle of conditioned reflexes. Every parent is familiar with the role of perceptive conditioning in the development of conscience because parents try to instill a certain type of behavior into a stubborn child by means of rewards, or discourage undesirable behavior by means of (mild) punishment. There was a time when it was fashionable for psychologists to disapprove strongly of spanking, but some of them have since then changed their minds on this issue. Although Proverbs recommends corporal punishment (13:24; 19:18; 22:15; 23:13-14; 29:15), it is simply not an issue anymore in many Western countries, because it is forbidden by law.

Whatever form of punishment is administered, it must be done promptly and consistently; that is, once you have made reasonable threats, follow through on them! The punishment must also be explained to the child, so that he knows for what misbehavior he is receiving the punishment, and how the measure of punishment relates to the measure of misbehavior. Furthermore, all punishment should be counterbalanced by *rewards,* that is, praise for the child, or even material rewards, whenever the child exhibits the desired behavior.

Today we have plenty of evidence to show that children who have been brought up with a greater degree of moral "freedom" (this word is a misnomer in this case!) commit more offenses and crimes than those who have had a firmer, more "conventional" upbringing. But as noted above, a firmer upbringing means punishment (now and then) *plus explanation.* Because Man has a spiritive idionomy, he can consider his actions, understand why something he does is good or bad, and see what harm his bad behavior does to other people. Moreover, he has a heart, by which, if he is truly born again, he can see why certain behavior amounts to "sin against God." Thus, for a child receiving a Christian upbringing, the conscience is formed in accordance with the standard of the revealed Word of God: "Fathers, do not provoke your children to anger, but bring them up in the discipline and instruction of the Lord" (Eph. 6:4).

It is precisely because the conscience can be *de*formed during the process of upbringing that people can, through a process of conditioning, acquire (sensitive) "guilt *feelings,*" as even higher animals are able to do (if we may indeed use the same term for what the latter are experiencing). Many of us recognize the behavior of a dog that "feels guilty." However, it is very important to clearly distinguish sensitive feelings of this sort from concrete *guilt* in the *ethical* sense. We may speak of guilt only when a concrete norm, which authoritatively applies to us, has been infringed. This (objective) guilt may or may not be accompanied by a (subjective) *feeling* of guilt. A "seared" conscience (cf. I Timothy 4:2) can bear a tremendous load of guilt without the person experiencing any *feeling* of guilt. In summary, guilt may or may not be accompanied by a feeling of guilt, and a feeling of guilt may or may not stem from genuine guilt.

On the other hand, a "weak" conscience (cf. 1 Cor. 8:7, 10, 12) could easily lead to the piling up of a feeling of guilt without there being any actual concrete guilt as far as the transgression of God's commandments is concerned. In some Christian families all sorts of taboos are instilled in the children, taboos which are in no way derived from the Bible but which are sometimes very hard to overcome in later life. Although people have become *rationally* convinced that the behavior which was once forbidden is no longer a problem (such as women not wearing hats anymore in church), they may still have a "bad conscience," a feeling of guilt on a sensitive level, when exhibiting this kind of behavior.

It is also for this reason that a good, thorough, genuinely biblical upbringing is so difficult and at the same time so important. The author of the book of Proverbs was not only familiar with spanking but could also, in intimate conversation with his child, say: "My son, do not forget my teaching, but let your heart keep my commandments ... trust in the Lord with all your heart, and do not lean on your own understanding. In all your ways acknowledge him, and he will make straight your paths. Be not wise in your own eyes; fear the Lord and turn away from evil" (Prov. 3:1, 5-7).

Heart and Love

The essence of the relationship between God and Man, and also of that between a man and his neighbor, is love (Matt. 22:37-39; John 13:34-35; see also Deut. 6:5; Lev. 19:18). If a person loves, this means that his heart goes out to God and to his fellow man. This idea is expressed in innumerable biblical passages.

I will begin by discussing *horizontal* love between a man and his neighbor. In this regard we can distinguish between (a) one-sided love or love of one's neighbor (German: *Nächstenliebe*; Dutch: *naastenliefde*), and (b) mutual love. When psychologists discuss love of neighbor, they like to speak of *altruism* (from Latin *alter*, "the other one"), or *pro-social behavior,* by which they mean behavior that leads to positive social consequences. This certainly sounds a lot different from love, a term possessing certain ethical overtones that fall outside the viewpoint of the psychologist. His own definition has the advantage of leaving the *motives* and *disposition* of the pro-social person out of consideration for the time being. We know all too well that a person can act pro-socially with the noblest of motives, but also from the most vicious or malevolent of motives, or with something in between, for example out of a sense of duty.

In any case, there are some very self-seeking motives that lie between these two extremes. On the one hand, help and charity of all kinds often require from the person involved only a small sacrifice, while on the other hand they may lead to honor, celebrity, prestige, and rewards (cf. John 12:43, which shows that some people "love the glory that comes from man more than the glory that comes from God"). This is *calculated* pro-social behavior. *Genuine* love of one's neighbor is very different; the greater the sacrifice demanded, and the fewer the readily visible advantages, the more genuine the love of neighbor is.

A striking example of such behavior is provided in the parable of the Good Samaritan (Luke 10:25-37):

(a) The Samaritan was not responsible for the condition of the wounded man. By contrast, in today's world, much pro-social behavior is in fact based on a feeling of guilt.

(b) There was no one forcing the Samaritan to help. Much assistance from neighbors occurs in the face of social pressure. The Samaritan's act was entirely voluntary and even non-conformist, since leaders in that society (the priest and the Levite) had already failed to help.

(c) The Samaritan was not prompted by any feeling of solidarity, for the wounded man belonged to a nation other than his own with which his own people lived on a footing of hostility (cf. John 4:9b).

(d) The Samaritan's act involved major outlays of time, exertion, risk, and money, without any reward. The Samaritan did not ask for anything in return for what he did, and did not receive anything either.

Does Genuine Neighborly Love Exist?

The question can now be asked: Is such love of neighbor actually to be found in the real world (apart from Jesus Christ; cf. 2 Cor. 8:9)? Many psychoanalysts and behaviorists have simply denied this possibility. Presupposing evolutionist ideas such as the "struggle for existence" and the "survival of the fittest" (expressions which go back to Herbert Spencer [1820-1903]), these thinkers *could not* do otherwise than maintain that human behavior is downright self-seeking. Christian thinkers can agree with this claim up to a point, but not on the basis of a belief in the evolutionary imperfection of Man. Rather, the basis is that Man, though originally created good, fell into sin by his own free choice (Gen. 1-3).

Even in the case of the Christian who is truly born again but in whom the sinful nature is still present, it is questionable whether one will ever come across an entirely disinterested act of a self-sacrificing disposition. The Apostle Paul clearly brings out the problem in what he said of Timothy, "I have no one like him, who will be genuinely concerned for your welfare. For they all seek their own interests, not those of Jesus Christ" (Phil. 2:20-21).

The truth of this statement is amply illustrated by an embarrassing example, which involved forty theological students who were instructed to go to a particular building to perform certain tasks there. The situation had been set up in such a way that some of the students had to hurry to get there in time. For several of the students, the task included giving a lecture on the Good Samaritan before the faculty and the other students! All the subjects in the experiment, on their way to the building, had to go directly past a man who was groaning and obviously in distress (although in reality he was an accomplice of the people conducting the experiment). The number of students who stopped to help the man in distress proved to be pitifully small (only three). The rest of them, like priests and Levites, rushed past the man in distress so that they would be on time for their interesting and honorable lecture on the Good Samaritan.

No matter how imperfect our readiness to help may be, it can be *learned* to a certain extent. This realization is of great importance when it comes to raising children. Helpfulness in children can be fostered by rewarding them afterwards in material or social ways. However, if the rewards are promised to them beforehand, this will have a bad effect, for the children will then be trained to judge their own behavior wrongly. They will imagine that they are doing something for the promised reward instead of out of love for their neighbor. As a result, they will not be quite so eager to help in situations where there is no reward in sight. When children are being raised, it is important to foster their ability to enter into the feelings of others, and thus to offer help not for reward but simply to relieve suffering and give joy.

Setting a good example is of immense importance here. Children are quick to imitate an example, especially when they see the positive results of extended helpfulness. Moreover, children imitate our *actions* far more readily than our *words*: if Dad can talk nicely about love of neighbor but never puts it into practice himself, his children generally will not do so either. Still, research has shown that Dad's words do have an influence: they affect the *words* his children will afterwards offer about love of neighbor to other people. People who talk a good line breed people who talk a good line.

On this subject, see Matthew 23:3-4 where Jesus gives this advice: "Do and observe whatever [the scribes and Pharisees] tell you, but not the works they do. For they preach, but do not practice." Paul has this to say to the church in Rome: "In passing judgment on another you condemn yourself, because you, the judge, practice the very same things... You then who teach others, do you not teach yourself?" (Rom. 2:1-3, 20-23). He shows Timothy how to be a good role model for others: "Set the believers an example in speech, in conduct, in love, in faith, in purity." (1 Tim. 4:12, 15-16); but this was based on what Timothy had learned from Paul: "You have followed my teaching, my conduct, my aim in life, my faith, my patience, my love, my steadfastness" (2 Tim. 3:10-11, 14).

Theories about Helpfulness

Quite apart from all these good, and often bad influences, and apart from the continued effect of sin on human life, which cannot be denied, we must admit that helpfulness does indeed occur. Many people, including non-Christians, can often be extremely helpful, even to perfect strangers, while remaining anonymous themselves, and deriving no benefit other than inner satisfaction from what they have done. Although we may be dealing with unbelievers in such cases, we may never hold such helpfulness in contempt. Even Christ loved the rich young man for his honesty and sincerity. Still, such "good" qualities do not in themselves earn anyone the right to inherit eternal life (Mark 10:21-22).

Nevertheless, helpfulness does occur. Self-interest undoubtedly plays some role in it, since a person is always inclined to gain the greatest possible advantage with the least possible expense. In psychology, this point is brought out through the *costs and profits* theory: we put energy into helping others only to the extent we get a profit from it. However, this theory does not manage to explain the heroic instances of the love of neighbor in which the costs are extraordinarily high, including even the sacrifice of one's own life, while the benefits are extremely low, that is, no more than inner self-satisfaction.

The *sensitive* theory, which tells us that helpfulness is proportional to "the ability to empathize," comes closer to explaining genuine helpfulness. This theory focuses on our ability to identify with the distress of another person. The more we manage to identify and the greater our own discomfort, the greater the effort we make to lessen both our own discomfort and that of the other person by helping him or her. Research has demonstrated that this ability to empathize can be stimulated in children and adults. When this is done, helpfulness increases.

General Norms

However, the spiritive theories that are used to explain helpfulness are, in my view, even more important. Such theories relate helpfulness to *norms*. It appears that what we are concerned with here is not so much vague, general social norms but very personal norms. Many people do not know how to handle general norms. For example, they do not know how to choose between "Love your neighbor" and "Do not meddle in other people's business." They think that the Golden Rule of Matthew 7:12 ("Whatever you wish that others would do to you, do also to them") is good enough.

Another problem is that people often do not *like* to be helped. Jesus said, "It is more blessed to give than to receive" (Acts 20:35); some people seem to take this to mean that they should *hate* to receive anything, because it places them in a position of dependence.

At the same time, many people are not very eager to *receive* certain forms of help simply because that might morally oblige them on occasion to offer help in return. People often feel threatened in their freedom of action if they feel obligated to perform a service in return, and so they may say: "Let's *not* go visit the neighbors, because then we will also have to invite *them* for a return visit pretty soon."

Personal Norms

Personal norms are much clearer than general norms. Most people have a rather clear view of their own moral obligations and responsibilities to offer help in specific situations. For example, if a person in a specific situation constantly succeeds in shifting the responsibility onto someone else, he can indeed imagine that he has a strong sense of duty, but if he himself is never responsible, he does not have to do his duty at all.

In some such way, even certain Christians may accept for themselves the highest biblical norms, and yet turn out to be poor help-providers because they have so little sense of responsibility. When it comes right down to it, they constantly declare that those fine biblical norms do not apply to the specific situations in which they find themselves. Notice again how sinful inclinations (*direction*) and purely mental factors (*structure*) are intertwined here.

It is *here* where we come to the crux of the whole matter. The question of personal responsibility forces us to confront the attitude of the *heart* toward God. Genuine love of one's neighbor can only emanate from a genuine love of God. "If anyone says, 'I love God,' and hates his brother, he is a liar; for he who does not love his brother whom he has seen cannot love God whom he has not seen. And this commandment we have from him: whoever loves God must also love his brother. Everyone who believes that Jesus is the Christ has been born of God, and everyone who loves the Father loves whoever has been born of him. By this we know that we love the children of God, when we love God and obey his commandments" (1 John 4:20–5:2).

Notice the two-way argument of the Apostle: if you love God, you will also love your brother; and if you love your brother, you may know from this that you also love God. Love toward God and love toward one's neighbor are inseparable. This necessarily implies that an unregenerate heart can never demonstrate genuine brotherly love.

Heart and Faith

Even this matter, Man's intimate love relationship to God—in other words, *religion* in its true sense—has been made the subject of psychological study. Such study takes place in a discipline called psychology of religion (German: *Religionspsychologie;* Dutch: *godsdienstpsychologie*). Of course there are also researchers in all sorts of other disciplines— philosophers, theologians, historians, ethnologists, sociologists, and even neurobiologists—who have occupied themselves with this tricky subject. Earlier we observed that Man's religious relationship to God is, in its true essence, not susceptible to scientific analysis (see also previous volumes *Wisdom for Thinkers* and *What Then Is Theology?*). Nevertheless, scientists of all kinds have done their utmost to get a handle on the phenomenon of religion.

Just to show you how difficult this is, I point out that even in response to what is supposedly the simplest question of all, namely, how religion is properly to be defined, the most divergent answers have been given. This confusion should not surprise us. It is precisely when scientific researchers occupy themselves with religion, which is the heart of the matter, as well as a matter of the *heart,* that their own hearts' involvement is at its highest. Therefore, the scientific investigator is nowhere more subjective than when the object of his study is religion.

In this area of study too—or perhaps I should say, precisely here—researchers have indeed pleaded for scientific open-mindedness, but from a Christian standpoint we see that it works just the other way around. You can only talk about Man's religious relationship meaningfully when you realize to what extent you yourself are involved in that relationship (taking "religion" in its broadest sense as Man's *ultimate commitment,* his directedness to some Final Ground). It is only the religious person, out of his personal experience, who knows anything about those very aspects of the religious relationship about which nothing sensible can be said in any strictly scientific sense. The religious person does not just *think* that he experiences the higher world and is in touch with it—he really *does* experience it and *is* in contact with it, whether it be the world of God *or* the world of the gods (idols, ideologies). As the French theologian Blaise Pascal (1623-1662) said, the heart has its own reasons for believing this.

Apart from this, we realize that, if someone who calls himself "truly scientific," proposes limiting himself to the objectively observable facts, he has a perfect right to do so. But then he must not expect to be able to study religion. At best he will be studying the empirical, and therefore least interesting and least essential, aspects of religion. He could be compared to someone who proposes to study an automobile but does not believe in gasoline: perhaps such a person would be able to make some nice observations about the appearance of the automobile, but the *essence* of the vehicle—its driving capacity—would escape him. In a similar way, scientific students of religion have become absorbed in looking at religious ideas, forms of conduct, rituals, feelings, theology, confessions of faith, church institutions, and ceremonies—without grasping that, while they were focusing on all these things, they were only studying the *immanent* phenomenon of *religiosity.*

Religiosity is extremely interesting, and we cannot encourage psychologists enough to study it. However, religiosity deals only indirectly with the *transcendent* religious relationship between Man and God (or the gods, the idols). All those *immanent*-religious things actually do touch that relationship, but they cannot be equated with it. Precisely that which surpasses these things, that which is beyond scientific investigation, is what really matters in regard to religion.

True and False

At the same time, we shall have to admit that many psychologists in recent decades have also gained some awareness of these things. If they had listened to the Bible it would not have taken them quite so long to learn to make the basic distinction between external immanent religious conduct and the inner *transcendent* religious experience of the heart. In today's terms one would speak of the distinction between *extrinsic* and *intrinsic* religiosity (Gordon W. Allport). Extrinsic religiosity is religiosity "on the outside," which is a matter of social status (of "belongingness") and of self-interest ("What can religion do for me?"). Moreover, extrinsic religious persons are of themselves often very authoritarian, heavily weighed down with all sorts of prejudices, and very confident that their own group is superior (cf. Theodore Adorno *et al., The Authoritarian Personality*).

Interestingly, there are people of this kind to be found in both liberal (modernist) and extremely conservative denominations. It appears that the properties of such people really can be traced back to the same personal needs of security and belonging (see the discussion of Abraham Maslow in chapter 5). They accept their own denomination's views regarding faith in a rather offhand manner, and conceal their timidity and uncertainty behind their religious self-conceit and the way they look down on other denominations. This is a work of the flesh (Gal. 5:20).

It appears to be much more difficult to provide a personality description of the *intrinsically* religious person. The reason for the difficulty is that his religious experience cannot be traced back to some few conspicuous sensitive or spiritive characteristics. Rather, it is a matter of the *heart*, to which all other needs and values in life have been completely subordinated. Human beings of this kind do not talk so much about a comfortable life, pleasure, ambition, social recognition, abilities, and so forth, as they do of redemption, forgiveness, love, and helpfulness. The intrinsically religious person is not characterized by certain mental qualities but rather by a *relationship* with God (or the gods). But of course this relationship has a definite *influence* on the person's mental life.

Interestingly, the genuinely religious person proves not to be "neurotic" or "psychically unhealthy," as Freud and others had thought, but instead he turns out to be more "spiritually healthy" than the extrinsically religious person, because he is less fixed, less legalistic, more flexible, less "sectarian." He is able to stand up more courageously for his own convictions, but he is at the same time less dogmatic about them, and is less inclined to glorify his own group (denomination). Of course, Christians have long been familiar with this distinction, but it is gratifying to see that non-Christian psychologists have also been discovering such insights.

In this discussion, of course, we must continue to bear in mind that only marginal phenomena of religiosity can be investigated by means of observation and experiment. Thus, the researcher can, as a matter of principle, make no distinction, for example, between the believing Christian, who lives in communion with God, and the occult mystic who, in the demonic world, obtains all kinds of experiences that the Bible forbids (cf. Deut. 18). As a rule, the worldly psychologist will look upon *both* these individuals as intrinsically religious persons, whereas the difference between the two, considered from a Scriptural point of view, is as wide as the heavens. The psychologist will say that *both* are in a religious relation with the "higher world." The Christian psychologists will reply: "But then it is a question of *two* higher worlds that are opposed to one another." He does not know this on the basis of any psychological research as such, but on the basis of the divine Word-revelation.

Thus, we need to ask ourselves the question as to what it means, from a Scriptural standpoint, to be truly religious. *True religion is communion with God, service to God, worship of God, devotion to God,* as these are only possible in the case of the born-again, redeemed, believing person, who lives in the power of the Holy Spirit: "I appeal to you therefore, brothers, by the mercies of God, to present your bodies as a living sacrifice, holy and acceptable to God, which is your spiritual worship" [note, your rational service; NIV: true and proper worship]—in short: your religion (Rom. 12:1). With the aid of some philosophical and psychological concepts, we can now distinguish the following elements:

(a) The *perceptive* aspect: Religion is first of all a *consciousness* or *awareness* of God's presence, rooted in the heart, based on God's Word-revelation, and fostered by the operation of the Holy Spirit.

(b) The *sensitive* aspect: This religious perception is *affectively* and *emotionally* colored, or loaded. Thus, we can speak of religious joy, exaltedness, harmony, peace, and of being deeply touched *or* of experiencing religious awe, of shying away, of feeling fear, *or* of a mixture of these. It all depends on how one knows God—if at all—and on what the condition of the heart is at a given moment.

(c) The various *spiritive* aspects: The *cognitive* recognition, acknowledgment and understanding of what is perceived of God, the *creative* way in which one's communion with God is given shape, and the *conative* dimension, i.e., the way one makes decisions about how to serve and worship God. It is very important to realize that awareness and feeling *without* revelational knowledge is mysticism, whereas knowledge *without* awareness and feeling is dogmatism. Or, as it sometimes has been put, the Word without the Spirit creates Pharisees, and the Spirit without the Word creates fanatics.

(d) This entire *immanent* religious experience, which is a matter of the whole person, and thus involves all the human idionomies, is concentrated in the *transcendent* human *heart,* the center and focal point of human existence.

These four points concern Man's vertical relationship. However, we must remember that this vertical dimension cannot function without the horizontal one. There is no true love toward God that is not accompanied by true love of neighbor. Therefore, I also quote this very practical definition of religion: "Religion that is pure and undefiled before God, the Father, is this: to visit orphans and widows in their affliction, and to keep oneself unstained from the world" (James 1:27).

Chapter Ten
THE ABNORMAL PERSONALITY

Having discussed some aspects of the normal human personality in chapters 8 and 9, we now turn to the *abnormal* personality. What I have in mind here is not the *positively* abnormal, that is, exceptionally gifted person, but the *negatively* abnormal person, that is, the person with a "mental disorder," the person who is "different from others," "disturbed," "mentally ill" (or, as some would say, "crazy" or "insane"), or whatever terminology one might care to use.

Of course, we immediately run into a problem when we initiate such a discussion. What is meant here by normal and abnormal? What are the norms or standards by which we should judge such a matter? Who decides who is normal or abnormal? If a person believes he is Napoleon, or refuses to venture into the street because he is afraid of open spaces (*agoraphobia*), or feels compelled to wash his hands fifty times a day, or can only get sexual satisfaction through contact with, for example, a woman's shoe, he is of course not normal. Not many people would debate that. But suppose a person thinks he is a prophet of the Hindu god Vishnu, or suppose that, because of his fear of heights (*acrophobia*), he does not wish to live in a high-rise apartment, or suppose he can only find sexual gratification with someone of the same gender, is such a person also to be judged as not normal?

The cases in the second group are not quite as clear as the cases in the first. At the very least, we can say that there is a sliding scale between normal and abnormal. And perhaps each one of us has things (whether they are little or not so little) in which we are (somewhat) abnormal.

The Statistical Norm for Abnormal Behavior

What norm determines whether behavior is normal or abnormal? Some people would answer that only a *statistical* norm could do so.

"Normal" is then simply the average behavior of a group: normal is what most people do. The problem with this way of thinking is that there are so terribly *many* mental disorders to be found in Western society that, if you follow the statistical norm idea, you would almost have to call the neurotic personality normal, and the exceptionally well-balanced and well-adjusted personality abnormal.

As a matter of fact, there are millions of people in the Western world who have been to a psychotherapist some time or another, and millions of others who reside in psychiatric institutions. If we go back some decades in history, we could find such people taking up the majority of the hospital beds. This situation has changed since then because hospital stays nowadays have become shorter, other sorts of clinics have been established, and much better medication is available so that patients can be treated at home.

Here we are talking only about the most serious of disturbances. If we go on to consider *all* mental disorders that are sufficiently serious to interfere with daily living, we would have to conclude that, roughly speaking, perhaps no less than *one-third* of the population appears to suffer from them, in both industrialized and so-called primitive societies.

The Social-Cultural Norm

Another possibility would be to appeal to the *social-cultural* norm, according to which abnormal behavior is behavior that is considered not socially acceptable. Then we would be talking about the behavior of people who do not fulfill their social roles, who do not conform to current morals or who do not live up to certain expectations regarding their behavior. However, here too we would run into many problems. After all, we might think that people from the East often behave "strangely," but does that mean we can therefore characterize them as "crazy"? Even within our own society we say quite freely of all sorts of people whose behavior or clothing is eccentric that they are "nuts," but does this mean that they *really* are mentally ill?

In a society that is being de-Christianized, it may well be that prayer and church attendance will one day come to be viewed as "crazy," but does such a judgment mean that Christians really *are* "crazy"? In any event, Christians and other abnormal persons, such as political dissidents, have been shut up in psychiatric institutions under totalitarian regimes, such as the former Soviet Union. This shows that the social-cultural norm is highly inefficient, if not outright dangerous.

The Personality Norm

We are on better ground when we consider what is known as the *personality norm.* People do differ from one another in the structure of their personalities, and because some people are mentally dysfunctional, they exhibit abnormal behavior. According to this norm, abnormal behavior is characterized especially by two norms:

(a) We call a person mentally abnormal if there is a *perceptive-cognitive* aberration, i.e., if the person has a distorted picture of reality. For example, he might have an unreasonable fear of spiders, he might hear strange voices, or he might be convinced that he is President Reagan.

(b) We call a person mentally abnormal if there is a *sensitive* aberration, e.g., if he feels ill at ease, unhappy, depressed, or frightened. Or perhaps he cannot sleep, he has no appetite, or he has all kinds of ailments, aches and pains.

These two groups of symptoms make proper adjustment to everyday life very difficult and point in a general way to the presence of one or more mental disorders. However, even this personality norm is only a relative matter. All of us, at one time or another, have suffered from unreasonable fears or delusions, and we all feel depressed at times. Usually we can cope with these conditions, but many people cannot. Somewhere between these two groups we have to draw the (necessarily vague) line between the mentally healthy and mentally unhealthy. (Etymologically speaking, the terms sane and insane mean exactly the same as mentally healthy and unhealthy, but these words have negative connotations nowadays.)

Moreover there is also the fact that some people lead a completely normal life and then suddenly exhibit completely abnormal behavior, without having felt the slightest twinge of fear or guilt beforehand. In such cases, it is precisely the *absence* of these feelings that can serve as an indication of a mental disorder. Or consider the example of a person who is particularly fearful, not because he is mentally disturbed but because he is actually facing a concrete danger ("There is a lion in the road!" [Prov. 26:13]). Or perhaps the person is guilt-ridden, not because he is mentally disturbed but because this feeling relates to a very concrete fault committed against his neighbor, or against God ("Against you, you only, have I sinned and done what is evil in your sight, so that you may be justified in your words and blameless in your judgment" [Ps. 51:4]).

The Christian Norm

Best of all, in my view, is the *Christian norm*. This norm takes into account not only the *situational* aspects of mental disorders to which the social-cultural norm points, but also the *personal* aspects to which the personality norm points. But this norm includes even *more*. On the basis of our Christian psychological view of Man, I wish to indicate the following:

(a) *Perceptive* factors: The mentally abnormal person is not in (good) contact with reality, and demonstrates this by responding to situations in ways that are neither effective nor realistic.

(b) *Sensitive* factors: The person does not know how to adjust to new situations with sufficient self-control and discipline, but instead experiences undue fear or depression.

(c) *Spiritive* factors: His actions are often harmful to himself or to others; he cannot or will not always assume responsibility for them. His goals in life, when judged by God's norm, will not be very valuable, but insofar as he has them, he does not try to reach them within the limits laid down by God's norms, *or* within reasonable limits set by society. As a result, what he attains does not provide him very much satisfaction.

(d) The *heart*: Above everything else, it is not possible for a person to function at his best apart from a personal fellowship with God the Father, and with Jesus Christ as his Savior and as the Lord of his life. Outside of that fellowship, a life in accordance with God's norms is not even possible.

This does not mean, however, that we could characterize all unbelievers as mentally disturbed. On the contrary: we all know unbelievers who are mentally healthy, and believers who are mentally disturbed. Again, I point here to the extremely important distinction between *structure* and *direction*. Someone may lead a life with the Lord (i.e., the *direction* of his heart is in order), and yet, in spite of this, disorders may arise in his mental idionomies (dealing with *structure*) that make him mentally unhealthy. And of course, the opposite is also possible: his mental idionomies may function in a healthy manner, whereas his heart may be turned away from God.

Structure and direction cannot be separated, but they must always be distinguished. This will help us to avoid the awful mistake of many Christians who assume that when a believer is fearful or depressed, this *must* be due to a disturbed relationship with God. This is usually not only factually wrong, but, what is worse, it also aggravates the condition of the patient. Besides his mental disorders, he is now also burdened with a feeling of guilt, thanks to people around him who are perhaps well intentioned but unwise and badly informed.

Explanations of Abnormal Behavior

The *explanations* of abnormal behavior are just as complicated as was the discussion of norms for abnormal behavior. In the course of history, psychologists have, as a rule, looked to one of what I call the human-structures to find a fitting explanation for mental disorders. However, precisely because they were usually trying to reduce abnormal behavior completely to one single idionomy, they could never do justice to the full nature of mental disorders.

On the basis of what was established in chapter 6 and 7, we can now understand how this works:

(a) The *organic model* tries to reduce all mental disorders to *physical-biotic* causes, or somatic (bodily) disorders. In this way, mental problems are treated as if they are nothing but physical and/or physiological problems.

(b) The *behavioristic model* looks for the causes of such disorders in the *perceptive* idionomy, and claims that feelings of fear and guilt can be attributed to conditioned responses to stimuli from the environment.

(c) The *psychoanalytical model* looks to the *sensitive* idionomy in its hunt for the causes of behavioral disorders; specifically, it looks for all sorts of (psychical) youthful conflicts and repressions.

(d) The *humanistic model* prefers to look for causes in the *spiritive* idionomy, and maintains that mental disorders arise when people are hindered in their search for self-actualization.

(e) In addition to all of these we have the *society-critical model,* which seeks the causes of behavioral disorders not so much within the person's *mental* idionomies but rather in the person's environment, or, to cast the net more widely, in society—for example, in factors such as oppression and poverty.

Of course, the *Christian-psychological model* finds traces of truth in each of these models. There are indeed some undeniable physical-biotic, perceptive, sensitive, spiritive, and social causes underlying most if not all mental disorders. However, it is precisely through a Christian view of Man that we can render an adequate account of this diversity of causes, and bring them together in meaningful coherence.

What is important above all is that we can take the human *heart* into consideration, along with its orientation toward or away from the living God. Therefore, when it comes to mental disorders, Christian psychology has room for certain concepts that scarcely play any role at all in non-Christian theorizing, such as responsibility, confession of sins, service, faith, hope, and love. We will come back to this matter in more detail later in this and in the following chapters.

The Medical Model

In this context, the *medical model,* which is so popular today, deserves our special attention. In fact, it is adhered to by both psychoanalysts and behaviorists, as well as by those therapists who have been inspired by their views. According to this model, the mentally disturbed person is *ill* (sick, unhealthy, insane), and therefore must be treated *medically.* Ever since this way of speaking has become established, people are comfortable with such terminology as *psychiatric illnesses* and *psychiatric patients.* They also talk about the *psychiatrist* and the *psychotherapist,* both of which terms mean literally "soul-healer" (from the Greek *iatros* and *therapeutèr,* "healer, physician").

All of this is really no more than common parlance today, even though it has become somewhat typical: when you have a mental disorder, you need "healing." Strictly speaking, however, we can only speak of a *medical model* when two things are being asserted:

(a) There are such things as distinct psychiatric *illnesses* or *diseases,* each of which has its own causes, symptoms, and course, just as we know them in somatic medicine (take the flu as a simple example).

(b) Because the patient is ill, he *therefore* bears no responsibility for his condition (just like someone having the flu can hardly be held responsible for this). The patient must not be preached at but must instead be *healed.*

As to the first point, however, the question is raised more and more frequently today whether such distinct *psychiatric illness-units* can really be said to exist. When it comes to mental disorders, it appears that *the same* causes can lead to very *different* disturbances, and also that the same disturbances can arise from very different causes, depending on the circumstances and the patient's personal characteristics . The situation is much more complicated than what we encounter in somatic medicine. In connection with mental disorders we must deal not only with viruses, bacteria, hereditary disorders, and so forth, but also with problems arising in marriage and family relationships, at work, in society, and in the church. People suffer because they have been hurt, disappointed, or frustrated, and they also suffer from grief and from all kinds of baggage acquired in their youth—too much or too little attention, parents who were either too strict or too lax, or who were constantly fighting, or got divorced, and so on.

"Mentally Ill"

Thus, when it comes to the question of whether or not specific mental illnesses exist, the medical model has gradually played itself out. But what about the second point, i.e. the responsibility of the patient (or the lack thereof)? Is it still possible to call someone "mentally ill" in a general sense? And does such a person have no responsibility whatsoever for his being in such a sick condition? We will have to be much more careful with the characterization "mentally ill" than the medical model in the past has often been.

For example, to begin with, we must not call the constitutionally disturbed person who is designated a *psychopath* "mentally ill," but at most "mentally handicapped." Such a person cannot be cured, for his disorder is anchored in his constitution; all we can do is try to teach him—which is what we attempt to do in Christian counseling—how he must *live* with his handicap as a Christian; in other words, how he may be able to "handle" it. To reach this goal, the psychopath has to be open to the possibility that he has a problem. Usually he is *not* open to this, which is one of the very characteristics of the psychopath.

Some of the psychopath's patterns of behavior happen to fit in poorly in the society of which he is a part, whereas in certain other societies he might not be conspicuous at all. However, there are other behaviors of the psychopath which go against *God's* norms, and that is a much more serious matter, which must be made clear to him in the course of counseling—as far as he is open to this.

In addition to the difference between ill and handicapped, there is a second distinction we must make between "*being* ill" and "*feeling* ill," or, to use more precise terminology, between being ill objectively and being ill subjectively. For example, a person could have a nasty tumor without being ill from it. That is to say, such a person might not feel miserable and might be able to live in a normal way—at least for a certain length of time—whereas someone else may feel very ill without the doctor being able to find a somatic cause. In such a case the doctor begins to look for the cause within the mental structures.

In addition to this, there is another distinction to be made, namely, between the psychopath and the *neurotic* person. In general, the psychopath does not feel miserable and is not wrapped up in himself, but only comes into collision with his surroundings. However, the neurotic person does feel miserable; he makes a problem of his nature and "suffers from his very being." The causes of his suffering might lie in one or more of his human structures, or quite directly in his heart. This is a matter for the counselor to find out, but he will have to begin by taking the subjective illness of the neurotic person seriously.

Some counselors are very much inclined to shy away from the concept of illness, because they make the same mistake as the advocates of the medical model; they think that if we call the neurotic person "ill," we *thereby* absolve him of responsibility for his situation. But this is not necessarily the case at all. Even when it comes to somatic illnesses, the person, no matter how ill he may be, is often himself responsible for his infection or for the ravages that his profligate lifestyle has produced in his body.

Three Reasons

There are at least three reasons why it makes sense to speak of mental illnesses. In the first place, some medical doctors have claimed that *all* illnesses of the body have (secondary) *mental* causes. Such claims have been made even for a genuinely infectious disease like tuberculosis, and also for cancer, which is a disease of considerable current interest. What I am saying is that, in exactly the same physical-biotic and social conditions, the one person may get tuberculosis or cancer, while the other does not, because of *mental* differences.

In the second place, it should be noted that all bodily diseases have at least some mental *after-effects*, such as disappointment, depression, fear, or anger. The biotic and mental aspects are interwoven to such an extent that it simply does not make sense to speak of biotic illnesses while at the same time throwing out the concept of mental illnesses. In any case, even though we may speak of illness, that fact does not relieve the person of all responsibility. People are often—although not always—responsible for both their physical and mental ailments, at least in part. This interconnectedness of the biotic and the mental, makes a rigid separation between medicine meant for the body on the one hand and psychotherapy or pastoral care on the other hand just as objectionable as a dichotomy between body and soul (or spirit). In a certain sense *all* the human structures—and especially the heart—are involved in *all* illnesses or disorders. And so there is nothing wrong with speaking of mental illness, as long as in doing so we are not taking away from human responsibility.

There is still a third reason why it makes sense to speak of mental illness, namely, illness in the sense of "not being able to cope with the situation." The psychopath is maladjusted, and the neurotic person has drifted into conflict situations. It is exactly the same way with bodily illness. Someone who is suffering from the flu cannot continue to walk around but has to stay in bed, and the heart patient cannot climb mountains anymore. There is always a relationship between two factors: the person's subjective tolerance level, or what he can manage, how much he can take (German: *Tragkraft*; Dutch: *draagkracht*, lit.: "strength to carry"), and the objective load or burden he has to carry, that is, how much he has to endure (German: *Traglast*; Dutch: *draaglast*, lit.: "burden to carry").

If we go back to our somatic example again, the heart of a heart patient has a lower tolerance level than the heart of a healthy person, which is why we say that the heart can take or stand less. The burden that such a person could carry is considerably smaller, and so he must refrain from mountain climbing and stay down in the valley. But if his tolerance level becomes higher again, that is, if his heart recovers, then he could once again carry a greater burden. This is the simple principle: make sure your burden never surpasses your strength, otherwise you will collapse.

It would appear that it is exactly the same way with mental problems. What we face in such cases is essentially the mental tolerance level on the one hand, i.e., what the person can mentally *handle*, and on the other hand the load or burden to be endured, i.e., what comes at him from the outside, such as the attacks of illness on his body (especially brain injuries), as well as the difficult situation around him. If someone is struggling with mental disorders, then, if the burden is too great for him to bear, there is not enough mental energy available to cope with his bodily illness and/or his circumstances. His tolerance level is too low, and/or his burden is too heavy, which amounts to the same thing: the person is unable, for the time being, to get the better of his problems. But as long as his tolerance level (that is, his physical and mental strength) surpasses the burden he must endure, everything goes smoothly.

Nevertheless, even people who have the highest possible tolerance level can get into a situation where the burden outweighs their physical and/or mental strength. In such a case, what is the person to do? He tries to compensate for his problems by building up certain *defense mechanisms*, as we shall see; he tries to increase his tolerance level in a forced and unnatural way. As a result, he becomes neurotic, but it is possible for him to hold out in this way for some time. If the situation gets still worse, however, he will eventually *break down*. He will collapse and become *psychotic* (in popular parlance, he will "go crazy" or "go insane"). When he is in such a situation, he will no longer be able to cope with even the lighter loads that he was able to handle before.

However, we see here at the same time—by way of anticipation of our subject—a clear hint of certain procedures to be followed in counseling. In such a situation, the aim of counseling (assuming it is at all possible) is to *raise the tolerance level*, physically, mentally, and spiritually, of the person involved, and/or to reduce the *biotic-mental and social burden* the person has to carry.

Forms of Mental Disorders

I will now offer a brief outline of the most important symptoms of mental disorders, starting again from the various human structures. Of course there are many symptoms that have to do with several human structures at the same time; therefore, at some points, our distinctions will seem somewhat artificial. Note carefully that in the case of the higher idionomies, the *lower ones are also involved*, but the opposite is not necessarily true: the symptoms of which we speak in connection with the lower human structures cannot always be directly related to the higher ones.

Here follows an outline of some important symptoms:

1. *Physical-biotic disorders*: We think here especially of various kinds of brain damage, or of hormonal disturbances and somatic diseases with important mental symptoms, such as diabetes.

2. *Perceptive disorders*: See especially also points 4 and 5, but at this point, we will speak only of motor disorders, because the (reflex) movements originate in the perceptive structure. Catatonia is the word we use to describe certain of these disorders, which are characterized by an excess of bizarre motions or even motionlessness, sometimes for hours or even days at a time.

3. *Sensitive disorders*: Here we think of:

(a) *Fright*: A vague, indeterminate anxiety, which can sometimes produce panic, without one's knowing just what it is that one is afraid of. This is accompanied by over-activity of the sympathetic nervous system, with palpitation of the heart, shortness of breath, sweating, dizziness, and nausea.

(b) *Depression*: Excessive dejection or despondency, often accompanied by self-accusation and a sense of inferiority; we call this a disorder if the depression is excessively deep and persists for a long time or continues to get worse.

(c) Here we can also mention *neurasthenia* (lit., "weak nerves"), that is, mental instability, irritability, or brooding.

4. *Cognitive disorders*: In this category I would include the following:

(a) *Bizarre thought-life*: Thoughts are often incoherent, strange, or rambling.

(b) *Partial amnesia*: The patient either forgets quickly certain things he has just recently observed or he can no longer recall events that happened long ago.

(c) *Dissociative disorders* such as *depersonalization*: This is loss of one's personality, which means that the patient sees himself more and more as a stranger; he loses his consciousness of self and becomes subject to *split* (or *multiple*) *personality disorder* (often confused with schizophrenia).

5. *Imaginative-creative disorders*: The patient imagines all sorts of things. For example, he may suffer from:

(a) *Phobia*: An unreasonable, crippling fear of something which is in fact harmless, such as a fear of certain animals (spiders, mice), of open or closed spaces, of crowds, of heights, of the dark.

(b) *Hysteria*: See chapter 5, under "Depth Psychology."

(c) *Hallucinations*: These may be experienced as visions or voices, without there being any sensory stimuli from the outside.

(d) *Delusions*: Persistent errors from which one cannot be dissuaded, for example:

(i) About *oneself*: Delusions of illness, delusions of self-condemnation, delusions of grandeur (a phenomenon which is sometimes called *megalomania*).

(ii) About *possessions*: Delusions of poverty or riches.

(iii) About *social relations*: The idea that your partner is disloyal or unfaithful to you, that all sorts of chance occurrences have a bearing on *you*, especially *paranoid* (morbid-suspicious) delusions, such as delusions of persecution.

(e) *Confabulations*: These fabrications, often in the case of amnesia, serve to fill a gap in memory; they are often quickly thought up and quickly forgotten, only to be replaced by others, and are not to be confused with delusions, to which such a person clings fanatically.

(6) *Conative disorders*: Here I must make special mention of:

(a) *Compulsive disorders*: The patient may feel impelled to:

(i) Think things he does not really *want* to think (compul sive thoughts or obsessions);

(ii) Do things he does not really *want* to do (compulsive actions); he repeats these actions endlessly and with pain ful precision, for example, washing his hands extremely thoroughly dozens of times per day;

(b) The *falling away of inhibitions*: This produces impulsive, violent motions and inappropriate utterances;

(c) *Sexual disorders*: Sexual gratification is sought by means of deviant activities, including such familiar examples as transvestitism, exhibitionism, masochism, sadism and pederasty.

(7) *The heart*: Here are included disturbances that affect the inmost depth of the personality, i.e., *existential* disorders. The person is frustrated about the meaning and purpose of life, and/or feels guilty because he has not realized all of his potential (depression), or he keeps trying compulsively to reach the "true" fulfillment of his life.

A number of the mental disturbances that are listed above used to be combined under the outdated term *neurosis*. It included symptoms such as fright, depression, neurasthenia, depersonalization, phobias, hysteria, compulsive disorders, as well as those in category 7, which was called an "existentialist [or, more properly, existential] neurosis."

Of course the list given above is extremely concise, but it still provides us, I believe, with an adequate summary of the variety of important symptoms, a summary that can be useful for the remainder of our discussion.

Mentally Disturbed Conditions

The symptoms that I have just listed are often found to be linked together. Accordingly, I will describe certain *conditions,* to be encountered in patients in whom we find a very distinct complex of symptoms occurring together.

It is important to distinguish here between more *permanent* conditions and more *temporary* ones. In the former case, we are talking about conditions that are probably inborn, or became embedded in the character at a very young age. We would then speak of personality disorders, and the persons affected are called *psychopaths,* or perhaps also *sociopaths.* These are people with a very difficult character. As a result they are constantly coming into conflict with their environment, hence the term "sociopath." They themselves may find this annoying, but they blame their environment rather than themselves.

There are many different possible kinds of psychopathic personalities, varying from excessively happy people to extremely brooding, cold, stand-offish, bizarre, compulsive, paranoid, or hysterical people. The psychopath, in a more restricted and more commonly used sense of the term, is the *anti-social* psychopath, i.e., the person without much of a conscience, without morals, without much of a feeling of responsibility or guilt. Sometimes such a person may seem to be a real "gentleman" or "lady," but in essence he or she will be an insensitive, unempathetic, aggressive figure who has never learned to consider the feelings of others, or to put up with disappointments, or to subject themselves to norms, or to postpone the fulfillment of their desires. Such a person easily becomes involved in criminal conduct.

In addition, as I indicated earlier, there are *temporary* conditions that, in the life of the person involved, have a definite history with specific causes. We can classify these conditions roughly to the extent that *biotic* and *mental* causes play a role in their genesis. We then come up with four categories:

1. *Biotic conditions*: Here, not only the direct cause but also the main symptoms are biotic; however, there are all sorts of important mental side-effects. (In a certain sense, of course, this can be said of all bodily sicknesses.) Here we might think of a concus-

sion of the brain, or brain injury, and meningitis, but there are also such illnesses elsewhere in the body, such as diabetes, as I have mentioned above.

2. *Biotic-mental conditions*: The direct cause is *always* biotic, and it is situated in the nervous system, but the symptoms are first of all of a mental nature. I am thinking here of all sorts of forms of "insanity" (professionals would use the term *psychoses*), but also of such conditions as cerebral hemorrhaging, inflammation of the brain tissue, and brain tumors.

3. *Mental-biotic conditions*: We usually call these conditions *psychosomatic*. Here we are concerned with all sorts of bodily disorders that have come about under the influence of the autonomic nervous system, and whose causes are first and foremost mental. Such conditions may exist, for example, when there is palpitation of the heart, high blood pressure, migraine headaches, stomach or intestinal ulcers, heartburn (stomach acidity), constipation, bronchial asthma, hiccups, itching, dermatitis, rheumatoid arthritis, pain in the lower back, muscle cramps, paralytic seizures, facial twitches, diabetes, obesity, bladder and menstrual problems, impotence, frigidity, or pain during sexual intercourse. Note that all of these ailments could be inborn, or they may well have purely somatic causes. Just what the cause really is in a concrete situation can only be established by the physician or medical specialist.

(4) *Mental conditions*: These are conditions in which biotic factors sometimes clearly play a role but in which the specifically biotic causes are not yet known, or not very clearly specified. Here I have in mind all sorts of conditions in which hallucinations, delusions and/or depression play a leading role, or certain neurotic conditions such as stuttering and the hyper syndrome, that is, being "hyper" (nervous debility or neurasthenia).

Chapter Eleven
CAUSES OF MENTAL DISORDERS

I have already pointed out that one and the same cause can bring on many mental disorders, and that one and the same mental disorder can have many different causes. Usually there are whole *complexes* of causes. Moreover, there is also the matter of *interaction* between external (situational) causes and the person's own *susceptibility* (personal factors). Earlier I spoke about the relationship between the (objective) weight of the burden to be carried and the person's (subjective) tolerance level (physical and mental strength). There are interactions between the person and his environment, but there are also interactions between the various human structures within the person. What is more, we must always bear in mind that *all* of these interactions occur under the guidance of the human *heart*, especially as far as the spiritive aspects are concerned.

Personal Factors

In previous chapters, I have made use several times of the formula

$$B = f\ (R, P, S),$$

that is, human behavior is a function of religious, personal, and situational factors. R (religious factors), P (personal factors), and S (situational factors), are grouped together, although we must always remember that they are not on the same footing: R has to do with *direction* (the directedness of the heart), whereas P and S have to do with *structure*. We could express this in the formula

$$B = f\ (D, St),$$

in which D stands for direction, and St for structure.

I will now take up the various factors in this order: P, S, and R. First of all, when we consider the *personal factors* (P), we must distinguish between inborn (= constitutional) and acquired factors. I will go through the various human structures one at a time.

In the first place, there are the *physical* and *biotic* factors. These always have to do with the brain, whether directly or indirectly. As for the *inborn* factors, we could include here hereditary disorders, brain injuries, and metabolism illnesses. When it comes to *acquired* factors, there are all sorts of brain injuries that could be mentioned. For certain metabolic disorders, we can point to hereditary factors (e.g., an inborn tendency toward diabetes) as well as acquired factors (e.g., obesity increases the likelihood of diabetes).

In the second place, there are (*perceptive* and) *sensitive* factors. The *inborn* factors in this case will frequently be related to the biotic, but it is not clear in each case just *how* they are related. I especially wish to discuss here our *temperament*, about which something was already said above in chapter 6. Each temperament has its weak sides, which can contribute to the emergence of mental problems; please remember for instance that the highest percentage of neurotic disorders occurs in the melancholic temperament. As for the *acquired* factors that a person develops *within himself*, I think especially of the *defense mechanisms* which people use in order to deal with their anxiety and fears. (Fear is always being afraid of something tangible, whereas anxiety is being afraid without anything specific that one is afraid of.)

Defense Mechanisms

Sigmund Freud maintained that the defense mechanisms to which I have just referred are always unconscious, but the truth is that we are often well aware (or at least half-conscious) of the fact that we are suppressing emotions, disguising them, explaining them away, or working them off on others, and so, in such situations, we (half-)intentionally deceive ourselves. In other words, we are more responsible for our defense mechanisms than psychoanalysts would be prepared to admit. Here again, what goes on in the mental idionomies cannot be severed from the *heart*. The principal defense mechanisms are:

(a) *Repression*: Here we have the pushing aside of unpleasant memories. It can be quite effective, but it is also quite morbid. Sometimes, for example, after wartime experiences, there is even a genuine loss of memory. Often the repression is so unsuccessful that the person affected winds up suffering from all kinds of irrational anxieties.

(b) *Rationalization*: This happens when a person thinks up a rational (intellectual) "explanation" during or after the event to make sense of a situation that otherwise would bring about anxiety or disappointment. What occurs is cognitive dissonance (see the discussion in chapter 8 above). If it becomes morbid, the person affected becomes more and more deeply entangled in a web of self-deception.

(c) *Reversal,* or turning something into its opposite: A person may camouflage emotions or motivations by exaggerated expressions of their very opposite. Exaggerated reaction against immorality *can* indicate the suppression of one's own sexuality (although this is not always necessarily the case), just as too much concern for someone can be a mask for hostility toward that person. Likewise, bravado can camouflage fear, and so forth.

(d) *Regression*: This occurs when a person relapses into an earlier (and often childish) form of life in order to cope with intimidating situations in an effort to obtain, for example, the sympathy of the people around them (e.g., by crying pitifully). Another form of regression is observed when people are imprisoned or held hostage, or are in some similar situation of helplessness, and begin to *identify* with their oppressors, just as little boys do with their stern fathers.

(e) *Projection*: This is the opposite of identification which I have just mentioned. Instead of transferring the admirable traits of the other onto oneself, one transfers one's own *undesirable* traits onto the other. Relevant here is Genesis 3:12-13, where Adam blames Eve for his eating of the forbidden fruit, and Eve in turn blames the serpent. Fear of failure leads one to cast the blame on another.

Fear of one's own aggressiveness leads one to pin that aggressiveness on the other. Fear of one's own sexual impulses leads one to attribute those impulses to others (cf. the description of rationalization above).

(f) *Transference*: Repressed or suppressed feelings are redirected toward another person where this is possible with a greater degree of safety. For example, you may be furious at your employer, but you hold your anger in and take it out on your wife. Or you work off your longing for children by showing great affection for a lapdog or a neighbor's child. Perhaps some phobias are actually fears that are transferred on some other, "safer" object than the original one.

In general, neurotic disorders could be regarded as exaggerated forms of defense mechanisms, by which a person suppresses his anxieties and fears and provides himself with a certain measure of security, but at the cost of a certain amount of freedom of movement. The man with a phobia *has* to flee, and the woman with a compulsion to wash her hands *has* to wash them. If the stress increases, the defense mechanisms need to be strengthened, and eventually the elastic is stretched too far. Then it snaps; we call this *decompensation*, a phenomenon in which the person affected breaks down under his anxieties and becomes psychotic ("insane"). In a certain sense, this psychosis is also a form of *defense*, but there is a very high price to be paid for it: the person affected loses his sense of reality and of his own personhood.

Spiritive Factors

In the third place, there are the *spiritive factors* that may cause certain mental disorders. The *inborn* factors here cannot be separated from the somatic factors or from one's temperament, both of which have been discussed above.

In connection with the *acquired* factors, in which case the *inborn predisposition*, as always, plays a large role, we can point to problems in all facets of our spiritive life. Note once again the order of the various spiritive aspects: problems revolve around:

(a) Difficulties with *thinking*; These include brooding over things and getting stuck in one's own reasoning (*logical* aspect).

(b) Difficulties with *authority*: There may be problems either with exercising it or with subjecting oneself to it (*formative* aspect).

(c) Difficulties with putting one's thoughts into *words* (for instance, stuttering), which causes insecurity (*lingual* aspect).

(d) Difficulties with developing or maintaining satisfactory social *relations* (*social* aspect).

(e) Difficulties with the discerning of *value* or the management of valuable possessions (*economic* aspect).

(f) Difficulties with the lack of *harmony* in one's life (living at less than one's best) (*aesthetic* aspect).

(g) Difficulties with accepting one's own life story (experiencing *remorse*) (*juridical* aspect).

(h) Difficulties with giving or accepting *love* (*ethical* aspect).

(i) Difficulties with establishing and maintaining fellowship with *God* (*pistical* aspect).

Situational Factors: Micro-Level

Mental problems that a person experiences in interaction with his surroundings can be distinguished in terms of three levels, which we might call (a) the micro-level, (b) the meso-level, and (c) the macro-level.

Let us look, first of all, at the *micro-level,* that is, the situation of the moment. In everyone's life, sudden and unexpected calamities may happen, severely testing one's level of mental tolerance. Such an ordeal creates stress. There are three special categories of factors that can cause stress:

(a) *Fear/anxiety,* whether a fear of something specific, or a vague, undefined feeling of anxiety (fright). Consider what I have said about this matter earlier in the discussion of defense mechanisms.

(b) *Frustration,* that is, (the feeling of) being obstructed in the effort to reach a particular goal. People may feel frustrated in all sorts of situations and may respond to them in any one of a number of different ways. For example:

(i) They become *restless* and *tense,* and begin to smoke, drink, or bite their nails.

(ii) They make fools of themselves by retreating into a *fantasy world* where they imagine they are still able to reach their goal (think of the pornographic pictures on the walls of the barracks of enlisted men).

(iii) They become *aggressive* toward the thing or the person causing the frustration, or perhaps even toward something that has nothing to do with the frustration (see above, for the discussion of transference). Thus, an entire community can work off its frustrations on selected targets, such as black people, or Jews, or migrant workers who have entered the country illegally.

(iv) They may become totally *apathetic*, hopeless, helpless, and depressed, so that they just cannot cope any longer.

(c) *Conflict*: for example, you have to make a very difficult choice between two things:

(i) You want both things very badly (for instance, you are in love with both Jill and Joan).

(ii) Your desire to *avoid* both things is equally strong (for instance, to take care of your aged mother or to leave that task to others and live with the resulting bad conscience).

(iii) Maybe you want something and do not want it at the same time (for example, you do *not* want to do what your parents tell you that you should do, but neither do you want to hurt your parents. The toddler badly wants to pet the big furry dog, but at the same time he is afraid of it).

These are some examples of conflict situations, which, under serious conditions, can bring on stress.

Situational Factors: Meso-Level

Second, there is the *meso-level*. Here I am thinking not only of *events* that bring on stress but also of the more or less permanent environment of which we form a part. We all know that the family in which we have been brought up has exerted a tremendous influence on us. Of course, the predisposition of the child, and the responsibility of the teenager and of the young adult also play a major role here. In addition there are factors to be noted in the upbringing itself that may serve to foster *or* hinder the child's normal development.

Just *what* those factors are is a question about which there has been much debate. In the twentieth century the pendulum has swung back and forth. For a time it was thought that love, warmth, pampering (with the elimination of punishment) was *the* remedy of choice for all the emotional problems in children. But then came a time in which all those things were considered fundamentally wrong. Instead, all that mattered was sternness, discipline, strict regularity, and firm consistency (Benjamin Spock). On the basis of Scripture we should have known all along that both of these points of view are wrong, even though many Christians have often not been aware of this. What really matters in the raising of children is the *balance* of love and warmth on the one hand, and consistent discipline on the other.

By the way, it is also true that many Christians have not been sufficiently aware of the difference between an *authoritative* parent, that is, one who exercises proper authority, and one who is *authoritarian* or domineering. The latter is a parent who proposes to "break" the child's will (what a horrible expression!), tries to bend the child to his will, or keeps the child feeling small and dependent, while forcing upon it all sorts of unexplained group norms. In contrast, the *authoritative* parent tries to guide the child's will and behavior, but does not avoid discussion with the child, does his best to explain and lovingly clarify what he has in mind in raising the child in a particular manner, tries to "understand" the child when it is being obstinate, respects the child's own will and ways and interests, but resolutely resists the child when it is disobedient, using both arguments and force, while requiring the child to co-operate in a disciplined way.

Research shows that authoritarian parents produce much more aggressive children than authoritative parents. Curiously enough, authoritarian parents are much more like very indulgent (permissive) parents in the way they bring up their children than they realize or would wish to admit! Even psychopathic, neurotic, and psychotic disorders can be brought on by the wrong kind of upbringing, that is, either too authoritarian or too permissive.

In addition to the influence of parents, the birth order of the children also plays a role in the parental home. In terms of what happens in the development of the child, it sometimes makes a big difference whether it is an only child, the oldest, the second, the middle, or the youngest child. Each of these positions in the family has its advantages as well as its disadvantages, which, especially if accompanied by an unfavorable predisposition, can have a significant adverse effect on the child's development.

Even the meso-environment of the adult still continues to exercise a favorable or unfavorable effect upon him. A great many problems arise within the marriage relationship, whether because of poor sexual adjustment or because the partners devote too little time and attention to one another, or because they lead separate lives, have conflicting interests and goals, argue too much, and/or do not know enough about each other or themselves. And then there is the possibility of infidelity. Very difficult children could also be a problem for the parents themselves and undermine the marriage.

Of course, in addition there are legions of labor problems, especially when the economic situation is bad. I am thinking here of unemployment, not enjoying one's work, conflicts with one's employer or employees, carrying heavy or burdensome responsibilities, long working hours, serious failures in one's work. It is clear that, if a person has a particularly unfavorable predisposition, worries of these kinds can lead to serious mental problems.

Last but not least, many Christians suffer from problems in their church: dissension, envy, jealousy, power conflicts, quarrels between leadership and members, or between the members themselves, creation of factions, and sometimes even division. In the latter case, many Christians do not even wish to choose sides. They *flee* as it were from the battle-ground, just to protect themselves from all kinds of anxiety, stress, distress, depression, etc.

Situational Factors: Macro-Level

Third, there is the *macro-level,* that is, present-day Western society, of which we are all a part. Society, too, leads to all sorts of frustrations: traffic congestion, long waiting periods, not enough money for popular luxury articles, social failure in a highly competitive economic world, and the experience of meaninglessness, of alienation. Thus, there are countless factors in our society that tend to make certain people neurotic.

We may be members of a number of different kinds of groups that no longer have any connection with one another. Modern mobility made possible by the automobile, train, and airplane exposes us to all sorts of superficial contacts, which only increase our solitariness and loneliness. At the same time, we often miss the sense of security we used to get from our circle of friends, our street, our neighborhood, and our church. Even the family is no longer a stronghold of safety and security: the various members of the family have too many divergent interests, no longer undertake much work together, are too independent, and are away from home too much because of increased prosperity. Moreover, parents have little authority anymore. This problem of authority gnaws away at *many* social structures.

In our modern society it is much more difficult to attain adulthood than it once was. Dutch psychiatrist Jan Hendrik van den Berg (1914-2012) guessed that modern young people reached adulthood between the ages of thirty and thirty-five. Adult life has become very complicated. Moreover, many important aspects of adult life have become invisible to the children. Nowadays the father's work is usually done away from home. People are no longer sick at home or die at home, nor are babies born at home; all these things occur in the hospital. Moreover, death is not talked about anymore; the funeral is put into the hands of strangers, and the modern burial place is camouflaged. As a consequence, modern Man can easily react neurotically to death when it does suddenly show itself.

Moreover, society is utterly hard and pitiless; advertising is aggressive. In a world that boasts of freedom, employers are unyielding. Anyone who does not fit in or is different from others cannot survive. Wherever you look today, society is intimidating. People have far too much contact with far too many other people, with the result that they often become afraid, suspicious, and dependent, not to mention immature. Our prosperity has made all of these things worse rather than better, for it has made the individual too independent and self-reliant. Often he cannot stand it, and it makes him fearful and utterly lonely.

Religious Factors

Fears, feelings of guilt, depression, psychosomatic disorders, thoughts of self-condemnation, loss of inhibitions, and confusion—all of these can be the consequences of purely personal factors. But it would be a major error *always* to trace them back to these, for they may also have to do with a person's *relationship to God.* In this case, a feeling of guilt may be caused by real concrete guilt. Self-condemnation is no illusion but is genuine and justified. The fears and depressions such a person experiences are real, for they may be based on a consciousness of future divine judgment.

Many biblicistic Christians make the serious mistake of thinking that *all* mental problems are due to sin, or a weak relationship with God. As I have said before, in this way they aggravate people's problems by causing them to develop unwarranted feelings of guilt. However, other Christians commit the opposite error: they think that mental problems *never* have anything to do with sin or a weak relationship with God. Under the influence of the medical model, they can only think of illnesses, for which the patients allegedly can never be held responsible. Nothing could be further from the truth. In Christian forms of counseling, the matter of sin has to be brought up. Although it does not happen in every instance, a life of sin can cause both somatic and mental diseases (read carefully Ps. 32:3-5; Matt. 9:2; John 5:14 in context). Therefore, when elders have to deal with illness in the church, they must always find out whether sin is perhaps playing a role (which is not necessarily the case) (James 5:14-16; cf. Matt. 9:1-2; John 5:14).

Of course we are very well aware of the fact that there are all sorts of religious delusions. And we also realize that personal and religious factors—or, to put it another way, *structure* and *direction*—are sometimes closely intermingled. The evangelist or pastor has to be aware of the fact that genuine guilt, for example, may be mixed together with false guilt feelings. That is, the guilt feelings may enormously surpass the seriousness of the committed sin(s). Nevertheless, guilt feelings as such must always be taken seriously because they may, and often do, point to concrete guilt. If we try to alleviate the guilt feelings without any confession of the guilt involved, we do the patient no good.

This is why it is so unfortunate that so many Christian psychotherapists today have been educated at secular universities only. As a consequence, they know how to deal with the guilt feelings, but not with the guilt (or they leave this to the pastor, a procedure which sometimes is very confusing for the client, and thus quite irresponsible). I have met several clients who were very afraid of having "sinned against the Holy Spirit" (cf. Matt. 12:31-32), and who told me that even their *Christian* psychotherapists were not able to explain this problem to them.

Three Errors

Some (not all) clients need precisely this: to be helped in their relationship with God. It is unlikely that this is their only problem; they may exhibit all kinds of mental disorders. Again, *structure* and *direction* have to be carefully distinguished here. But in many cases their main problem lies in their relationship with God. At least, this is what the clients themselves believe, a fact which has to be taken seriously.

In this connection, I wish to point out three mistakes that we may encounter. (I have mentioned them already in passing, but I will here bring this material together):

1. *Secular* psychotherapists often—although not always—try to break down the Christian client's relationship with God, because they believe (as a consequence of their own prejudices) that his "neurotic religiosity" is the actual problem. Of course, this can only make matters worse for a believing client.

2. *Christian* psychotherapists often (although not always) focus only on the mental disorders for which they have been trained at university, and belittle or ignore what they call "theological" problems because they have not been trained to handle them; at best they leave them to the pastor.

3. Other Christians, usually pastors and counselors who are not trained psychotherapists, make the opposite mistake. They focus only on the "theological" aspects by reducing the client's mental disorders entirely to faith problems. They belittle or ignore the client's mental problems because they have not been trained to handle them; in cases where somatic problems are involved, they leave these to the physician.

We have to realize that by far *most* Christian patients, or clients, or whatever you call them, fall into the hands of one of these three kinds of help providers. *None* of these three groups knows how to distinguish between *structure* and *direction*. This means that in all three cases, if the psychotherapist or counselor is able to offer the client any help at all, it is limited. This does not prevent these three groups of counselors from boasting about many cases of spectacular healing. In the remainder of this chapter and in the next chapter, we will see why this is the case.

Especially to counselors in the first two groups, I would like to say that if the client's basic problem is not mental disorders but specific guilt, he does not need any treatment for his guilt *feelings*. What he needs is the gospel (good news) of Jesus Christ, who, as our substitute, took upon himself the judgment for the sins of all those who believe in him. It is by faith, and by faith alone, that such a person can be delivered from his fear and guilt. Moreover, there may even be some occult influences in the picture, in which case the person will need some specific spiritual care (I leave this matter aside here).

To the third group of counselors I would like to say that if the client's problems also involve sensitive and spiritive as well as social factors, the person will need in addition some broader assistance (professional psychotherapy, perhaps medication). Many biblicistic counselors are guilty of neglecting the somatic and mental aspects of their clients' problems, thus aggravating their condition.

In summary, it is difficult to say whether it is worse for Christian clients to fall into the hands of the first, second, or third group. Perhaps after all, the second group is the least damaging, as long as it works closely with pastors and counselors.

Mental Therapies

Now that we have briefly discussed the symptoms and causes of mental disorders, we can undertake a discussion of the therapies, the modes of treatment. This will not be an easy matter to discuss, for there are literally hundreds of different kinds of psychotherapy, all of which differ from one another to some degree, although the actual differences are often slight. Let us try once again to get an overview by starting from the various human structures.

Here follows an outline of important therapies:

1. *Physical-biotic therapies*: Without going into this matter very extensively, I will mention psychosurgery (removal of healthy brain tissue to modify a patient's behavior), electric shock treatment (application of electric shocks, perhaps to bring someone out of a depression) and psychopharmacotherapy, with its many narcotics (sleeping pills), tranquilizers, and anti-psychotic and anti-depressive medicines. In some situations, such as a crisis, biotic therapies can be very helpful, but they are not aimed at the purely mental sides of the problem. Moreover, they often have very adverse side-effects.

2. *Perceptive therapies*: These are the behaviorist therapies that acknowledge hardly anything other than unconditioned or conditioned reflexes. Behavioral disorders are then seen as wrongly acquired reflexes, which can be unlearned in therapy, while new behavioral patterns can be acquired by conditioning.

3. *Sensitive therapies*: These are the psychoanalytical therapies, which look for the causes of all conflicts in a person's *unconscious. Mental illnesses* arise when people can no longer live with the conflicts that have built up inside themselves, often from early youth.

4. *Spiritive therapies*: These are the therapies that place more emphasis on cognitive processes (*cognitive therapies*), or on free self-actualization on the part of the client (*humanistic therapies*), or which may even involve all sorts of (Eastern) mystical methods and techniques such as transcendental meditation, yoga, and the like (*mystical-transcendent therapies*).

Of course, there are countless mixes between these various categories of therapy. One such mixed form is group therapy, of which there are again a great many forms and varieties.

Do Psychotherapies *Help*?

For decades there has been conflict over the question whether all these different psychotherapies really *help*. Can they indeed solve mental problems? Are they able to offer a lasting improvement? And which of them work best? Or could it be that they are equally good—or equally bad? Besides, who is qualified to determine what is good and what is bad? All of these questions are very important for the psychotherapists, for the patients, and for the system that pays for the treatment.

The discussion of these questions began when some psychologists back in the 1950s claimed that people recovered *spontaneously* just as readily as they did from psychotherapy. In other words, when it comes to the question whether or not to receive treatment, it is six of one and half a dozen of the other? Since that time, research into the effectiveness of psychotherapies has been undertaken on a large scale, and it can be said that the results up to this point are quite curious.

Let us agree first of all (for the time being!) on what we understand by "improvement." What I mean by it is a lessening of fear and anxiety, of psychosomatic disorders, of addiction, of psychopathic behavior, and of stress—or, to put it in more positive terms, improvement in one's sense of dignity, improvement of one's adjustment to circumstances, of one's personality characteristics, of social behavior, and of performance at work or school.

If we define "improvement" in this way, it appears today that, in any case, *psychotherapy is more effective than no therapy.* Moreover, the positive effect of psychotherapy is quite substantial, almost comparable to that of school instruction or of medicine. But just as surprising is a second conclusion: *the one therapy is hardly more effective than the other.* Whether you are looking at a given therapy's theoretical background or its technical approach, it does not appear to make all that much difference.

Now, this does not mean that it makes no difference whatsoever what psychotherapists do with their clients. That it does indeed make some difference is evident from a comparison of serious therapies on the one hand with ordinary recreational training, or group discussions, or informal gatherings and so forth, on the other. *Placebo* treatments clearly also have a therapeutic effect when compared with no treatment at all. But it became evident that a serious psychotherapeutic treatment was twice as effective as a placebo treatment. Thus, on the one hand it appears as though anything one might do for a patient will help, but on the other hand concrete, systematic treatment is much more helpful yet.

Still, strange as it may seem, it does not matter very much what kind of treatment it is. Whether it be talk-therapy or action-therapy, individual or group therapy, long or short therapy, or therapy administered by a person with a lot of experience or none at all, it all makes only limited difference. The only thing that really matters is for the therapist to employ a concrete, well-defined treatment.

How are we to explain these startling conclusions? It would appear that there is no other conclusion to be drawn than this: in placebo treatments, to a certain extent, and in serious psychotherapies, to a much larger extent, certain elements known as *curative factors* are present; *all* psychotherapies have these in common, no matter how much they may differ from one another in theoretical starting points or methodology. It seems that what really matters is not the things in which the various therapies differ, but the ones they *agree on*. These are the factors of which the therapists themselves are often not very aware, since they are inclined to put much more emphasis on the aspects in which *their* approach differs from the approach used by competing psychotherapists. Yet those points of difference appear to be the very things that make no difference to the effectiveness of the treatment.

The really beneficial factors that are present in good measure in psychotherapies are also found in everyday life. That is why so many people recover *spontaneously*, which means, in fact, that they recover either because of stimulating changes in their surroundings, or because they become more mature, or because they get help from pastors, physicians, friends, relatives, and so forth.

Hence it appears that psychotherapy can be understood as a kind of "process of social influence," which does not differ all that much from other processes that might be mentioned, such as upbringing, schooling, hygiene, and the aid of friends. However, in psychotherapy, the social influencing that takes place is more directed, and more systematic than in ordinary life. Now, exactly *what* those very important beneficial factors are is a matter about which a productive discussion sprang up in the 1970s. But before we enter comment on that discussion, I want to say something in the following chapter about where the Christian psychologist stands with regard to all these matters.

Chapter Twelve
THE CHRISTIAN AND PSYCHOTHERAPY

We have seen, on the one hand, that the theoretical starting points of the various psychotherapies do not make all that much difference in terms of their effectiveness, but on the other hand, that the Christian who undergoes psychotherapeutic treatment can be sure that he will often come into contact with the worldviews and ideologies underlying them. He might well form the impression that they *are* very important, and as a result, they could become harmful to him after all.

Therefore, it is a good thing to bear in mind that all the secular psychotherapies we have mentioned fail to appreciate that the *heart*, or Man's relationship to God (or, the gods), directs all the mental idionomies. In other words, they fail to recognize the deepest cause of all mental problems, for that cause lies in the heart, that is, in the relationship of the person to God (or to idols). This is directly related to another important matter: secular psychotherapies—as well as many "Christian" sorts of treatment, for that matter—do not distinguish between *structure* and *direction*.

Secular and Christian Therapy

One implication of this realization is that those secular therapies *as such* are, in principle, unusable in Christian counseling. It makes no difference whether we are speaking of perceptive, sensitive, or spiritive therapies, of structure or direction. In other words, every one of them fails to appreciate the true nature of Man as we know it from God's Word-revelation, and *therefore* misconceives the nature of his problems. To get an impression of the views that underlie psychoanalysis, behaviorism, and humanistic and existentialist psychology, in particular, one need only read again the relevant sections in chapter 5.

Christian counseling must take a course that is fundamentally different. Of course, it is aware of the *mental* causes of some *somatic* ailments and is also aware of the somatic causes of some *mental* disorders. Likewise, it is acquainted with situations and occurrences that are almost too much to bear mentally. But it also takes into account that more is going on. The simple reason for this is that what is truly human in Man is not the sensitive or even the spiritive. Secular psychotherapy is convinced that it can grasp the *whole* person in its concepts and frameworks, and that it can scientifically analyze Man's essential nature. In a similar fashion, it considers itself able to "cure" the person who is "mentally ill." But it fails to realize that all *immanent* aspects and idionomies of Man find their unity in his *transcendent heart*.

This heart is *not* susceptible to scientific analysis. The knowledge that the Christian psychologist possesses of the heart, like his knowledge of anything else that is transcendent, is not derived from secular science but from a Christian anthropology, that as such is rooted in a biblical worldview. Hence counseling, properly so called, is not *scientific* in nature, but should be regarded as a Scriptural *conversation from heart to heart* within the framework of *Christian social living* on the part of two persons, the counselor and the counselee, in their personal and communal relationship to God.

This is not to say that Christian psychologists could never learn anything from secular psychotherapies. On the contrary, if secular therapists are capable of bringing about the kinds of improvements—albeit limited ones—described earlier, we have every reason to be pleased. To put it even more strongly, neglecting the many useful insights of secular psychotherapy is only detrimental to the client (whether or not he or she is a believer). Christian psychotherapy does not have to re-invent fire and the wheel. After all, it is connected to the entire development of psychology and psychiatry during the last two centuries. However, I repeat that the insights which are the most fundamental with respect to Man, and which therefore have the most value for psychotherapy, are not derived from secular science, but from a Christian anthropology which is based upon God's revelation.

Thus, although we may be *pleased* with important secular insights, for the Christian counselor these can never be sufficient. He can never be satisfied with relieving people of stress, phobias, or addictions, or with rehabilitating them for society again if he does not also try to touch their hearts in the process. To a certain extent, people are responsible for getting into stressful situations, for becoming addicted, or for part of their psychopathic behavior, and so forth, no matter how many extenuating circumstances might be brought forward on the basis of factors such as their constitution, organic disorders from which they suffer, a difficult environment, bad upbringing, or a corrupt society. People are always responsible to their fellow human beings, and above all to God. They are neither physical-biotic machines to be repaired, nor robots, nor puppets, but images of God.

In Christian counseling, people must be made aware of the responsibility they bear. It is precisely when they are living in fear and stress that they are more open to hearing the gospel message, and therefore also to finding the supreme path to restoration. It is true that a Christian social worker and a Christian physician or psychotherapist cannot spend all their time evangelizing; in fact, when they are working in a secular environment, they are not even *allowed* to evangelize. Yet, the closer the person's problems are to his heart—as is the case with so many mental problems—the more important it is that the counseling he is offered be truly *evangelical* in the broad sense of the term (without any reference to any denomination whatsoever).

Again, the Curative Factors

In this discussion about psychotherapies, it is very important to point out that the Christian counselor can consider the application of secular psychotherapies that appear to be helpful, *not* because of the worldview in which they are rooted or because of their methodologies, but because of certain *curative factors*. For a long time, the proponents of these therapies usually had little awareness of these factors. Nowadays, we are not only aware of these factors, but we are also gladly making use of them in whatever therapies we are using.

It is important to understand that not a single psychoanalyst or behaviorist (or, for that matter, a theorist of any particular type) can ever claim that *his* therapy is better *because* it is psychoanalytical, or behaviorist, or whatever. The theoretical orientation of a therapy appears to have hardly anything to do with its success. Therefore no one can maintain that Christian counseling would be less effective than secular counseling. If the goal is indeed to get rid of abnormal behavior or to bring about a readjustment to society, then it is clear that the *same* curative factors play a role in Christian counseling as in secular psychotherapies. We shall soon see that these curative factors have been available for many centuries in the Bible. If it is true that secular therapies do achieve a certain measure of (outward) success, it is because, as it turns out, they are employing nothing other than age-old biblical wisdom, though often in garbled form.

Thus, if what we are seeking is the person's outward improvement, Christian counseling is of at least as much value as the secular therapies. But in fact we believe it is superior. This is in the first place because it employs the curative factors in a pure way by making direct use of biblical wisdom in this area. In the second place, Christian counseling treats the *whole* person, both the various human structures, and also the heart, in which these idionomies find their unity. In his heart, Man is in either a good or a bad relationship with God, or in a relationship with idols. Whatever one might say of the Bible, one would at least have to grant that it is a book that claims to teach how people should live. Christian counseling differs from other therapies in that it takes the superior, divine wisdom of this book seriously, precisely when the thing that really matters is to teach troubled people how to start living differently and better, according to God's intentions for their lives.

Provided they use the Bible properly, People of the Book make the best counselors, whether they are professionals or not. As a matter of fact, even non-Christian psychologists now know that professional therapists on the whole are not very much more effective than non-professionals are. In principle, most spiritive stress and most behavioral problems could be resolved by any wise and spiritually minded church member. But what we find all too often is that many Christians are quick to run to a psychotherapist or a psychiatrist—even a non-Christian one.

It reminds me of the words of the Apostle Paul; I take the liberty of varying them a little: "When one of you has a mental problem, does he dare go to a secular shrink instead of the saints? Or do you not realize that the saints will judge the world? And if the world is to be judged by you, are you incompetent to solve mental problems? Do you not know that we are to judge angels? How much more, then, matters pertaining to this life! So if you have such cases, why do you lay them before those who have no standing in the church? I say this to your shame. Can it be that there is no one among you wise enough to solve the mental problems of the brothers and sisters, instead of them going to shrinks, and that to unbelievers?" (cf. 1 Cor. 6:1-6).

I make one important exception here. In certain serious cases, medication is absolutely necessary as a kind of "first aid." As we know, medication can only be prescribed by psychiatrists and other physicians. But even then, when a specialist is called on for help, pastoral help is *never* rendered superfluous. A physician addresses himself to the possible physical-biotic basis of the problem, whereas a psychologist who may be called in addresses himself to the mental aspects of the problem. But the person who provides pastoral care will address himself to the innermost depth, the I (Ego), the heart, the personality. Of course, the very best thing would be for the "specialist" himself to be pastorally equipped, but it is also possible—although not ideal—for him to work closely with a pastoral counselor.

Pastoral Care and Psychology

There has been a good deal of discussion about the proper relationship between psychology and pastoral care. Let us now distinguish four models drawn up by Christians:

1. The *dualistic model* limits pastoral care to problems of faith, and leaves all mental problems to the (secular) psychotherapist. This standpoint is very popular among Christians who are psychologists, especially because many of them work at so-called neutral institutions, where no other position would even be permitted. Yet this pragmatic view can easily be refuted. We simply *cannot* divorce problems of faith from mental problems. A person's biotic and mental disorders should never be considered as detached

from his heart's relationship to God. This observation applies not just to the person seeking help, the client, but also to the counselor, who, as a Christian, may *never* be content with giving *neutral* advice. Biotic and mental disorders influence his spiritual life, and disturbances in his spiritual life in turn affect his biotic and mental functioning. How could these things be treated separately?

2. The *biblicist model* limits psychology to physiological problems at most, since in this area, where medication can be effective, no harm can be done. It assigns the whole area of faith and mental problems to the pastor or to a counselor who does not have psychological training. But here we also encounter an objectionable separation, namely, between physical-biotic disorders on the one hand, and mental problems on the other, or—to put it in the traditional terminology that is usually also preferred by biblicists—between *body and soul*. Here, too, we see a failure to appreciate the unity of the person, for somatic ailments *always* have spiritual (and thus pastoral) aspects, and mental or spiritual problems in fact *always* have roots in the physical and biotic idionomies.

3. The *integrationist model* at least recognizes the objectionable divisions made by the previous two models. But often it does not seem to recognize with sufficient clarity the status of secular psychology. Thus, it will not do to try to integrate or blend supposedly "neutral" psychology with biblical ideas, for current psychology is simply not neutral (cf. chapter 1). In its roots it is even anti-biblical. What we want, and need, is not a blending of anti-biblical psychology with biblical ideas, but a psychology that is itself faithful to the Bible, one which, from the ground up, is constructed on a Christian anthropology and a Christian philosophy of sickness and healing.

4. The model I am advocating here tries to follow a *different route*. It does not pit Christian counseling against secular psychology; it does not subject either one of them to the other, but distinguishes between the two. It screens and critically assesses secular psychology and takes over what is useful in it, while at the same time transforming it. All of this is *possible* because this model has a radically Christian anthropology available to it, based on a Christian-philosophical view of reality and knowledge (I refer the reader once again to my *Wisdom for Thinkers*). Such a Chris-

tian anthropology and the resulting psychology can function as a "sieve" to catch and sift many good elements out of the porridge of secular psychology. This radically Christian psychology aims to be both thoroughly scientific and thoroughly pastoral.

The Good Therapist

This book is intended to be a popular psychological introduction to the topic—not a practical manual for counselors. Nevertheless, when something as practical as counseling is discussed, practical questions will unavoidably arise. One such question is this: What are the requirements that must be met by a good (Christian) counselor?

First of all, the counselor has to be called to his task by the Holy Spirit (compare Acts 20:28). Second, he or she must be completely devoted to the service of the client, in utter obedience to the Lord and his Word. He must have an aptitude for applying that Word in the counseling he offers (cf. the example I gave earlier about the "sin against the Holy Spirit"). He must have a practical wisdom and knowledge of life, a warm heart for those in need of help, a great amount of empathy, a self-effacing disposition, a living faith, and a cheerful heart. He must live an exemplary life, have an exemplary family, a good reputation with non-believers, and a deep sense of the responsibility that accompanies being a leader and of the account that he must render to God (cf. the elders in 1 Tim. 3:1-7; Titus 1:5-9; 1 Pet. 5:1-5).

Actually, this list of qualities—including even the very first point—should be applicable to *all* more mature Christians. *Every* believer who meets these requirements will come into contact with counselees—in fact he or she will not even be able to avoid people that need help (Rom. 15:14; Gal. 6:1; Col. 3:16). However, among the believers there will be some who have special gifts and a special calling for the work of counseling.

Before prospective counselors conclude that they require lengthy training for their work, they should be reminded again that trained, professional therapists do not appear to have a great deal more success than inexperienced "amateurs" who are warm, sympathetic, mature, and willing to listen. Our churches should be full of such Christian amateurs. However, this is not to say that such "amateurs" could not profit tremendously from knowledge of Christian psychology, that is, knowledge based on biblical revelation and enriched with the critical, systematic findings of the acute Christian observer. Here are a couple of examples that have already been touched on in this book. It is useful to know something about:

(a) The possible somatic causes of mental problems (so that, if necessary, the client may be sent in time to the physician).

(b) The theory of temperaments (especially the relationship between temperament and character, in relation to the work of the Holy Spirit).

(c) The ongoing influence of unconscious feelings and reflexes (often learned in the client's youth), and the tactical approach to them.

(d) The nature of fallacies (sophisms) with which people deceive themselves, and how to expose them.

(e) The difference between sensitive (impulsive) and spiritive (conscious-normative) motivation.

(f) The influence of (false) attributions.

(g) The relationship between needs, desires, and values.

(h) Cognitive dissonance.

(i) Aggression.

(j) The relationship between conformism and a person's own responsibility.

(j) Extrinsic and intrinsic religiosity.

The Ground Plan for Counseling

From what has been discussed up to this point, a number of guidelines for Christian counseling follow almost automatically. The first rule for counseling is that the counselor must constantly guard against *too* quickly indicating a *single* cause as the *only* explanation for a particular problem. In reality, what he is facing is an enormous *interaction* of biotic, mental, and situational factors. Therefore, the counselor must always ask himself these questions:

1. What *biotic* (somatic) factors could be playing a role here? As I said, if the counselor suspects the presence of somatic factors,

he must send his client on to a physician (unless he is a physician himself).

2. What *stress*-causing factors are present in the client's micro- and/or meso-environment (for example, marriage, family, work, or church), factors that might lead to fright, frustration, and/or conflicts? Here *social* help must be made available; if possible, the social situation must be made more bearable.

3. What kind of *temperament* and *character structure* does the client have? What (exaggerated) *defense mechanisms* and what *fallacies* (sophisms) has he developed? How does he feel about his *past,* and especially about his *parents*? How does *society* (the macro-environment) and its social structure contribute to his problems? Here *mental* assistance must be provided, that is to say, *instruction* is particularly needful.

4. What *religious* factors are playing a role in the situation? Here the *gospel* must be presented to unbelievers, and *pastoral* help needs to be offered to believers.

Of course, these four points are thoroughly interwoven with one another in practice. We must also remember that they can be broken down into two elements:

(a) *The burden to be borne,* consisting of *biotic* factors (especially acquired brain injuries) and *social* factors. The counselor must try to *reduce* this burden (and this is especially where the physician and the social worker come into the picture).

(b) *The tolerance level* (strength), which consists of *biotic* factors (bodily constitution and the condition at the moment), *mental* factors (see point 3 above) and *religious* factors. The counselor must try to *increase* this tolerance level (and this is especially where the physician, the psychotherapist and the pastor/evangelist can be helpful).

Of course too much professional dispersion of effort does not work in the client's favor. It may instead lead to rivalry between specialists, or to an erroneous separation between somatic (physical-biotic) problems and mental-spiritive problems, *or* between physical-mental problems and spiritive problems. Because such professional dispersion of efforts does take place, the client is often forced to turn to two, or even three, counselors. All of this could be avoided, of course, if more *unity* in the provision of help were provided, as follows:

(a) Broader *instruction* of counselors, so that the various specialists will have more knowledge of one another's fields.

(bBetter *cooperation* among the counselors, by forming *teams* of physicians, pastors, and, if possible, social workers and psychotherapists, all of whom should be Christians. These teams should engage in intense communication with one another and, whenever possible, should work together in the same building, a center for providing counseling and assistance.

The Atmosphere for Counseling

Earlier we saw that psychotherapies seem to work because they start—often unconsciously—from a number of curative factors which they all have in common. These factors can actually be traced back to ancient biblical wisdom, and therefore are put into practice in their entirety and in the biblical way only in Christian counseling. I will now deal briefly with these curative factors, which includes the proper atmosphere for counseling.

The first thing that is necessary is an intense, confidential, *helping relationship*, which is something like the relationship between parent and child. If the counselor is to have such a relationship, he must radiate a certain authority. The client must be assured of privacy, and be confident that the counselor has only his wellbeing in mind. The counselor listens to him with never-flagging attention and with empathy, making a constant effort to understand what the client is trying to say. Of course, in Christian counseling this special relationship is based on the *divine* love that is bestowed on the counselor by the Holy Spirit (Rom. 5:5). Because of this love *and* the involvement of the Holy Spirit, there is a real spiritual unity and communion in prayer between the counselor and the client, provided that both are Christians (Eph. 4:3; James 5:14-16). If the client is not a Christian, it means there must be a deep neighborly love on the part of the counselor (cf. Rom. 12:7-8; Gal. 6:10).

The second thing that is needed is what secular psychologists call a *theoretical framework*. The counselor must work with a theory, which, according to secular psychologists, in reality is a myth. That it is a myth, or that it has such and such contents, does not really matter, just so long as the counselor and the client *both* believe in it. The myth will then clear up the client's problems and point to a possible solution, so that what the counselor and client are doing is given meaning. What a difference there is between such an approach on the one hand, and what the Christian counselor does on the other hand! The Christian counselor starts with Scripture—not with a human theory, even less with a myth, but with the inspired and infallible Word of the living God.

The Bible does not give us a concrete, explicit and specific answer to any and every practical, pastoral question, but it does give us an infallible framework, which, at least on a general level, offers an explanation for a life lived according to God's thoughts—the kind of life that is best suited for the client's well-being.

A third element—and it is extremely important—is *arousing hope*. The client, by "going into therapy," becomes motivated. He believes in the possibilities of counseling and begins to expect help from the counselor, especially if the latter is an expert with a high reputation. These expectations on the part of the client can already contribute to his recovery; thus, in themselves, they constitute a curative factor. In this context it must be understood that when Christian counseling takes place, the counselor points away from himself and his methods in order to direct his client's heart to God. The client may have great expectations of his counselor, but at the same time he must see that his counselor, too, is only a human being with limited insight and limited capabilities. Yet the counselor points to a perfect Book and an almighty God who, by his Spirit, can bring about a total renewal of life. It is hope in God and in his promises, and in the operation of his Spirit (which far exceeds human help), that serves as the "starter motor" that is able to get Christian counseling under way (cf. Lam. 3:24-26; Ps. 42:5, 11; 43:5).

Special Counseling Procedures (1)

Psychotherapists have engaged in heavy debates about *catharsis*, as it is usually called, by which we mean the venting of intense, pent-up emotions, a process that is also called *abreaction*. One psycholo-gist will argue that this reliving of earlier emotions in an emotional way is very important, whereas another will maintain that a strict-ly intellectual approach to one's emotions should be taken.

This longstanding conflict between feeling and understanding can only be overcome within a viewpoint that leads both understanding and feeling back to the *heart*, by which ultimately both are governed. The mere venting of feelings provides in itself no solution. After all, the human heart is an inexhaustible fountainhead of sinful (sensitive) feelings *and* (spiritive) thoughts. This faucet must not be turned on unless there is a very good reason to do so. The Bible clearly warns against carelessness in this area (see Eph. 4:26, 29, 31). When it comes to these matters, everything depends on having an understanding counselor so that, under his intelligent guidance, the emotions can be released in a very wholesome way. One of the most important results of this process is that the client learns to *forgive* the people against whom his emotions are directed—not because those people deserve it, but so that the client, who was bound to the people he hated, may receive his freedom back.

A second curative procedure is to give directions and advice to the client, to convince him, and to map out goals with him. When the counselor engages in these sorts of things, it is to make it clear that it is only with God and his Word that good counsel is to be found (see Ps. 32:8; Prov. 19:20-21; 21:30; 27:9). The counselor needs to convince his client—for his own good—that he must learn to follow biblical directives, and so he tries to reorganize his client's behavior in a biblical sense (cf. Eph. 4:22-24; Col. 3:8-10).

Directly connected with this is the third curative procedure: the client needs *insightful instruction*. First of all, the counselor must give his client *information* about his diagnosis and the proposed plan of treatment. For example, he must make it clear to his client that the behavior in which he is currently engaged is unconsciously injurious to him, and that he is afflicted with distorted ideas about reality, and so forth. Wrong ideas lie at the root of many problems, and those mistaken ideas must be tracked down by the counselor and corrected in the light of biblical revelation so that a "renewing of thought" (Rom. 12:2; Eph. 4:23) may take place.

Thus the counselor brings his client to *self-examination*. The client needs to gain insight into himself, his motivations and his feelings. This is made possible for him when the counselor places him before the mirror of God's Word (cf. James 1:23-25). It is not just a question of seeing into oneself but of being seen into by God and of learning from his Word about one's heart, one's thoughts, and one's offensive way (Ps. 139:23-24 [NIV], thereby coming eventually to the point of *confessing one's guilt*. This renewing of thought teaches the client to confess his personal sins, to forgive others, and to live his life relying on God's forgiveness and acceptance. Self-examination that is directed entirely to the person himself can make him miserable. Therefore the heart must be directed to Christ (Rom. 7:7-27).

Special Counseling Procedures (2)

Another way to gain insight is through *feedback*. The counselor sums up the impressions that the client's behavior produces in himself and in others. Through this process, the client is taught to look at himself from the viewpoint of others, and in this way he gains more insight into himself. Of course, in Christian counseling it is very important that the counselor, when he undertakes this task, does not emphasize his own, subjective opinion, but makes it clear what really matters. "Your behavior comes across to me thus and so; however, what is most important is not what *I* think about it or how *I* experience it, but what the Bible, the authoritative Word of the living God, says about it."

The counselor must be able to function as a personal *example* of a mature, well-adjusted, functioning human being. It is a normal and healthy phenomenon for us, whether consciously or unconsciously, to adopt the values, attitudes, and behavior of a person whom we believe we can respect. From the counselor the client can learn how to remain calm, even in the midst of an outburst of rage, how to overcome impulsive forms of behavior, and how to make a choice when confronted with confusing alternatives (of course this is something which demands vast self-control and self-confidence on the part of the counselor. It is even more important for the counselor not only to function as an example himself but also to be in a position to point his client to the great example, Jesus Christ (see Rom. 8:29; 13:14; 2 Cor. 3:18; Gal. 4:19; Phil. 2:5).

It is absolutely essential that the counselor instill in his client a conviction about the *meaning of life* and about one's responsibility and dedication. The client must learn to face up to the possibilities, limitations, and inevitabilities of human existence so that he will be able to arrange his life accordingly. In life, every human being has to make all kinds of decisions on his own, and so each one must *learn* a certain measure of independence. In this connection, the Christian counselor will raise the question of what, according to the Bible, the meaning of a human life is when ordered in accordance with God's Word and directed to his glory and his service (see Judg. 5:31; Isa. 40:31; Prov. 4:18; 1 Cor. 1:9, 24; 2 Cor. 4:4-6; Eph. 3:16-19, 4:13; Phil. 1:21; Col. 2:2-10, 3:1-3; 1 Tim. 3:16).

Finally, I wish to draw attention to the *correction* that can take place naturally when the client, on the basis of his good relationship with the counselor, comes to the realization that his life really can be different. This realization brings about a change in all the bitterness and unresolved conflicts in his personal life. In his relationships, the client was previously rejected, oppressed, and so forth, but in his new experience with his counselor he discovers what it is like to be liked, loved, and accepted.

Of course these discoveries will require a lot of time, for the client needs opportunities to practice being in a new, loving, and meaningful relationship before he starts trying out his new attitudes in public, where he will find on the one hand less love, but on the other less criticism. Moreover, it is very important that the client be a member of a strong and loving community of Christians, or that he be received into one. Above everything else, the client must develop a new and close communion with Christ and with God the Father. He must learn to throw himself unconditionally upon God with his brothers and sisters in Christ. He must also be willing to take risks with his fellow human beings in general, and he must dare to exhibit new attitudes and behaviors. If he does so, God will reveal himself in his faithful love, and the client will know from his own experience that God loves him and accepts him in Christ.

Conclusion

In essence, the same curative factors that are apparently effective in secular psychology are also present in Christian counseling. But there are also some major differences when it comes to fill-ing in the content. Secular therapies operate from a human, or humanistic, viewpoint. They have been developed strictly for and by human beings; therefore they cannot help but be human-centered. Moreover, they remain bound to the immanent life and circumstances of the client; they cannot bring in the transcendent dimension. Christian counseling, on the contrary, operates from the divine perspective: Christ is always at the center. For that reason alone, each and every one of the curative factors looks different within the framework of Christian counseling.

In addition, there are differences of principle to be noted. As I said, the Christian counselor does not work from a myth, but from God's self-revelation. He does not arouse any false hopes but offers real, realistic hope in the living God. He does not allow any or all emotions to pour out in uncontrolled fashion (abreaction), but brings them under control and accompanies the venting of the emotions cognitively and in the light of Scripture. He encourages self-examination, but in doing so he directs attention not to himself but to the great example for all who are now or who will become believers—Jesus Christ. He does not impart to his client a meaning of life that he himself has made up, but shows his client the true meaning of life with God.

It turns out that the Bible speaks expressly about all the basic ingredients (i.e. curative factors) of counseling. Moreover it is clear that in the Bible these curative factors always have an essentially different *directedness* to them than what secular psychotherapy is able to give them. Thus, we should not say that the curative factors are *adopted* from secular therapy; it would be better to say that they are actively transformed and *converted*. Of course it should be remembered that they came from the Bible in the first place. Therefore, we could also argue that the reverse is true: it is secular psychotherapy that has adopted the curative factors from Christian traditional pastoral care.

Do not accept the argument of some biblicists that a diseased tree cannot bear good fruit (Matt. 7:16-19; cf. 12:33), and that therefore there is *nothing* we can learn (much less adopt) from secular psychology. This argument is used by people who themselves accept out of necessity all kinds of secular wisdom, for instance, from their medical doctor. Does this mean that secular medical wisdom is "neutral," whereas secular psychological wisdom is not? I am afraid that behind this kind of thinking very often the age-old dualism of body and soul still exerts its influence. Moreover, Jesus is not speaking of scientific thinking but of certain *persons* who are evil trees; this means that wicked people cannot please God. However, in secular psychology and psychotherapy a lot of age-old biblical wisdom has been preserved, and many useful insights, which originated not in wicked hearts but in *God's* creation itself. *All truth is God's truth* (Arthur F. Holmes). Wicked people are not truthful. But some of their insights may be truthful, because these insights do not belong to them at all, but to God and his creation.

Because secular psychotherapy is (historically speaking at least) a de-Christianized form of pastoral care, it is naturally the enemy of Christian psychotherapy. Still, even from our greatest enemies we can learn something. By making a serious critical examination of secular models and by evaluating them, we can bring some useful elements to light, which otherwise would not so easily have come to our attention—such as the curative factors—which we can then absorb in purified form into a Christian psychology, in the sense of working them into it.

Christian psychology in its entirety includes among its assumptions the conviction that even the greatest enemy of Holy Scripture can, by his utterances, unintentionally make us aware of facets of the whole of *God's* creational truth, which formerly escaped our attention. But the most important thing to bear in mind is that Christian psychology is based on a conviction about which its enemies will *never* be able to teach it anything. This is the persuasion that no science will ever really understand anything about the human person if the person is not seen in the context of his or her relationship with God as a creature and image-bearer of God, and, in the case of the Christian, as a son or daughter of God, who is the Creator, Preserver, and Redeemer.

CONCISE BIBLIOGRAPHY

Adams, J.E. 1986. *A Theology of Christian Counseling: More than Redemption*. Grand Rapids, MI: Zondervan.

Berg, J.H. van den. 1961. *The Changing Nature of Man: Introduction to an Historical Psychology*. New York: Norton.

Berg, J.H. van den. 1974. *Divided Existence and Complex Society: An Historical Approach*. Pittsburg: Duquesne University Press.

Brain, C. 2002. *Advanced Psychology: Applications, Issues and Perspectives*. Cheltenham: Nelson Thornes.

Carter, J.D. & Narramore, S.B. 1979. *The Integration of Psychology and Theology: An Introduction*. Grand Rapids, MI: Zondervan.

Chambers, O. 1995. *Biblical Psychology: Christ-Centered Solutions for Daily Problems*. Grand Rapids, MI: Discovery House Publishers.

Clouser, R.A. 2007. *Knowing with the Heart: Religious Experience and Belief in God*. Eugene, OR: Wipf & Stock.

Colman, A.M. (ed.). 2009. *A Dictionary of Psychology*. 3rd ed. New York: Oxford University Press.

Coon, D. & Mitterer, J.O. 2008. *Introduction to Psychology: Gateways to Mind and Behavior*. 12th ed. Stamford, CT: Wadsworth Publishing.

Crabb, L.J. 1997. *Understanding Who You Are: What Your Relationships Tell You about Yourself*. Colorado Springs, CO: Navpress Publishing Group.

Dooyeweerd, H. 1979, 2003 (repr.). *Roots of Western Culture: Pagan, Secular, and Christian Options*. Lewiston, NY: Edwin Mellen Press.

Farra, S.H. 2012. *From Sigmund Freud to Viktor Frankl: How Psychiatry Became Human*. Amazon Digital Services (e-book).

Farra, S.H. 2013. *The Biblical Model of Human Psychology*. Farra Publishing. (Amazon Digital Services, e-book).

Fernald, L.D. 2007. *Psychology: Six Perspectives*. Thousand Oaks, CA: Sage Publications.

Frankl, V.E. 2004. *On the Theory and Therapy of Mental Disorders: An Introduction to Logotherapy and Existential Analysis*. New York: Brunner-Routledge.

Frankl, V.E. 2006. *Man's Search for Meaning: An Introduction to Logotherapy.* Boston: Beacon Press.

Hergenhahn, B.R. 2005. *An Introduction to the History of Psychology.* Belmont, CA: Thomson Wadsworth.

Johnson, E.L. & Jones, S.L. (eds.) (with Collins, G.R., Myers, D.G., Powlison, D. & Roberts, R.C.). 2000. *Psychology & Christianity: Four Views.* Downers Grove, IL: InterVarsity Press.

Jones, S.L. & Butman, R.E. 1991. *Modern Psychotherapies: A Comprehensive Christian Appraisal.* Downers Grove, IL: InterVarsity Press.

Johnson, E.L. (ed.) 2010. Psychology and Christianity: Five Views. Downers Grove, IL: IVP Academic.

Kirwan, W.T. 1984. *Biblical Concepts for Christian Counseling: A Case for Integrating Psychology and Theology.* Grand Rapids, MI: Baker Book House.

Korchin, S.J. 2004. *Modern Clinical Psychology: Principles of Intervention in the Clinic and Community.* New York: CBS Publishers.

LeDoux, J.E. 1998. *The Emotional Brain: The Mysterious Underpinnings of Emotional Life.* New York: Simon & Schuster.

Lommel, P. van. 2010, 2011 (repr.). *Consciousness beyond Life: The Science of the Near-Death Experience.* San Francisco: HarperOne.

Mandler, G. 2007. *A History of Modern Experimental Psychology: From James and Wundt to Cognitive Science.* Cambridge, MA: MIT Press.

McMinn, M.R. 1996. *Psychology, Theology, and Spirituality in Christian Counseling.* Wheaton, IL: Tyndale House.

Milgram, S. 1974. *Obedience to Authority: An Experimental View.* San Francisco: HarperCollins.

Myers, D.G. & Jeeves, M.A. (eds.) 2002. Psychology Through the Eyes of Faith. San Francisco: HarperOne.

Ouweneel, W.J. 2014a. *Wisdom for Thinkers: An Introduction to Christian Philosophy.* Jordan Station, ON: Paideia Press.

Ouweneel, W.J. 2014b. *Power in Service: An Introduction to Christian Political Thought.* Jordan Station, ON: Paideia Press.

Ouweneel, W.J. 2014c. *What Then Is Theology?: An Introduction to Christian Theology.* Jordan Station, ON: Paideia Press.

Powlison, D. 2010. The Biblical Counseling Movement: History and Context. Greensboro, NC: New Growth Press.

CONCISE BIBLIOGRAPHY

Popper, K. & Eccles, J.C. 1977, 1984 (repr.). *The Self and Its Brain: An Argument for Interactionism*. London: Routledge.

Swaab, D. 2014. *We Are Our Brains: A Neurobiography of the Brain, from the Womb to Alzheimer's*. New York: Spiegel & Grau.

Troost, A. 1983. *The Christian Ethos: A Philosophical Survey*. Bloemfontein: Patmos.

INDEX OF NAMES

INDEX OF SUBJECTS

www.ingramcontent.com/pod-product-compliance
Lightning Source LLC
Chambersburg PA
CBHW072102020426
42334CB00017B/1608

* 9 7 8 0 8 8 8 1 5 2 5 8 9 *